Traffic Management

**POLICE
FOUNDATIONS
PROGRAM**

John Grime and Laurence M. Olivo

2000

EMOND MONTGOMERY PUBLICATIONS LIMITED

TORONTO, CANADA

Printed in Canada.

Edited, designed, and typeset by WordsWorth Communications, Toronto.
Cover design by Susan Darrach, Darrach Design.

We acknowledge the financial support of the Government of Canada through the Book Publishing Industry Development Program (BPIDP) for our publishing activities.

Canadian Cataloguing in Publication Data

Grime, John
    Traffic management

(Police foundations program)
ISBN 1-55239-072-1

1. Traffic violations — Canada. 2. Traffic regulations — Canada. 3. Traffic accident investigation — Canada. I. Olivo, Laurence M., 1946– . II. Title. III. Series.

HV8079.5.G74 2000   363.2'332'0971   C00-931690-6

To my wife Helen Grime,
for her patience, understanding, and tolerance.
John Grime

To Joyce Moore,
best friend and greatest supporter.
Laurence Olivo

Contents

LIST OF FIGURES   ix

PREFACE   xi

■ *Chapter* 1   **BACKGROUND TO FEDERAL AND PROVINCIAL MOTOR VEHICLE LAW   1**

Overview of Court Jurisdiction Over Motor Vehicle Law   1

Chapter Summary   8

Key Terms   9

Review Questions   10

Notes   13

■ *Chapter* 2   **THE HIGHWAY TRAFFIC ACT: DEFINING TERMS   15**

Introduction   15

Definition of Vehicle, Section 1   16

Chapter Summary   25

Key Terms   25

Review Questions   26

■ *Chapter* 3   **LICENCES AND PERMITS   29**

Introduction   30

Vehicle Permits   30

Summary of Permit Requirements   30

Vehicle Classes   39

Vehicle Class Description, O. Reg. 340/94, S. 2(1), Table   40

Driver's Licences   42

Chapter Summary   53

Key Terms   53

Review Questions   54

Notes   58

Chapter 4   RULES OF THE ROAD   59

Introduction   59

Rules of the Road: Speed   59

Rules of the Road   62

Vehicle Equipment Requirements   87

Chapter Summary   88

Key Terms   89

Review Questions   90

Notes   106

Chapter 5   MOTOR VEHICLE OFFENCES   107

Introduction   108

Motor Vehicle Stops   108

Suspect Apprehension Pursuits   111

HTA Offences   112

Compulsory Automobile Insurance Act   121

Criminal Code Motor Vehicle Offences   122

Turning "Reasonable Suspicion" into "Reasonable Grounds To
    Believe"   126

Chapter Summary   136

Key Terms   136

Review Questions   137

Notes   142

Chapter 6 COLLISION INVESTIGATION   143

Collision, Reconstruction, and Investigation   145

Steps in a Collision Investigation   145

Sketching, Measuring, and Diagramming a Collision Scene   161

Collection of Physical Evidence   167

Series of Events in Collision Reconstruction   191

Chapter Summary   195

Key Terms   195

Review Questions   196

Chapter 7 MOTOR VEHICLE OFFENCES ARISING FROM COLLISION INVESTIGATION   205

Introduction   206

Hit-and-Run Law   206

Careless Driving Offences   210

Chapter Summary   219

Review Questions   221

Notes   225

APPENDIX A   SHORT-FORM WORDINGS AND SET FINES FROM THE PROVINCIAL OFFENCES ACT   227

APPENDIX B   PROVINCIAL OFFENCE TICKET AND SUMMONS   249

APPENDIX C   SUSPECT APPREHENSION PURSUITS REGULATION   261

List of Figures

Figure 1.1   Procedural Routes for CCC Offences   4

Figure 2.1   Highways   19

Figure 2.2   Highway with Several Roadways   21

Figure 2.3   Intersection   22

Figure 2.4   Unmarked Crosswalk   23

Figure 2.5   Marked Crosswalk   24

Figure 3.1   10-Day Permit   32

Figure 3.2   In-Transit Permit   33

Figure 3.3   Dealer and Service Permits and Plates   34

Figure 3.4   Six-Day Temporary Use of Plates   36

Figure 3.5   Vehicle Class Categorized by Passenger Carrying and by Weight   41

Figure 3.6   What Class of Driver's Licence Is Required by the Driver of These Vehicles?   43

Figure 3.7   Non-Resident Plate and Licence Exemption   52

Figure 4.1   Right of Way—Uncontrolled Intersection   63

Figure 4.2   Overtaking Stopped Vehicle at Crossover   65

Figure 4.3   Overtaking Moving Vehicle Near Crossover   66

Figure 4.4   Right-Hand Turn   67

Figure 4.5   Left-Hand Turn   68

Figure 4.6   Wide Turns   70

Figure 4.7   Hand Signals   71

Figure 4.8   Yielding to Bus   72

Figure 4.9   Traffic Signals   74

Figure 4.10   Left Turn at Intersection with a Median Wider than 15 Metres   75

Figure 4.11   Right and Left Turns on Red Signals   77

Figure 4.12   Giving Way to Emergency Vehicle   81

Figure 5.1   Provincial Offence Ticket   114–116

Figure 5.2   Provincial Offence Summons   117

Figure 5.3   Measuring Reasonable Suspicion and Reasonable Grounds   126

Figure 5.4   Assessment of a Motorist with Regard to Alcohol Consumption   127

Figure 5.5   Breath Demands   130

Figure 5.6   Drunk Driving Offence Procedure at a Glance   135

Figure 6.1   Dangerous Goods Symbols   151

Figure 6.2   Barricades   154

Figure 6.3   Example of Intangible Reference Point   163

Figure 6.4   Example of Coordinate Measurement   164

Figure 6.5   Examples of Triangulation Measurements   165

Figure 6.6   Example of Triangulation Measurement Using "Off Road" References   166

Figure 6.7   Example of Measurement of Simple Road Configuration   167

Figure 6.8   Example of Measurement of Road Configuration Where Roads Not Aligned   168

Figure 6.9   Example of Measurement of Irregular Road Configuration   169

Figure 6.10   Tire Marks   171

Figure 6.11   Normally Inflated Tire   172

Figure 6.12   Underinflated (Overdeflected) Tire   172

Figure 6.13   Overinflated (Underdeflected) Tire   173

Figure 6.14   Change in Skid Marks   175

Figure 6.15   Front-Wheel Lockup   176

Figure 6.16   Rear-Wheel Lockup Skid   178

Figure 6.17   Effect of Camber on a Skid   179

Figure 6.18   Effect of Side-Wheel Lockup   180

Figure 6.19   One Wheel Not Locked   181

Figure 6.20   Wheels on Different Surfaces   183

Figure 6.21   Measuring a Yaw Mark   184

Figure 6.22   Yaw Marks—Critical Speed Marks   185

Figure 6.23   Flat Tire Mark   186

Figure 6.24   Unusual Skid Patterns   187

Figure 6.25   Measuring and Locating Skid Marks on Roadway   189

Figure 6.26   Metal Scars and Debris   190

Figure 6.27   Flips or Vaults   192

Figure 6.28   Overview of Events in a Collision Reconstruction   194

Figure 6.29   What Is Missing in This Sketch?   199

Figure 6.30   Two Collision Scene Diagrams   201

Figure 7.1   Hit-and-Run Table   209

Figure 7.2   Non-Reportable Motor Vehicle Accident Report   211

Figure 7.3   Ministry Motor Vehicle Accident Report   212–215

Preface

This text was written specifically for students in the Ontario Police Foundations Program offered through the Ontario Colleges of Applied Arts and Technology. It covers all of the prescribed Traffic Management curriculum in the Police Foundations Program, and it goes further. The authors are mindful that the expectations, needs, and practices of the various police services across the province differ, and that, as recruits, students may be expected to be familiar with some topics beyond those in the basic curriculum. For that reason, we have included other material, notably detailed presentation on licence and permit classifications and requirements, and information on collision investigation that goes beyond securing and controlling a collision site.

This text will also be useful for students studying in related fields. Paralegals learning to defend traffic offences will find the book very useful, as will those who are training to become litigation law clerks or motor vehicle insurance adjusters.

Many of the topics covered concern the analysis and description of physical events. While these can be and are conveyed in words, they can often be best understood with illustrations. For that reason, we have been lavish with illustrations that explain and clarify many of the topics covered in the text. To help students master material that is, at times, complex and detailed, we have provided lists, summaries, and suggested mnemonic memory aids to aid comprehension. To enforce what has been learned, there are review questions at the end of each chapter, together with discussion questions to allow students to develop and use their analytical and problem-solving skills.

Statements on the law are current to the date of publication. However, students should remember that the law changes constantly. They need to know the law, and how to find it in the relevant statutes and regulations, so that their knowledge is always up to date. Our approach is to teach the basic techniques of using legal materials to find the law and interpret it properly. Students are then given the opportunity to practise those techniques by doing problems at the end of chapters. To get into the habit of looking up the law, students should acquire and use with this book a consolidated version of the *Highway Traffic Act* and regulations, and a consolidated version of the *Criminal Code of Canada*.

Finally, we would like to thank our own students, whose feedback helped us to work through how best to present this material so as to make learning it a positive experience.

John Grime
Laurence M. Olivo
Toronto, 2000

CHAPTER 1

Background to Federal and Provincial Motor Vehicle Law

CHAPTER OBJECTIVES

After completing this chapter, you should be able to:

◆ Define and understand how precedent and *stare decisis* are used.

◆ Understand the significance of the hierarchy of courts to the operation of precedent and *stare decisis*.

◆ Know why precedent and *stare decisis* are less important in the lower courts where provincial offences are heard, and appreciate the significance of this for prosecuting motor vehicle offences.

◆ On the basis of the offence charged, determine the procedural route through the courts that a case will follow.

◆ Understand the relationship between a statute and the regulations made under it.

◆ Understand how to find topics in office consolidation versions of the *Highway Traffic Act* using the Act's general index, the table of contents to the regulations, and the general regulation.

OVERVIEW OF COURT JURISDICTION OVER MOTOR VEHICLE LAW

Provincial Law and Criminal Law

Laws governing regulations and offences involving motor vehicles are contained in the *Highway Traffic Act* (HTA) of Ontario and in regulations made under that Act. Some of the more serious operating offences are contained in the *Criminal Code of Canada* (CCC). Laws governing the rights of citizens to sue for personal injury and property damage arising from a motor vehicle collision are governed by provincial negligence law and motor vehicle insurance law. Although negligence and insurance law are not concerns of this text, a police officer, like any other citizen, can be summonsed to give evidence at a trial in a civil action for negligence, and his or her oral evidence, the contents of the officer's notebook, and the contents of an accident report prepared by the officer may all be relevant to the issues in a civil trial. An officer who is served with a summons issued under the Ontario *Rules of Civil Procedure* should notify his or her superiors and follow department procedures for responding to a civil summons.

Leaving aside negligence law, you should always be aware of whether the motor vehicle law you are dealing with is federal or provincial because the prosecution procedures are different.

The HTA and the regulations made under it are provincial law, and any offences under this law are provincial offences that are tried under procedures prescribed by Ontario's *Provincial Offences Act* (POA).[1] Although HTA offences may in some circumstances be tried before a judge of the Ontario Court of Justice, a trial is much more likely to take place before a justice of the peace (JP) in the Provincial Offences Court of the Ontario Court of Justice. Traditionally, JPs have not been lawyers and may not have received extensive legal training. That is now changing. Some lawyers are being appointed as JPs, and the training program for all JPs who hear traffic cases is now more extensive.

It is important for you to be aware of how JPs approach different categories of HTA offences. In courts above the JP level, judges sometimes give reasons for judgment that explain the legal basis for their decisions. These reasons can be read by other judges and lawyers and become **precedents** that other judges may then follow. As judges follow previous decisions, the law becomes consistent, relatively uniform across the jurisdiction, and predictable. To further ensure consistency, a judge who decides a case wrongly or contrary to precedent may find that one of the parties has appealed to a higher, appellate court. Once an appellate court decides the issue, its decision is binding on lower courts. The process of a precedent becoming binding is known as ***stare decisis***. Note that there is a difference between *stare decisis* and precedent. A precedent should be followed in a given jurisdiction by judges of the same level of court that gave the judgment and by lower courts. *Stare decisis* means judges of lower courts must follow decisions of higher courts within the same jurisdiction. With the exception of the Supreme Court of Canada, which can bind the courts in all provinces, judges in one province need not follow decisions of judges in another province, although decisions from courts in other provinces should receive consideration and deference, particularly if the court in another province is an appellate court. This means that in Ontario, a judge may give consideration to an Alberta case and may elect to follow the precedent, but the Ontario judge is not bound by the Alberta decision, even if the decision comes from the Alberta Court of Appeal. How *stare decisis* and precedent work is illustrated on the following page.

Unlike the practice in the higher courts, JPs rarely give written reasons for their judgments; consequently, the reasons why a JP decided a case in a particular way are not always clear. Further, without reasons it is impossible to build a consistent province-wide body of law because JPs are unaware of how other JPs in the province are deciding similar cases.

precedent
a case is one in which the judge has written reasons for judgment that set down a principle of law that other judges should follow in cases with similar issues and facts; if the precedent comes from a higher court, like a provincial court of appeal, it is binding on lower-level courts

stare decisis
the shortened version of a Latin maxim that means "let the decision stand"; requires that a decision of an appellate court must be followed by lower courts in similar cases

---

DOCTRINE OF STARE DECISIS AND DOCTRINE OF PRECEDENT

Supreme Court of Canada	Decision binds all courts in Canada
Ontario Court of Appeal	Decision binds all courts in Ontario
Superior Court of Justice	Decision binds the Ontario Court of Justice and should be followed by other Superior Court judges, but is not binding on them
Ontario Court of Justice	Decision of one judge of this court is not binding, but should be followed by other Ontario Court of Justice judges

Each JP tends to develop his or her own interpretations; the result is the likelihood of different interpretations developing in different areas of the province. This problem is compounded because neither the Crown nor the accused are likely to appeal a decision by a JP. Many accused do not bother using lawyers in these kinds of cases because the costs of hiring a lawyer are often too high for what is at stake.[2] Accused who do not hire lawyers are unlikely to be aware whether a decision could be appealed. Without appeals, consequently, appellate courts do not review these cases and are not in a position to create a more uniform or consistent interpretation of HTA law. As a result, these differences in approach go largely unchecked and can create some confusion. It is wise, therefore, for you to get to know the interpretive approaches of JPs in courts with which you deal regularly.

Offences under the CCC, such as offences involving impaired driving, are not provincial offences; they are criminal offences. CCC offences are dealt with through different procedures and different courts from HTA offences. Most CCC offences, including impaired-driving offences, are "dual procedure" offences (also called "mixed" or "hybrid" offences). The Crown initially has the right to decide to try the offence as a **summary conviction offence** or as an **indictable offence**. If the Crown chooses to proceed summarily, as it usually does, the trial is held before a judge of the Ontario Court of Justice. If the Crown elects to try the offence as an indictable offence, the procedural route depends on whether the offence falls into s. 553, 536, or 469 of the CCC, as the following list indicates:

◆ If the offence is listed as a "553" offence, the trial procedure is the same as if the Crown had elected to proceed summarily, but the Crown can ask for a longer sentence than it could have asked for if it had proceeded summarily.

◆ If the offence is a "536" offence, the accused has the right to elect to be tried by an Ontario Court judge alone, or by a Superior Court judge alone, or by a Superior Court judge and jury.

summary conviction offence
a category of offence in the CCC that is tried by a relatively uncomplicated procedure before an Ontario Court of Justice judge; sentences on conviction cannot be more than six months and a fine may not exceed $2,000

indictable offence
more serious offences than summary conviction offences; the trial procedure is usually more complicated than the procedure for summary offences, and may involve trial in the Superior Court, with or without a jury

■ **Figure 1.1   Procedural Routes for CCC Offences**

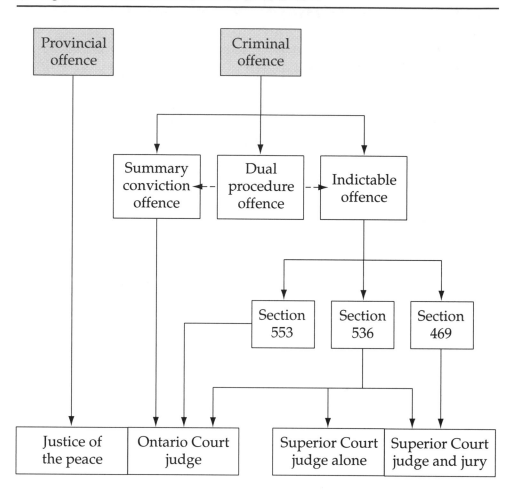

◆ If the offence is a "469" offence—most of which are very serious, such as murder—the trial goes before a Superior Court judge and jury.

The procedural routes for CCC offences are illustrated in figure 1.1.

The Relationship Between a Statute and Its Regulations

In order to work with a statute such as the HTA, you should understand the relationship between a statute and its regulations.

The HTA is statute law. It was passed by receiving a majority vote in the provincial legislature. Starting out as a "bill," it was introduced at first reading, debated at second reading, reviewed section by section in a legislative committee and, finally, voted on at third reading. If the bill passed by a majority vote, it received royal assent when it was signed by the lieutenant governor, and came into force on the day it received royal assent or on a date set out in the legislation (either a fixed date or a date set by the lieutenant governor). The enactment of legislation is a relatively slow process that ensures that each piece of legislation, whatever its merits, is carefully considered by members of the legislature.

Statutes are usually confined to general principles and statements. Because members of the legislature are not experts in every field, they are not capable of enacting statutory provisions that deal with legislative details or technical matters; nor does the legislative agenda allow the time it would take to deal with technical details. For example, the section of the HTA requiring the driver of a motor vehicle on a highway to wear a seat belt is a general principle that the elected members of the legislature can debate and vote on without needing an extensive background in safety engineering or medicine. But specifying who should use what kind of seat belt and restraint system, and in what circumstances, is beyond the competence of members of the legislature. Instead, these technical details are dealt with by regulations. Where it is necessary to make regulations, the legislation grants power to more appropriate and knowledgeable bodies, usually as part of the statute itself. Such a delegation of power may be worded as follows: "The **lieutenant governor in council** may make regulations under this Act to: ... ." The powers to make regulations on various subjects covered by the statute would then be set out. A statute may also give this power to a minister or other government official. In reality, it is usually an expert employed in the civil service who exercises this power.

lieutenant governor in council
the legal and formal name for the provincial Cabinet (the federal Cabinet is called the governor in council)

For a regulation to be valid, the following conditions must be met:

◆ The regulation maker must be able to identify its statutory power to make a particular regulation. If, for example, there is no statutory power that permits regulations to be made prescribing the type of seat belts to be used in passenger automobiles or, more generally, prescribing the specifications for automobile safety devices, any regulation that prescribes the type of seat belts to be used would be invalid and of no legal effect. Because a regulation has no validity unless it is made under the regulation-making authority of a statute, regulations are sometimes referred to as "subordinate legislation."

◆ The regulation must also be officially signed by the Cabinet (the lieutenant governor in council) and proclaimed in force by publication in an official government publication called the *Ontario Gazette*.[3]

The regulation-making process is relatively quick: no vote or activity from the legislature is required. A regulation, once drafted and approved within a ministry, is routinely approved by the lieutenant governor in council, posted to the *Gazette*, and then considered to be in force. This allows for quick updating of the regulations and for experts to provide the necessary technical or scientific details. It is often a good idea, after reading a section of the HTA or other statutes, to check the regulations to see if the regulations provide further information.

Locating Topics in the HTA and the Regulations

Because police officers need to be familiar with many parts of the HTA and frequently use the Act, there are a number of "pocket book" or con-

> ## EXAMPLE OF A STATUTORY PROVISION AND THE AUTHORITY TO MAKE REGULATIONS UNDER THAT PROVISION
>
> s. 78.(1) No person shall drive on a highway a motor vehicle that is equipped with a television receiving set,
>
> (a) any part of which is located in the motor vehicle forward of the back of the driver's seat; or
>
> (b) that is visible to the driver while he or she is operating the motor vehicle. ...
>
> (3) The Lieutenant Governor in Council may make regulations exempting any class of persons or vehicles or any use of equipment or type of equipment from this section. ...

solidated versions of the Act that assemble the HTA and some or all of its regulations, complete with a table of contents and a subject index. Your instructor will specify which of the consolidated versions you should use. Without a consolidated version, you would need to have available to you the 1990 revision of the HTA (in the Revised Statutes of Ontario), all of the amendments to the HTA since 1990, the 1990 revised HTA regulations (in the Revised Regulations of Ontario), and all of the regulations made since 1990.[4] The publications containing all of this material would take up several feet of shelf space, weigh about 25 kg, and cost more than you would like to spend. A consolidated version of the HTA and the regulations is an attractive alternative to this. However, if you are using a consolidated version, note the date to which it is current. In some circumstances, it may be necessary to update the statute or the regulations to be sure there have been no changes since the publication of the consolidated version you are using.

HTA Table of Contents

The consolidated HTA begins with a table of contents that defines its part-by-part organization. Each part is titled and lists the sections dealing with the subject in that part. Note that just the sections are listed, not the subsections, clauses, or subclauses. This means that the table of contents is only a partial aid in locating topics; it merely skims the surface.

Example: Table of Contents of the HTA

Part 1	**Administration**
s. 2	Powers and Duties of Ministry
s. 3	Registrar of Motor Vehicles
s. 4	Deputy Registrar
s. 5	Power to Make Regulations re: Fees

HTA Index

A more specific aid is the index at the back of the Act. The index to the Act is a more detailed list of subjects by pointer words, which is arranged alphabetically by subject. For example, one set of pointer words is "number plates." Listed alphabetically under this heading are subheadings that are more specific pointer words, along with the section, subsection, and clause where the more specific topics can be located. For example, if you look at the entry for number plates, you will see a subheading on the more specific topic about number plates, "visibility and cleanliness," which refers you to s. 13(2).

Example: HTA Index

Number Plates:

> obstructions, s. 13(3)

> violations as to, s. 12(1)(a)-(f)

> visibility and cleanliness, s. 13(2). ...

Abbreviated Forms for HTA Offences

The *Provincial Offences Act* makes writing HTA tickets easier for an officer, by permitting the offence to be described by section number and an appropriate abbreviated description. This is referred to as the "short form" of the offence, or "abbreviated forms."

The short forms can also be used like an index or table of contents to quickly find an offence, together with its section number.

The abbreviated forms are authorized by the *Provincial Offences Act*, and are found in Schedule 43 to Reg. 950, RRO 1990, "Proceedings Commenced by Certificate of Offence." The abbreviated forms are listed in appendix A.

HTA Table of Contents Regulations

If the topic is very detailed, it may be the kind of topic that would be described in a regulation, much like detailed commentary supports a statement of principle. To locate a topic in the regulations, refer to the table of contents for the regulations. This table of contents is usually located in the consolidated version, following the main body of the Act. It is arranged alphabetically like an index, but is much shorter. For example, the kinds of motorcycle helmets that meet the required legal specifications would be found in the regulations. Scanning the table of contents for the regulations will show that there is a regulation about safety helmets.

Table of Contents Regulations

Title	RRO 1990	page
Safety Helmets	610	R27.1

HTA General Regulation

If a topic of fine detail cannot be located by pointer word in the table of contents for the regulations, find the general regulation in the index. The general regulation (O. reg. 596, RRO 1990, as amended by O. reg. 537/97) is a mix of miscellaneous topics and is located alphabetically under "g" in the table of contents for the regulations. Once the actual general regulation is located, scan the list underneath for the desired information. The pointer words in the table of contents for the regulations will show, for example, that no specific regulation covers the amount of damage to property that requires that the police complete a motor vehicle accident report. The general regulation should be consulted for this information.[5]

Example of a Provision in the General Regulation

s. 11 For the purpose of s. 199(1) of the Act, the prescribed amount for damage to property is $1,000.

Hint: In the consolidated version, you should stick a tab at the beginning of

1. the table of contents,
2. the index,
3. the table of contents for regulations, and
4. the general regulation (under "g" in the contents for regulations).

This will make it quicker and easier for you to look things up in the Act and regulations.

USUAL METHOD OF LOCATING A TOPIC IN THE HTA

1. Check HTA Index—general principles of law
2. Check HTA table of contents of regulations—for detail on general principle of law found in the HTA index
3. Check HTA table of contents for regulations, under "g" for General Regulation—collection of miscellaneous regulations

See appendix A, "Short-Form Wordings from the POA," at the back of the book.

CHAPTER SUMMARY

This chapter introduces you to some of the court structures and sources of law related to motor vehicle law. Motor vehicle law is primarily governed by the provincial HTA and by some sections of the federal CCC. This chapter explains that there are different ways to handle offences, depending on whether the offence is provincial or federal. The particular charge will determine which court hears the case, and what rules of procedure are applied. Provincial offences are often tried before JPs, where the doctrines of precedent and *stare decisis* are not followed as strictly as they are in the higher courts.

The nature of statutes and regulations and their relationship are explored, because knowledge of the regulations is as important as the statute itself in this area of law. How to look up and find statute sections and relevant regulations is explained so that you will be able to find the information from subject or topic headings easily.

KEY TERMS

precedent

stare decisis

summary conviction offence

indictable offence

lieutenant governor in council

REVIEW QUESTIONS

■ SHORT ANSWER

1. What are the principal sources of law in Canada governing motor vehicle offences?

2. If police officers have no direct involvement in civil lawsuits arising from motor vehicle collisions, why do they have to be aware of these lawsuits?

3. Why is it important to know that judgments from provincial offences court rarely come with written reasons for judgment and are rarely appealed?

4. Explain how the doctrine of precedent works.

5. How is the doctrine of precedent different from *stare decisis*?

6. Explain what route the following offences would take through the courts, including options available to Crown and accused:

   a. criminal negligence causing death (s. 220, CCC)

   b. driving while disqualified (ss. 259(4)–(5), CCC)

   c. first-degree murder (s. 231, CCC)

   d. speeding penalties (s. 128(14) HTA)

7. What is the relationship between a statute and a regulation made under it?

8. What is required for a regulation to be valid?

9. Using the HTA indexes and table of contents, find all the statute sections and regulations dealing with the following:

a. automobile trailers

b. fines for speeding offences

c. motorcycle helmets

d. lighting on bicycles

■ DISCUSSION QUESTION

1. There are significant differences between the provincial offences court and other courts when it comes to the trial of motor vehicle offences. Discuss, explaining what the differences are and why they are significant.

NOTES

1 For more information on the POA and the procedures used, see U. Capy and E. MacCarthy, *Provincial Offences* (Toronto: Emond Montgomery, 2000).

2 Drunk-driving offences and serious CCC offences provide an exception to this statement; here custodial time, loss of driving privileges, and heavy fines may make an appeal worthwhile. Also, because these offences cross economic class lines, there are a number of accused who have the financial resources to pursue appeals.

3 Every province has a gazette in which government proclamations and other announcements required by statute are posted. The federal government publishes the *Canada Gazette*, which performs the same functions at the federal level.

4 For more information on how to use the standard sources for finding and updating statutes and regulations, see generally M. Kerr, *Legal Research: Step by Step* (Toronto: Emond Montgomery Publications, 1998), pp. 3–16; and R. Carson, "Legal Research: An Introduction," in L. Olivo, ed., *Introduction to Law in Canada* (Toronto: Captus Press, 1999).

5 Dollar amounts are often described in the regulations rather than in the statute because regulations can be quickly changed to reflect the impact of inflation.

CHAPTER 2

The Highway Traffic Act: Defining Terms

CHAPTER OBJECTIVES

After completing this chapter, you should be able to:

Distinguish between the various definitions of "vehicle" in the HTA and understand the reasons for the variations in the definitions.

Understand the definitions of highway, roadway, and related terms used in the HTA and the reasons for those definitions.

Appreciate that although the definitions discussed in this chapter are key definitions, there are others in the HTA that you will need to look up from time to time.

INTRODUCTION

This chapter defines and discusses some key definitions in the *Highway Traffic Act* (HTA). These include definitions of conveyances of various kinds, such as

◆ vehicle, s. 1;

◆ motor vehicle, s. 1;

◆ commercial motor vehicle, s. 1;

trailer, s. 1;

bus, s. 1;

school bus, s. 175(1), reg. 612; and

school-purposes bus, reg. 612, s. 1(4).

Other definitions include geographical elements over which conveyances travel, such as

◆ highway, s. 1;

◆ roadway, s. 1;

◆ intersection, s. 1;

- ◆ crosswalks, s. 1; and

- ◆ pedestrian crossover, s. 1.

Finally, there are some definitions about stopping conveyances on highways, such as

- ◆ stopping, s. 1;

- ◆ standing, s. 1; and

- ◆ parking, s. 1.

DEFINITION OF VEHICLE, SECTION 1

This definition includes motor vehicles, such as cars, trucks, trailers, farm tractors, and road-building machinery (including steam rollers and graders). The definition also includes vehicles that operate by any other form of power, including muscular power, such as bicycles and horse-drawn carriages. The definition of vehicle is used in connection with "rules of the road" and is very broad so that drivers of a wide variety of vehicles can be made subject to the rules of the road. Streetcars and motorized snow vehicles (snowmobiles) are explicitly excluded from the definition, primarily because they are covered by other legislation. For example, snowmobiles are regulated under the *Motorized Snow Vehicles Act* (RSO 1990, c. M.44).

Definition of Motor Vehicle, Section 1

This definition includes automobiles, motor-assisted bicycles (mopeds), and motorcycles (which includes motor scooters), unless otherwise indicated in the HTA. It also includes other vehicles propelled by anything other than muscular power. However, the following vehicles are not included in the definition:

- ◆ **snow**mobiles,

- ◆ **f**arm tractors,

- ◆ self-propelled **i**mplements of husbandry (such as **r**eapers and combines),

- ◆ **r**oad-building machinery,

- ◆ **s**treetcars, and

- ◆ **t**raction engines.

You can remember what is excluded by using the mnemonic "snowfirst."

This definition is generally used for rules regarding vehicle permits, driver's licences, and equipment requirements. It is narrower and more restrictive than the definition of "vehicle."

Definition of Commercial Motor Vehicle, Section 1

A commercial motor vehicle is a vehicle that has a truck or delivery body attached to it. "Delivery body" is not defined, but it can be assumed that it is a vehicle primarily for carrying cargo or objects rather than people. Other vehicles specifically included in the definition are

◆ ambulances,

◆ hearses,

◆ fire apparatus,

◆ buses, and

◆ tractors used for hauling on highways.

This definition is not based on the purpose or function of the vehicle, but on its structure or physical description. Therefore, if someone uses a hearse as a domestic family vehicle, it is still defined as a commercial vehicle because of its physical description and structure. This definition is used in the HTA to describe the type of motor vehicle that requires commercial motor vehicle licence plates. Commercial plates have a different colour (black, rather than blue, on a white background) and the number sequencing is different from that for passenger motor vehicles. With respect to vans, if there is a seating capacity of 4 or more passengers, the van is considered a passenger motor vehicle; if there are fewer than 4 seats, the van is considered a commercial motor vehicle. If a van has more than 10 seats and is used for transporting people, it is considered a commercial vehicle, but will also be defined as a bus.

Definition of Trailer, Section 1

A trailer is any vehicle drawn on a highway by a motor vehicle, but excludes the following, which you may remember by using the mnemonic "MMIST":

◆ a **m**otor vehicle being towed,

◆ a **m**obile home,

◆ an **i**mplement of husbandry (for example a hay wagon),

◆ a **s**ide car on a motorcycle, and

◆ any device or apparatus not designed to **t**ransport persons or property and that is temporarily drawn on a highway (for example, a portable cement mixer).

This definition describes vehicles that require trailer plates. Such vehicle must be pulled by a motor vehicle and pulled on a highway. If the vehicle does not fit the definition or is one of the exceptions, it does not require trailer plates.

Definition of a Bus, Section 1

A bus is a motor vehicle designed and used for carrying 10 or more passengers. This definition is used for the purpose of determining who must have a bus driver's licence.

Definition of School Bus, Section 175(1), Regulation 612

As in the definition of bus, the definition of school bus has two parts: a definition by physical description, and a definition by use. A school bus is chrome yellow in colour. It has the words "SCHOOL BUS" marked on the front and rear and the words "DO NOT PASS WHEN SIGNALS FLASHING" on the rear. It also has red flashing lights at front and rear. A school bus is used for transporting children anywhere for any reason, or transporting developmentally handicapped adults to or from a training centre. Buses that fit this definition must meet the safety equipment requirements and the rules for operation of this equipment when loading or discharging passengers, and drivers must meet licensing requirements specific to school buses.

Definition of School-Purposes Bus, Regulation 612, Section 1(4)

The definition of school-purposes bus covers buses of any colour that are operated by or under a contract to a school board for the transportation of children anywhere for any reason. It also includes chrome-yellow school buses. This definition is broad enough to cover any driver who will be in charge of transporting children.

Definition of Highway, Section 1

road allowance
a continuous strip of land dedicated for the location of a public highway, usually one chain, or 66 feet, wide; the actual roadway may be considerably narrower, but the whole width of the road allowance constitutes the highway, within the meaning of the HTA

chain
a surveyor's measure, consisting of a chain or line that is 66 feet long

The term "highway" is described very broadly and includes a public street, avenue, parkway, driveway, square, place, bridge, viaduct or trestle that is intended for or used by anyone to pass over in a vehicle. It includes not only the space over which the vehicle moves, but also the land on either side of the roadway between the lateral property lines. In many parts of the province, **road allowances** that constitute the highway are one **chain**, or 66 feet, wide (33 feet on either side of the centre of the roadway). Where the roadway is narrower than the road allowance, private property owners may have encroached on the highway where it is not clearly delineated, planting lawns or shrubs on what is technically the road allowance and part of the highway. For practical reasons, on city streets, the highway includes the sidewalks on either side or, if there is no sidewalk, the shoulder or verge of the road up to the property line of properties adjacent to the highway. The illustrations in figure 2.1 will help you see that the highway consists of more than just the roadway itself.

■ **Figure 2.1   Highways**

City: Storefront to storefront

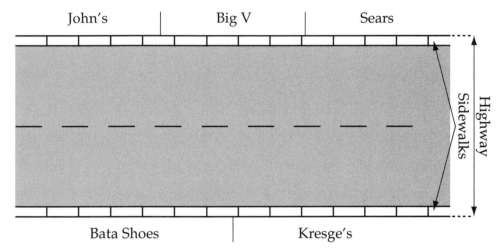

Suburb: Mid-lawn to mid-lawn

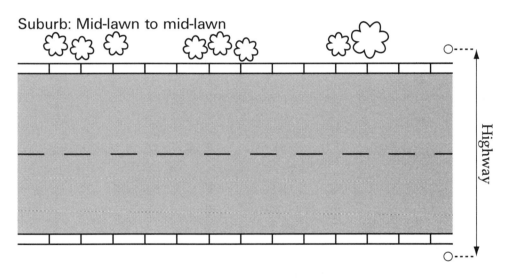

Country: Fence line to fence line

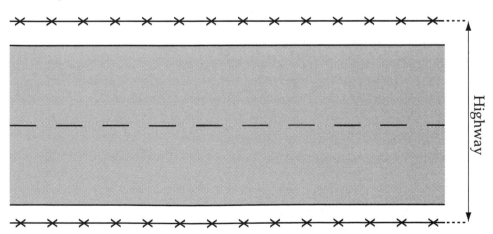

Definition of King's Highway, Section 1

The term "King's Highway" describes a class of highway, consisting of secondary and tertiary provincial highways designated under the *Public Transportation and Highway Improvement Act*. These highways are commonly known as provincial highways and are identified by numbered route signs posted along the highway.

Definition of Roadway, Section 1

The roadway is the travelled portion of a highway ordinarily used for vehicular traffic, and does not include the shoulders, even if they are paved. What is considered the roadway depends on the physical attributes of the road. For example, the roadway is,

◆ on a city street, the paved portion between the curbs on either side;

◆ on a street where there is no curb, the paved portion between the edges of the pavement on either side of the travelled portion; and

◆ on a gravel or snow-covered road, the travelled portion (note that this kind of road can change width, depending on how much of the right of way is gravelled or cleared of snow).

To summarize, a roadway is the travelled part of a highway. Where there are median dividers and exit and entrance ramps, a highway, like Highway 401, can include several roadways, as figure 2.2 illustrates.

The definition of a driver in s. 1 is restricted to someone who drives a vehicle on a highway. Therefore, if the term "driver" is used in the description of an offence, the location of the offence is restricted to a highway, as defined in the HTA. This means, that offences committed on private drives, driveways, or in private parking lots, including the parts used for traffic circulation, cannot be subject to charges under the HTA; a private parking area or drive is not a highway under the HTA (*R v. Mansour*, [1979] SCR 916).

Definition of Intersection, Section 1

An intersection is the area of the highway that falls within the extension of the curb lines or, if there is no curb, it is the area that falls within the extension of the lateral boundary lines of two or more highways that join one another at an angle, whether or not the highways cross each other. Note that if there are curbs, the definition seems to describe a roadway, yet if there are no curbs, the reference to lateral boundary lines seems to suggest the more encompassing definition of a highway rather than the narrower one of a roadway. The angle of an intersection can be oblique or acute, although we usually think of intersections as two highways crossing each other at right angles. See figure 2.3.

The definition of an intersection provides an important reference point for defining some driving offences. For example, the definition of intersection is invoked to describe the legal placement of a stop sign. A

■ **Figure 2.2   Highway with Several Roadways**

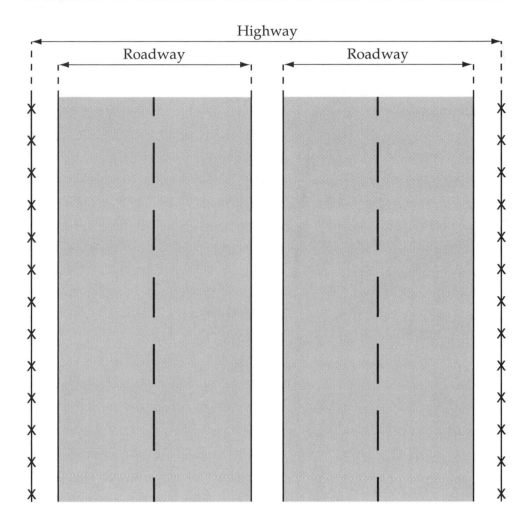

stop sign is probably only advisory if it is not placed where two highways intersect. For example, stop signs used in plaza or mall exits to highways are probably only advisory, and charges might not be laid successfully for failing to stop at such signs.

Definition of Crosswalks, Section 1

There are two kinds of crosswalks to consider: marked crosswalks and unmarked (imaginary) crosswalks. Unmarked crosswalks are defined as that part of a roadway *at an intersection* that forms the area within the boundary created by the connection of the lateral lines of the sidewalks on opposite sides of the highway. More simply, an unmarked crosswalk exists only where there is an intersection with sidewalks on opposite sides. One of the sidewalks, if it were to continue, would cross the road to meet another sidewalk on the opposite side. See figure 2.4 for an example. This definition determines the place at an intersection where a pedestrian may safely cross the highway.

■ **Figure 2.3 Intersection**

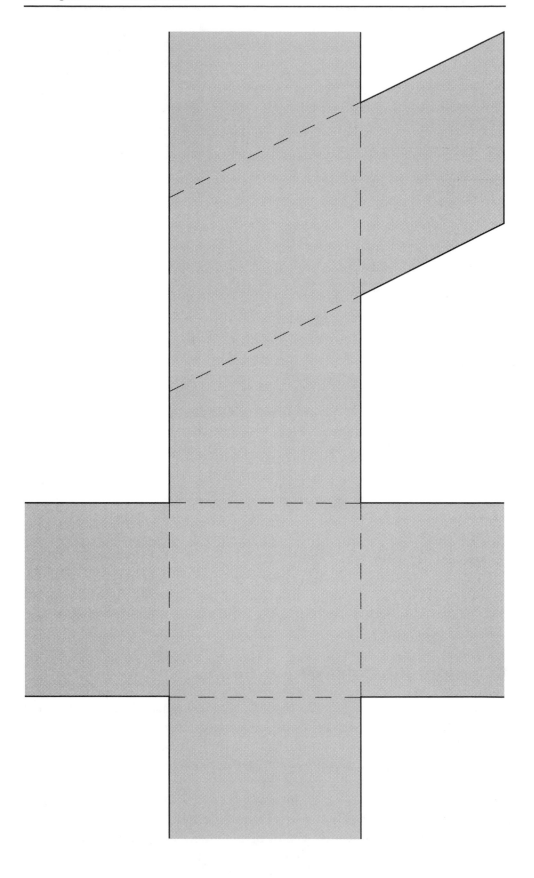

■ **Figure 2.4   Unmarked Crosswalk**

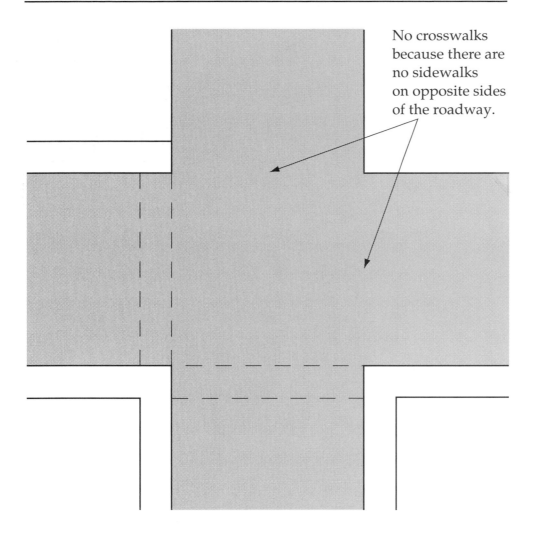

No crosswalks
because there are
no sidewalks
on opposite sides
of the roadway.

Three requirements:

1. at an intersection,
2. sidewalks on opposite sides, and
3. one of the sidewalks if projected must cross the road.

A marked crosswalk is any portion of a roadway, at an intersection or elsewhere, distinctly set out for pedestrian crossing by signs or markings on the roadway. Because a marked crosswalk can be posted at places other than intersections, the law requires that they be marked. See figure 2.5.

Definition of Pedestrian Crossover, Section 1

A pedestrian crossover is any portion of a roadway designated by a municipal bylaw for pedestrian crossing by signs on the highway, markings on the roadway, or both, as prescribed by the regulations. This type of crossing is generally found in large cities, and there are prescribed stopping and passing requirements with respect to these crossovers that do

■ **Figure 2.5 Marked Crosswalk**

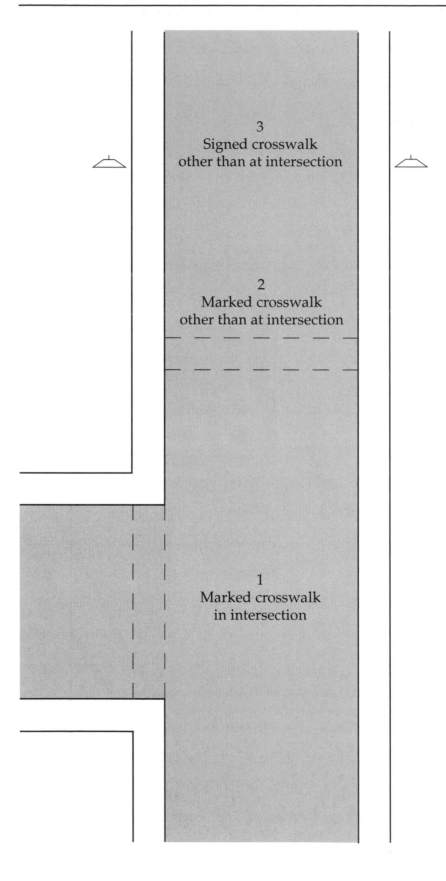

not apply to ordinary crosswalks. Usually, crossovers have signs, lights, or both suspended over the roadway, although these are not required by law.

Definition of Stopping, Section 1

A "no stopping" area on a roadway indicates that a vehicle may not stop for any reason, except to avoid traffic or when required by the police, signs, or traffic signals.

Definition of Standing, Section 1

A "no standing" sign means that a vehicle may not stop, except while picking up or dropping off passengers. Standing does not mean that a vehicle can stay to wait for passengers who are *going to be* picked up or dropped off.

Definition of Parking, Section 1

A "no parking" sign means that a vehicle may not be left standing, whether occupied or not, except when standing temporarily to pick up or drop off passengers. Like the definition of standing, a vehicle may not be left standing in a "no parking" area except when in the act of picking up or dropping off passengers.

CHAPTER SUMMARY

This chapter introduces you to some of the basic terms and definitions in the HTA that you need to understand and apply to driving offences permits. The general term "vehicle" is first defined, followed by its subcategories: motor vehicle, commercial motor vehicle, and various types of buses. The division of "vehicle" into subclasses is generally related to operator licensing requirements and, in the case of commercial vehicles and buses, to equipment requirements. The term "highway" is defined, along with its related component parts, including roadway, intersection, and crosswalk. These elements provide the necessary context for driving offences and collision investigation that concern police officers; they are discussed in more detail later in the book.

KEY TERMS

road allowance

chain

REVIEW QUESTIONS

■ TRUE OR FALSE

In the space provided next to each statement, place a "T" if the statement is true or an "F" if the statement is false.

_____ 1. A roadway includes shoulders.

_____ 2. A bicycle is a vehicle.

_____ 3. A self-propelled farm harvester is a motor vehicle by HTA definition.

_____ 4. A manure spreader, which is drawn along a highway by a truck, is a trailer.

_____ 5. The only exception to prohibited parking is for picking up or dropping off passengers.

_____ 6. A street car is a motor vehicle.

_____ 7. A portable cement mixer, which is pulled by a dump truck, is a trailer.

_____ 8. A road grader is not a motor vehicle.

_____ 9. When a motor vehicle with a designed seating capacity of 14 people is carrying 7 people, the motor vehicle is considered a bus as defined in the HTA.

_____ 10. In a residential area, the boulevard and sidewalk on either side of the roadway are considered part of the highway.

_____ 11. A compressor, which is pulled by a half-ton truck, is a trailer.

_____ 12. Whenever an offence refers to a driver in the HTA, the offence must occur on a highway.

_____ 13. A highway is all the area between the lateral property lines of the road allowance.

_____ 14. A motorcycle, a motor-assisted bicycle, a motor home, and a self-propelled cement truck are all motor vehicles as defined in the HTA.

_____ 15. An exception to prohibited stopping is the temporary loading or unloading of cargo.

_____ 16. A pedestrian crossover is only required to be designated by signs and a bylaw to be lawful.

_____ 17. A chrome-yellow bus with the words "SCHOOL BUS" on the front and rear and "DO NOT PASS WHEN SIGNALS FLASHING" on the rear that is used for transporting a children's hockey team to a weekend tournament is a school bus.

■ **SHORT ANSWER**

Briefly answer the following questions in the space provided.

1. How does a marked crosswalk differ from an unmarked crosswalk, and how do both differ from a pedestrian crossover?

2. List four vehicles with motors that are excluded from the HTA definition of motor vehicle.

3. Can you be charged for driving 80 km/hr in the traffic circulation area of a private parking area in a plaza? Why or why not?

4. What is the difference between a highway and a roadway under the HTA?

5. If a half-ton truck is used only for personal use can it be classed as a passenger automobile rather than a truck?

6. How does a "school-purposes bus" differ from a "school bus"?

7. What towed vehicles are excluded from the definition of trailer in the HTA?

8. Is a trailer pulled by a bicycle considered a trailer within the meaning of the HTA?

9. Can an unmarked crosswalk be located on a highway, 250 m from an intersection?

■ DISCUSSION QUESTIONS

1. Nanette is skating down a city street on her rollerblades. She comes to an intersection and proceeds right past a stop sign without stopping. Can she be charged under the HTA? On what would this depend? Set out arguments for and against charging her.

2. Babette has a four-wheel vehicle that seats one person and has a flat, horizontal deck behind the seat. It also has a mast and a sail; there is no motor. Using wind power, she is able to drive around the city. Does she require a vehicle permit under s. 7(1) of the HTA? If so, what kind?

3. Babette has added a larger deck and seating for 11 passengers to her wind-driven vehicle. She has accepted a contract for driving children to and from school. She drives this vehicle out of a shopping plaza parking lot and ignores the stop sign where the lot enters onto a highway. Discuss how this vehicle should be classified and whether or not, based on these facts, Babette could be charged with failing to stop at a stop sign while driving it.

CHAPTER 3
Licences and Permits

CHAPTER OBJECTIVES

After completing this chapter, you should be able to:

Identify the circumstances where a vehicle may use a 10-day permit, "in transit" permit, or dealer and service permit.

Know what restricted permits and their plates look like, and where to find them on a vehicle.

Determine whether a permanent permit matches the number plate displayed.

Know that no plate may be attached unless there is a permit authorizing use of the plate.

Know the circumstances where a plate can be transferred from one vehicle to another.

Describe the buyer's and seller's obligations with respect to transferring ownership of a motor vehicle.

Know the procedure for transferring the ownership of a motor vehicle.

Know the elements of the offences concerning unlawful use of plates and permits and validation tags.

Identify the vehicle classes set out in the HTA.

Assign a vehicle to an appropriate vehicle class by weight, purpose, passenger carrying capacity, use, or other factors.

Know the levels and restrictions on graduated licences for G and M class licences.

Know how a driver progresses through the graduated licence system.

Determine which class of vehicle a licence holder of a certain class can drive.

◆ Know the elements of driver's licence offences.

Understand the circumstances when reverse-onus rules apply to an offence.

◆ Know when you can arrest for an offence or ticket for an offence.

◆ Identify the circumstances where non-Ontario plates and licences can be used by a person driving on the highway.

INTRODUCTION

In this chapter, we examine the requirements of the permit system for licensing different classes of vehicles and the requirements for different classes of operator's licences.

VEHICLE PERMITS

The permit is the document that licenses a vehicle to be used on the highways of the province and authorizes the attachment of metal number plates to that vehicle. There are two parts to a permit: the vehicle portion and the number portion.

The statutory basis for the requirement of permits is s. 7 of the *Highway Traffic Act* (HTA). It reads as follows:

s. 7(1) No one shall drive a motor vehicle on a highway unless,

(a) there exists a currently validated permit for the vehicle;

(b) there are displayed on the vehicle, in the manner prescribed by regulations, number plates issued in accordance with regulations showing the number of the permit issued for the vehicle; and

(c) there is affixed to the number plate displayed on the vehicle, in the manner displayed on the vehicle, in the manner prescribed by regulation, evidence of current validation ("**valtag**").

s. 7(5) Every driver of a motor vehicle on a highway shall carry,

(a) the permit for it or a true copy thereof; and

(b) where the motor vehicle is pulling a trailer, the permit for the trailer or a true copy thereof,

and shall surrender the permits or copies for inspection upon demand of a police officer.

valtag
short-form term for validation tag, which is attached to metal number plates to show that the plate is currently valid

SUMMARY OF PERMIT REQUIREMENTS

HAVE: Any driver of a motor vehicle on a highway must have a permit for the motor vehicle that authorizes the number plates on that vehicle.

DISPLAY: Except in the case of temporary permits, there must be two number plates that are affixed to the front and rear of a motor vehicle operated on a highway, and the rear plate must be currently validated in the upper-right-hand corner of the plate.

SURRENDER: The driver of a motor vehicle on a highway must carry the permit or a true copy of it in the motor vehicle and surrender it to a police officer for inspection on demand.

Restricted Permits

There are three types of restricted permits for motor vehicles and trailers: 10-day permits, "in transit" permits, and dealer and service permits and plates. All are authorized by s. 7(24) of the HTA and by reg. 628, ss. 11-13.

10-Day Permits

These permits are temporary and are valid for a 10-day period (O. reg. 628, s. 11). They are used when it is necessary to move a vehicle on a highway that does not have permanent plates and where permanent plates are not being sought (for example, where the vehicle is being sold in the near future, but needs to be moved to another part of Ontario). These permits are sometimes referred to as "trip" permits, although this is misleading because the permits can be used for more than one trip within the 10-day period for which they are issued. Anyone may obtain these permits for any reason and for any use in Ontario.

A safety standard certificate is not required to obtain a 10-day permit because it is not issued for a change of ownership; however, the vehicle must be insured. The permit is a heavy paper sticker that takes the place of the ownership part of the permit and the metal number plates.

It must be placed in a clearly visible portion of the windshield of the motor vehicle for which it was issued or, in the case of a trailer, to the windshield of the motor vehicle that is drawing the trailer. The expiry date is written on the back of the permit and is visible from inside the car. See figure 3.1.

If a motor vehicle or a trailer drawn by a plated motor vehicle is found on the highway with an expired 10-day permit, the violator is charged with driving a motor vehicle or drawing a trailer with no permit.

"In-Transit" Permits

This permit is available only to a manufacturer or to a dealer in motor vehicles or trailers (O. reg. 628, s. 12). The permit shall be used only for the original trip that the vehicle takes from the manufacturer to the dealer.

The paper permit must be placed in a clearly visible place on the windshield or on the rear of the trailer for which it was issued. It is not a metal number plate. The permit takes the place of the paper ownership and the number plate normally required. The place of origin and the destination are written on the back of the permit and are visible from inside the motor vehicle. A violator is charged with driving a motor vehicle or drawing a trailer with no permit. No safety standard certificate is required as these are used with new cars or trailers usually protected by warranty. See figure 3.2.

■ **Figure 3.1   10-Day Permit**

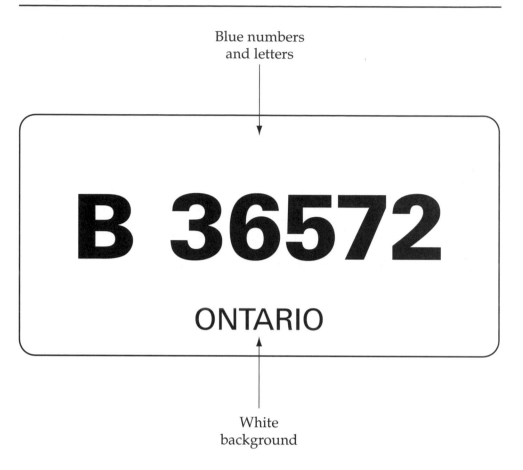

Blue numbers
and letters

B 36572
ONTARIO

White
background

Dealer and Service Permits and Plates

Dealer and service permits (O. reg. 628, s. 13) and plates are issued to

◆ a **m**anufacturer of motor vehicles or trailers;

◆ a **d**ealer in motor vehicles or trailers;

◆ a person engaged in the business of **r**epairing, customizing, or modifying motor vehicles or trailers; and

◆ a person engaged in the business of **t**ransporting motor vehicles or trailers.

You may wish to use the mnemonic "**mdrt**" to remember the classes of persons to whom this permit may be issued.

They may be used only

◆ on a vehicle for **s**ale that is owned by the permit holder;

◆ to fix, **t**est, or modify a vehicle by the person who owns the permit; and

◆ on a vehicle being **t**ransported by a person engaged in the business of transporting vehicles.

■ **Figure 3.2   In-Transit Permit**

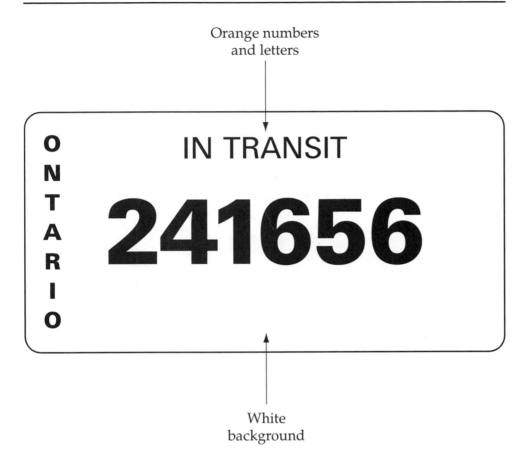

Orange numbers
and letters

IN TRANSIT

241656

ONTARIO

White
background

You may wish to use the mnemonic "**stt**" to remember the circumstances where the dealer permit and plate may be used.

The permit and plates may not be used on a new vehicle that is being rented. Only one plate is issued, with black letters and numbers on an orange background. The plate must be attached in a conspicuous position on the rear of the rear-most vehicle being towed or driven on a highway. This suggests that the permit may apply to more than one vehicle, if they are linked together for transit. Dealer plates must be validated, and the valtag shall be affixed to the upper-right-hand corner of the plate. See figure 3.3.

Non-Restricted Permits

We can now look at the requirements for permits and number plates in the ordinary course of events, and we will do this for a number of common vehicle transfer and acquisition situations. There are two points that will help you make sense of the rules about permits. First, generally you cannot affix number plates to a motor vehicle until you have first obtained a permit from the ministry that authorizes the plates for that vehicle. As a general rule, you should get the permit before attaching the

■ **Figure 3.3** **Dealer and Service Permits and Plates**

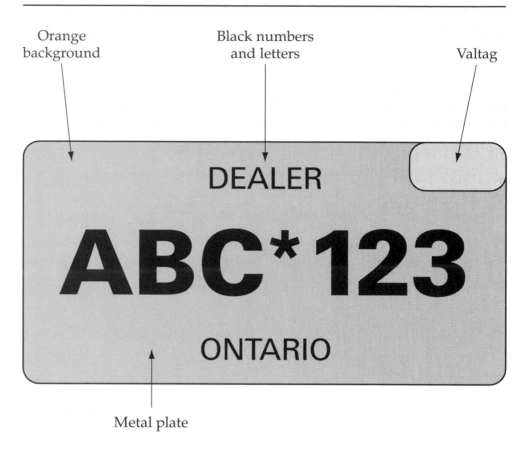

plates. Do not attach plates for which you have no authorizing permit. Second, number plates are issued to the person rather than the vehicle, which means that plates can be transferred by an owner from one vehicle he or she owned to another that he or she has bought. This means that if you buy a used or new car, you can transfer the plates to it from the car you previously owned, provided that you follow the rules prescribed in the legislation.

Seller's Obligations, HTA, Section 11(1)

The seller, on selling a motor vehicle, is not obliged to notify the ministry, but is obliged

◆ to remove the number plates from the vehicle;

◆ to retain the plate portion of the permit;

◆ on delivery of the vehicle to the new owner,

  ◆ to complete and sign the transfer application on the back of the vehicle portion of the permit, including the date of delivery, the date of the transfer, and the odometer reading; and

  ◆ to give this portion of the permit to the new owner.

The seller or transferor may retain the plates that he or she has removed from the vehicle and affix them to another car that he or she owns under certain circumstances described in the HTA and its regulations (HTA, s. 11(3)). The newly acquired motor vehicle must be similar to the class of vehicle from which the plates have been removed—that is, you can transfer a plate from one passenger automobile to another passenger automobile, but not from a passenger automobile to a commercial vehicle. In addition, you must meet the following requirements set out in reg. 628, s. 10(1):

◆ The number plate must be currently validated.

◆ The driver must have in his or her possession the following documents:

  ◆ The vehicle portion of the permit issued for the vehicle that you are driving, with the transfer application completed on the back, signed by both seller and purchaser. If the motor vehicle is new and has not had a previous owner or lessee, a copy of the bill of sale or other ownership document or a leasing document may be substituted for the vehicle portion of the permit issued for the vehicle (O. reg. 628, s. 10(4)).

  ◆ The plate portion of the permit corresponding to the plates you have transferred to the vehicle.

  ◆ A valid Safety Standards Certificate—that is, one issued within 36 days of the transfer. This is not required if the vehicle is new (O. reg. 628, s. 10(3)).

Buyer's Obligations, HTA, Section 11(2)

The buyer is obliged to apply for a new permit within six days of becoming the owner of a motor vehicle or trailer for which a permit was previously issued to someone else.

In general, if a person wants to take the number plates off one motor vehicle and transfer the plates to another motor vehicle, he or she should get a new registration permit authorizing the "old" plates to be used on the "new" motor vehicle before attaching the old plates to the new car. However, the new owner may use plates issued for one vehicle on another temporarily without notifying the ministry for up to six days after becoming the owner. To do this, the buyer must comply with the requirements set out in reg. 628, s. 10(6), which states that the buyer must carry the documents or true copies (see s. 10(1) of reg. 628). Figure 3.4 sets out the requirements in a visual format.

The following scenarios illustrate some of the most common situations that might involve switching plates. Note that for some of the situations, switching plates is prohibited.

TRANSFERRING PLATES FROM ONE VEHICLE THAT YOU OWN TO ANOTHER VEHICLE THAT YOU OWN Where you own two vehicles at the same time,

■ Figure 3.4   Six-Day Temporary Use of Plates

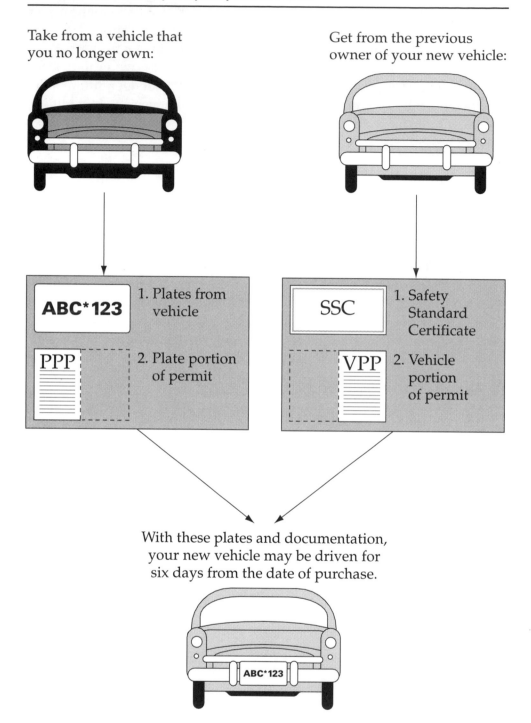

Take from a vehicle that you no longer own:

Get from the previous owner of your new vehicle:

ABC*123 — 1. Plates from vehicle

PPP — 2. Plate portion of permit

SSC — 1. Safety Standard Certificate

VPP — 2. Vehicle portion of permit

With these plates and documentation, your new vehicle may be driven for six days from the date of purchase.

ABC*123

you cannot use the six-day temporary use of plates provision because the plates are not from a vehicle that you no longer own, nor are they being transferred to a vehicle that you have purchased in the last six days. In this case, you must apply for a new permit authorizing the use of the plate on the vehicle before you can attach the plates to it and drive on the highway. Also, if you do this, you cannot transfer the plate back to the original vehicle by relying on the six-day temporary use rule.

TRANSFERRING PLATES FROM ONE VEHICLE THAT YOU HAVE JUST SOLD TO ANOTHER VEHICLE THAT YOU HAVE OWNED FOR A PERIOD OF TIME PRIOR TO THE SALE OF THE OTHER VEHICLE Where you owned two vehicles at the same time and sold one, you cannot use the six-day temporary use of plates provision if you did not obtain ownership of the vehicle to which you propose to transfer the plates within the last six days. Again, you can only resort to the six-day temporary use of plates provision if you bought the vehicle in the last six days and are using the plates within that six-day period. If stopped by the police, you will have to produce the old plate portion, the new vehicle portion, and a valid safety standards certificate.

TRANSFERRING PLATES FROM A VEHICLE YOU PREVIOUSLY OWNED TO A BRAND-NEW VEHICLE WHERE YOU ARE THE FIRST OWNER OR LESSEE Where you have sold one vehicle and then bought or leased another brand-new vehicle you *can* take advantage of the six-day temporary use of plates provision for six days from the date of purchase, after which you must obtain a new permit from the Ministry of Transportation. In general, a dealer will do this as a courtesy for a new owner, although this ability to obtain a permit in the name of someone else is a cause for some concern. During the six-day period, you are required to carry the plate portion of the old permit, a bill of sale, or a copy of the lease in lieu of the vehicle portion of the permit, since this car, because it is new, has never had a permit. No safety certificate is required because the car is new.

TRANSFERRING PLATES FROM A VEHICLE YOU PREVIOUSLY OWNED TO A USED VEHICLE THAT YOU HAVE JUST BOUGHT Where you have sold one vehicle and then bought or leased a used vehicle, you *can* take advantage of the six-day temporary use of plates provision for six days from the date of purchase, at which time you must obtain a new permit from the Ministry of Transportation. During the six-day period, you are required to carry the plate portion of the old permit, the vehicle portion of the permit, and a valid safety standards certificate.

TRANSFERRING PLATES BY A DEALER SELLING A "DEMO" MODEL WITH REGULAR, RATHER THAN DEALER, PLATES TO ANOTHER VEHICLE THAT THE DEALER BOUGHT IN THE LAST SIX DAYS If you are a dealer, you cannot do this because dealers or other persons entitled to use "dealer" plates are not entitled to take advantage of the six-day temporary use of plates provision. In this case, the dealer would have to apply for a new permit authorizing the use of plates on the car before it can be operated on the highway.

Plate and Permit Offences

Section 12(1) of the HTA sets out several offences involving the unlawful use of plates and permits. A person may be arrested for offences under s. 12 without a warrant. If a person is convicted of a s. 12 offence, he or she is liable to a fine of between $100 and $1,000, to imprisonment for not more than 30 days, or both a fine and imprisonment. In addition, the convicted offender may have his or her licence suspended for up to six months.

Defacing or Altering Plates or Permits, Section 12(1)(a)

It is an offence to alter or deface any number plate, permit, or valtag.

Use of Defaced Plates or Permits, Section 12(1)(b)

In addition to altering or defacing, use of an altered or defaced number plate, permit, or valtag is prohibited.

Unauthorized Removal of Number Plate, Section 12(1)(c)

It is an offence to remove a number plate from a vehicle or a trailer without the authorization of the permit holder. This offence is commonly related to the theft of a number plate.

Use of Unauthorized Number Plate, Section 12(1)(d)

It is an offence to use or permit the use of a number plate on a vehicle other than the number plate authorized for use on that vehicle. This section can be invoked to charge someone who abuses the six-day temporary use rule.

Unauthorized Use of Valtag, Section 12(1)(e)

It is an offence to use or permit the use of a valtag on a number plate displayed on a motor vehicle that is not the valtag furnished by the ministry for that vehicle.

Use of Valtag or Plate Contrary to the HTA and Regulations, Section 12(1)(f)

Anyone who uses or permits the use of a number plate or valtag other than in accordance with the HTA and the regulations is guilty of an offence. This provision can be invoked for any future amendments to the legislation or for amended or new regulations.

Seizure of Evidence of a Section 12 Offence, Section 14(1)

This section authorizes the seizure of evidence of an offence under s. 12(1). It says that a police officer may seize the number plate, valtag, or permit, and retain it until the facts in issue have been determined if the officer has reason to believe that a number plate, valtag, or permit

◆ is not authorized for that vehicle,

◆ was obtained by false pretences, or

◆ is defaced or altered.

This means that the items seized may be held until the trial has ended and the time for launching an appeal has elapsed. If an appeal is launched, the items may be held until the appeal is dismissed.

VEHICLE CLASSES

Motor vehicle classes for vehicles other than passenger automobiles are determined by passenger capacity, purpose, or weight, in the case of buses, and by weight, in all other types of commercial vehicles. These classifications are then used to determine the type of vehicle permit required and the class of licence that an operator must possess to operate a motor vehicle for each class.

Buses—Classed by Passengers

A motor vehicle is a bus if it has at least 10 permanent passenger seats. Buses with more than 24 passenger seats are a different class of motor vehicle than buses with 24 or less passenger seats. The two types of buses require different skills to operate and, therefore, require different driver's licences. The main reasons for differentiating between "big" and "little" school-purposes buses is simply to ensure that school-purpose bus drivers have been criminally screened.

Buses—Classed by Weight When it Does Not Have Passengers

A vehicle is not considered a bus for the purpose of driver's licence requirements unless the bus has at least one passenger. If there are no passengers on board, the weight of the bus is used to determine the class of driver's licence required by the driver. If, for example, a school bus carrying no passengers on a highway weighs only 9000 kg, the driver needs only a class G driver's licence to drive the bus lawfully on the highway. If a large bus carrying no passengers on a highway weighs 17 000 kg, the driver needs a class D driver's licence to drive the bus on the highway lawfully.

Weights and Vehicle Classes

The **towed weight** is the weight of the trailer and its load. The **gross weight** of a trailer and its load can be determined only by weigh scales of the type that you see on 400-class highways.

The **total weight** is determined from *either* the gross weight of the motor vehicle, trailer, and load *or* the **registered gross weight** of the motor vehicle, whichever is more. The registered gross weight is printed on the

towed weight
the weight of the trailer and its load

gross weight
the total weight of the motor vehicle, its trailer, and the load it is carrying; can be determined only by weigh scales

total weight
determined from either the gross weight of the motor vehicle, trailer, and load or the registered gross weight of the motor vehicle, whichever is more

registered gross weight
the weight of the vehicle and the load set out in the motor vehicle permit; the owner has prepaid the government to have the legal right to haul loads of that size in that vehicle on the highway

permit for commercial motor vehicles. This is the weight for which the owner has prepaid the government for hauling loads on the highway—a form of tax for highway carriers to defray the cost of repairing the damage caused to the roadway by heavy commercial vehicles. The registered gross weight is used to determine the class of the motor vehicle, even if it is empty and weighs far less than the registered gross weight. If the truck is loaded, and the actual gross weight according to the weigh scales exceeds the registered gross weight, the larger weight is used to determine the motor vehicle class, and the driver or owner can be fined for exceeding the weight for which he or she has prepaid. The registered gross weight allows enforcement officers to determine the class of motor vehicle simply by checking the permit.

The registered gross weight always applies to a motor vehicle, not a trailer. The registered gross weight for a truck tractor (the tractor of a tractor-trailer combination) will always exceed 11 000 kg because of the size it needs to be to pull heavy loads. This means that even when the truck tractor is being operated independently without a trailer, the registered gross weight will exceed 11 000 kg, and the driver in this case would need a class D driver's licence. The moment that the driver hooks the trailer onto his vehicle, the total weight of the trailer and its load must be considered. The permit for the trailer has the empty vehicle weight printed on it. If the empty weight of the trailer is not more than 4600 kg, the driver still only needs a class D driver's licence. When the trailer is loaded so that the total weight of the trailer and its load exceeds 4600 kg, the driver needs a class A driver's licence. See figure 3.5.

VEHICLE CLASS DESCRIPTION, O. REG. 340/94, S. 2(1), TABLE

Class A

A class A vehicle is any combination of a motor vehicle and towed vehicles, where the towed vehicles exceed a total gross weight of 4600 kg. This does not include a bus carrying passengers.

Class B

A class B vehicle is a school-purposes bus with a designed seating capacity of more than 24 passengers.

Class C

A class C vehicle is a bus with a designed seating capacity of more than 24, but not a school-purposes bus carrying passengers.

Class D

A class D vehicle is a motor vehicle that exceeds 11 000 kg total gross weight or registered gross weight *or* any combination of a motor vehicle

∎   **Figure 3.5   Vehicle Class Categorized by Passenger Carrying and by Weight**

Basis for classification	Vehicle class
Passenger capacity *If the vehicle is not actually carrying passengers, the basis for classification is weight.*	
Up to 24 passengers	E (Board of education)
	F (First aid and few)
More than 24 passengers	B (Board of education)
	C (Coaches and city buses)
Weight	
Up to 4600 kg towed weight	
Up to 11 000 kg total weight	D (Dump trucks)
More than 11 000 kg total weight	G (General vehicles)
More than 4600 kg towed weight	A (Allied Van lines)

exceeding 11 000 kg total gross weight or registered gross weight and towed vehicles not exceeding a total gross weight of 4600 kg. This does not include a bus carrying passengers that otherwise might fit the class D definition.

Class E

A class E vehicle is a school-purposes bus with a designed seating capacity of 24 passengers or less.

Class F

A class F vehicle is any ambulance or any bus with a seating capacity of not more than 24 passengers that is not a school-purposes bus carrying passengers.

Class G

Class G vehicles include the following:

◆   Any motor vehicle, including a motor-assisted bicycle (but not a motorcycle), that weighs less than 11 000 kg gross weight or registered gross weight.

◆   Any combination of a motor vehicle not exceeding a total gross weight or registered weight of 11 000 kg and a towed vehicle not exceeding a total gross weight of 4600 kg.

However, class G motor vehicles do not include a motorcycle, an ambulance when it is providing ambulance service under the *Ambulance Act*, or a bus when it is carrying passengers, even though these vehicles might otherwise fall within the weight limits that would make them class G vehicles.

Class D and G tow trucks consider the towed vehicle. A class D tow truck is one that, together with a towed vehicle with a total gross weight of less than 4600 kg, has a total gross weight or registered gross weight of more than 11 000 kg. A class G tow truck is one that has a total gross weight or registered gross weight of less than 11 000 kg. A class G tow truck keeps its class regardless of the weight of the towed vehicle. Generally, a towed vehicle weighing more than 4600 kg would require a driver with an A licence if the towed vehicle weight were taken into account (O. reg. 304/94, s. 2(2)).

A motor vehicle with a designed seating capacity of not more than 11 passengers would normally be a class F vehicle (small bus). However, if it is used for personal transportation without compensation, it is treated as a class G vehicle (O. reg. 304/94, s. 2(5)). See figure 3.6.

DRIVER'S LICENCES

In this section, we discuss the requirements for various classes of driver's licences, and what motor vehicles can be driven by a person with a particular class of licence.

Graduated/Restricted Licences—G1, G2, G, and M1, M2, M[1]

G1 Driver's Licence

Ontario now has a "graduated" system for obtaining a G licence. An individual must first obtain a G1 licence, then a G2 licence, before graduating to the final class G licence. In order to obtain a G1 licence, the applicant must pass a written test. Once he or she obtains the G1, the person may drive a class G motor vehicle (passenger car, van, or light truck) when accompanied by a driver with at least four years of driving experience and who is licensed to drive a class G vehicle. This accompanying driver must ride in the front passenger's seat beside the G1 driver. The back seat may hold as many passengers as there are seat belts for them.

A G1 driver must remain at that level for 12 months before he or she can graduate to the G2 level. However, if the G1 driver takes a recognized driver-education course, this period can be reduced by 4 months.

There are restrictions that apply to G1 drivers that do not apply to G drivers in general (O. reg. 340/94, s. 5). Drivers generally must have a blood alcohol level of less than .08 percent. However, a G1 driver must have a blood alcohol level of zero, and the accompanying driver must have a blood alcohol level that is less than .05 percent. G1 drivers also are prohibited from driving between midnight and 5 a.m. Also, they may not drive on any 400-series highway with a posted speed of more than 80 km/h. In addition, a G1 driver may not drive on any urban expressways.

■ **Figure 3.6   What Class of Driver's Licence Is Required by the Driver of These Vehicles?**

2000 kg   500 kg   1200 kg   800 kg

10 000 kg   5000 kg   15 000 kg   6000 kg

10 000 kg   3000 kg   8000 kg   4000 kg

12 000 kg   3000 kg

Procedure:

1. If the towed weight is more than 4600 kg,
    a class A licence is required.
2. If the towed weight is not more than 4600 kg,
    the total weight is considered.
3. If the total weight is more than 11 000 kg,
    a class D licence is required.
4. If the total weight is not more than 11 000 kg,
    a class G licence is required.

These include the QEW, the Don Valley Parkway, the Gardiner Expressway, the EC Row Expressway, and the Conestoga Expressway, except if accompanied by a licensed driving instructor.

In order to progress to the G2 class, the G1 driver must pass a road test. A driver who passes the G2 test enters that level and remains there for a minimum of 12 months. Like the G1, the driver's blood alcohol level must be zero. The G2 driver, however, may drive alone and without an accompanying qualified class G driver. The G2 driver may have as many passengers as there are operable seat belts provided in the vehicle. After 12 months, the G2 driver may take a comprehensive road test and obtain the G licence. The G2 driver has five years from the time he or she obtained the G1 licence to take the comprehensive road test for the G licence. If the person does not apply to take the test within five years of obtaining the G1 licence, he or she must start over again and apply for a G1 licence.

THE GRADUATED G LICENCE SYSTEM

G1 ⟶ G2 ⟶ G
written test   road test comprehensive   road test

The only differences between a class G and a class G2 licence are that for the G2 licence,

◆ the driver's blood alcohol concentration must be zero, and

◆ the number of passengers must be limited to the number of operable seat-belt assemblies.

Once the basic G class licence has been obtained, a class G driver can drive a class G motor vehicle, which includes

◆ any motor vehicle, including a motor-assisted bicycle (but not a motorcycle), that weighs less than 11 000 kg gross weight or registered gross weight; and

◆ any combination of a motor vehicle not exceeding a total gross weight or registered weight of 11 000 kg and a towed vehicle where the towed vehicles do not exceed a total gross weight of 4600 kg.

However, class G motor vehicles do not include motorcycles, ambulances when they are providing ambulance services under the *Ambulance Act*, or buses when they are carrying passengers, even though these vehicles might otherwise come within the weight limits that would make them class G vehicles (O. reg. 340/94, s. 2(1), table).

G2 drivers may drive any class G vehicle, except one equipped with air brakes, which requires training and a test.

G1 drivers may drive any class G vehicle, except heavy farm vehicles used by farmers for personal use transportation and for shipping and moving their crops to market; these vehicles usually have "farm" number plates. Such heavy vehicles would usually be class D, but if used for farm purposes, are deemed to be G. However, these vehicles do not include large combines and harvesters that are driven on a highway, because these are considered self-propelled implements of husbandry and are not defined as motor vehicles. This means that, despite such a vehicle's size, a driver need not have a driver's licence of any kind to operate it on the highway (O. reg. 340, s. 2(3)).

Class F vehicles—such as paddy wagons operated by police officers and ambulances—are deemed to be class G vehicles when they are not carrying passengers and being used as paddy wagons or ambulances. But G1 drivers may *not* drive them when they are being used as paddy wagons or ambulances (O. reg. 340/94, s. 2(3) and (4)).

Although a class G driver is limited in the vehicles he or she may drive, a class G driver can learn to drive any other class of vehicle as long as he or she is accompanied by a driver who is licensed to drive that particular class of vehicle.

M1 Driver's Licence

Anyone who wishes to drive a motorcycle must obtain a class M licence. Much like the class G licence, the M licence is also a graduated system; the driver must obtain the M1 and then the M2 before obtaining the M licence. To obtain the M1 licence, the applicant must pass a written test that will permit the applicant to learn to drive a motorcycle only. An M1 licence lasts for a minimum of 60 days and is valid for only 90 days. This means that the licence holder cannot take the road test for the M2 for at least 60 days from the date that the M1 was issued, even if the licence holder has taken a motorcycle safety course. However, the licence holder must take the test within 90 days; if he or she does not, the licence holder must apply for an M1 licence again.

There are specific operating conditions for M1 drivers (O. reg. 340/94, s. 7). The driver

◆   cannot carry any passengers on the motorcycle;

◆   must have a blood alcohol level of zero;

◆   must drive the motorcycle only during daylight hours (one half hour before sunrise to one half hour after sunrise);

◆   cannot drive on highways with speed limits in excess of 80 km/h, except highways 11, 17, 61, 71, 101, 102, 144, and 655; and

◆   must pass a road test to progress to the M2 licence.

M2 Driver's Licence

Once the driver has passed the road test, he or she progresses to the M2 level, where he or she must remain for a minimum of 22 months. This period may be reduced to 18 months if the M2 licence holder completes an approved motorcycle safety course, which can be taken at any time while the driver is classed as an M1 or M2 licence holder.

The nighttime driving restriction is lifted for M2 drivers, but the M2 driver must have a blood alcohol level of zero. Once the driver has completed the minimum M2 licence period, he or she may take a comprehensive road test to qualify for a class M licence.

Holders of an M2 driver's licence can also drive a class G motor vehicle under the conditions that apply to a class G1 driver's licence.

Once an M2 driver has passed the road test and has become an M licence holder, he or she may lawfully drive any motorcycle and may also drive a class G vehicle under the conditions that apply to a class G1 driver.

RELATIONSHIP BETWEEN CLASS M AND G LICENCES

M1 ⟶ M2 ⟶ M
M2 = G1
M = G1

Duration of Graduated Driver's Licences

G1 Lasts a minimum of 12 months (8 months, if lessons taken) and a maximum of 5 years.

G2 Lasts a minimum of 12 months and is valid for the remainder of the five-year period for which the G1 licence was valid.

M1 Lasts a minimum of 60 days and a maximum of 90 days.

M2 Lasts a minimum of 22 months (18 months, if lessons taken) and a maximum of 5 years.

Penalties for Violating Conditions of a Graduated M or G Licence

If a person is convicted of violating the conditions of the graduated licence system, he or she will be notified that his or her driver's licence has been suspended. The suspension will last for 30 days from the date that the licence is surrendered or 2 years from the date the licence is suspended if it is not surrendered.

The graduated system described here replaced the "learner" system that existed before 1994. It now takes much longer to obtain an unrestricted licence, and there are more restrictions on level 1 and 2 drivers than there were on learners. Although there have been some problems with the graduated system—long waits for road tests, for example—there is evidence that jurisdictions using graduated licensing systems boast a reduction in collisions among young drivers. The graduated system had a policy aim to reduce collisions among young drivers, but the reduction in collisions has been across the spectrum of drivers, regardless of age.

Non-Graduated Driver's Licences

Once a driver has obtained a G licence, he or she may go on to obtain other licences to drive other classes of vehicles. There is no graduated system for these licences; the only requirement is that a learner have an accompanying driver with a class of licence for driving that class of vehicle. For example, a person seeking a class A licence must have a person with a valid class A licence with him or her while driving a class A vehicle.

Class A Licence

A driver with this licence may drive

a class A vehicle, which is any combination of a motor vehicle and towed vehicles where the towed vehicles exceed a total gross weight of 4600 kg, but does not include a bus carrying passengers (which requires a B, C, E, or F driver's licence, depending on the size of or purpose of the bus; or

a class D and G vehicle (O. reg. 340/94, s. 2(1) table).

Class B Licence

A driver with this licence may drive

any school-purposes bus with a designed seating capacity of more than 24 passengers; and

any class C, D, E, F, and G vehicle.

Class C Licence

A driver with this licence may drive

any bus with a designed seating capacity of more than 24, except a school-purposes bus carrying passengers; and

any class D, F, and G vehicle.

Class D Licence

A driver with this licence may drive

◆ a motor vehicle that exceeds 11 000 kg total gross weight or registered gross weight;

any combination of a motor vehicle exceeding 11 000 kg total gross weight or registered gross weight and towed vehicles not exceeding a total gross weight of 4600 kg; and

◆   any class G vehicle.

However, a D licence holder may not drive a bus carrying passengers that otherwise might fit the class D definition. A bus that weighs over 11 000 kg cannot be classified as a class D vehicle once a passenger climbs aboard. Now the driver requires the appropriate bus licence.

Class E Licence

A driver with this licence may drive

◆   any school-purposes bus with a designed seating capacity of 24 passengers or less, and

◆   any class F or G vehicle.

Class F Licence

A driver with this licence may drive

◆   any ambulance;

◆   any bus with a seating capacity of not more than 24 passengers; and

◆   any class G vehicle.

However, an F licence holder may not drive a school-purposes bus carrying passengers.

Air Brakes

The Z endorsement on any class of driver's licence authorizes the holder of the licence to drive the class of vehicle he or she is otherwise permitted to drive if it is equipped with air brakes. The endorsement is not a separate class of licence; rather, it is in addition to the existing class of driver's licence. For example, the holder of a D licence who obtains an air-brake endorsement will receive a DZ licence, showing that he or she can drive a class D vehicle equipped with air brakes. To obtain a Z endorsement, the applicant must attend classroom instruction and pass an examination.

There is an easy way to calculate all the classes of motor vehicles that a driver is legally licensed to drive on a highway in Ontario: the "Big Eddie" acronym, set out in the box on the following page.

The "Big Eddie" acronym is used to help remember the order of the right-hand column.

To calculate all the classes of motor vehicles that a driver is legally licensed to drive on a highway in Ontario, use the two columns above with the system that follows:

THE "BIG EDDIE" ACRONYM

A	B	(Big)
B	E	(Eddie)
C	C	(Can)
D	F	(Fool)
E	A	(All)
F	D	(Dumb)
G	G	(Guys/Girls)

1. Note the class of driver's licence in the driver's possession.

2. Locate the letter that denotes the class of driver's licence in both of the above columns.

3. Lay your pen so that it joins the same letter in both columns.

4. The driver can legally drive the class of motor vehicle for which he or she is licensed and any *pair of letters* below the pen.

EXAMPLE OF HOW TO USE THE "BIG EDDIE" TECHNIQUE

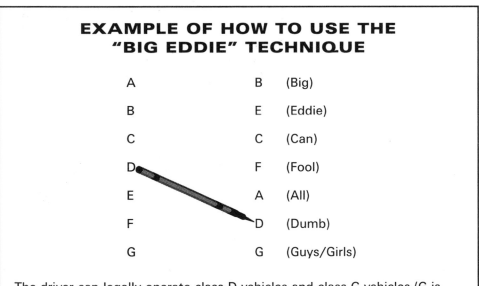

A		B	(Big)
B		E	(Eddie)
C		C	(Can)
D		F	(Fool)
E		A	(All)
F		D	(Dumb)
G		G	(Guys/Girls)

The driver can legally operate class D vehicles and class G vehicles (G is the only *pair* of letters below the pen).

Despite the class limits on licences, any class of "Big Eddie" licence (B, E, C, F, A, D, and G) is authority for a police officer to drive any class of motor vehicle, including those equipped with air brakes, except for a motorcycle, on a highway in an emergency in the course of his or her duty. For example, a police officer is allowed to drive a large bus in an emergency with a class G licence. Similarly, a mechanic is also permitted this liberty while road testing a vehicle in the course of servicing it. Again, motorcycles are excluded.

The "Top" Licence

The holder of a class ABMZ driver's licence can drive any motor vehicle on the highway.

Driver's Licence Offences, HTA, Section 32

Once a licence is issued, in addition to driving within the licence restrictions, the licence holder is required to have the licence in his or her possession when driving, and to surrender it for inspection by a police officer or other designated person.

Section 32(1) says that no person shall drive a motor vehicle on a highway unless the motor vehicle is within a class of motor vehicles for which the person holds a valid driver's licence. If a licence holder is convicted of driving a class of vehicle that he or she is not entitled to drive, he or she is subject to a fine of not less than $200 and not more than $1,000. If a streetcar is driven on a right of way that is on a highway, even though it is not a motor vehicle within the HTA definition, the operator must, nevertheless, have a driver's licence (HTA, s. 32(2)).

Section 33(1) requires every driver of a motor vehicle or streetcar to carry a driver's licence at all times while in charge of a motor vehicle, and to surrender it for reasonable inspection on the demand of a police officer or an officer appointed for carrying out the provisions of the HTA. If a person is unable or refuses to surrender his or her driver's licence in accordance with s. 33(1) or (2), he or she shall give reasonable identification of himself or herself, and, for the purposes of s. 33(3), the correct name and address shall be deemed to be reasonable identification. Failure to comply with s. 33(3) can lead to an arrest.

If a citizen is driving a motor vehicle on a highway, the citizen is lawfully required to identify himself or herself if a police officer demands this information. This is one of the few instances when a citizen is lawfully required to identify himself or herself to a police officer. If an officer asks the person to identify himself or herself and the person tells the officer orally who he or she is, the officer cannot arbitrarily decide that the driver is not who he or she claims to be. The officer must have reasonable proof that the person is lying in order to arrest the person. This proof may require some investigation. Remember that the citizen has the right to remain silent and is not obliged to answer these investigative questions, and refusal to answer the questions is not proof that the person is lying. The refusal may lead to suspicion, but the officer needs more than suspicion for grounds to make an arrest.

If the driver is arrested, he or she is released once the correct identification has been obtained. With the name and address, the driver can be given a ticket for failing to surrender his or her driver's licence and for failing to identify himself or herself.

**ARREST AUTHORITY:
NOT HAVING OR SURRENDERING A
LICENCE OR NOT IDENTIFYING YOURSELF**

◆ A person *cannot* be arrested for failing to have or failing to surrender a driver's licence, but a person can be charged.

◆ a person *can* be arrested for failing to identify oneself after failing or refusing to surrender his or her driver's licence.

The authority to arrest is for failing to identify, and is intended to secure the person until he or she can be identified.

Authority for Use of Non-Ontario Plates and Licence

The issuance of Ontario plates and licences is tied to provincial residents. Residents of the province only may apply for vehicle permits and licences. Non-residents may, in general, drive vehicles on Ontario highways for limited periods of time. For these purposes, s. 15 (plates) and s. 34 (permits) of the HTA distinguish between residents of another province and residents of another country. The non-resident exemptions and conditions are set out in figure 3.7.

Non-Resident Exemptions and Reverse-Onus Requirements

Since the early applications of the *Canadian Charter of Rights and Freedoms* to criminal or quasi-criminal proceedings, the accused is no longer required to prove anything under a reverse-onus requirement in a statute, because reverse-onus rules have been held to be contrary to the Charter. An example of a reverse-onus clause in criminal law follows: in circumstances where the Crown proved that a person was inside premises unlawfully, the accused is presumed to have been there for the purpose of committing an indictable offence. It is then up to the accused to prove that he or she was not there for the purpose of committing an indictable offence. Under the Charter, however, the Crown must now prove every element of the offence, without the accused having to prove that he or she had not done something. This is described as the accused's right.

However, s. 47(3) of the *Provincial Offences Act* (POA) places the burden of proof on the accused to show that an exemption under ss. 15 and 34 of the HTA operates in his or her favour. Although this is clearly a reverse-onus clause, the courts in Ontario have accepted that driving is a privilege, rather than a right, so the reverse-onus provision is deemed lawful. This means that a driver in Ontario is presumed to require an Ontario driver's licence and Ontario number plates and that the onus is on the person to prove entitlement to the exemptions in ss. 15 and 34.

Figure 3.7 — Non-Resident Plate and Licence Exemption   *Know for Exam*

Authority to drive in Ontario

	With out-of-province plates (section 15)		With out-of-province driver's licence (section 34)	
	Non-Ontario resident	New Ontario resident	Non-Ontario resident	New Ontario resident
From other province	One who resides in another province and who does not reside in or carry on a business in Ontario for more than six consecutive months in a calendar year.	One who no longer resides in another province and is a new resident of Ontario must obtain Ontario plates within 30 days. (Needs S.S.C.)	One who resides in another province and who is at least 16 years old and has a valid driver's licence from that province can use his or her driver's licence so long as it is valid.	One who no longer resides in another province and is a new resident of Ontario must obtain an Ontario driver's licence within 60 days.
From other country	One who resides in another country and who does not reside in or carry on a business in Ontario for more than three months in a calendar year.	One who no longer resides in another country and is a new resident of Ontario must obtain Ontario plates within 30 days. (Needs S.S.C.)	One who resides in another country and who is at least 16 years old and has a valid driver's licence from that country can use his or her driver's licence in Ontario for no more than three months in a calendar year.	One who no longer resides in another country and is a new resident of Ontario must obtain an Ontario driver's licence within 60 days.

CHAPTER SUMMARY

This chapter deals with the law and procedures for issuing motor vehicle permits, plates, and driver's licences, and outlines related offences under the HTA. The classification of motor vehicles is explained in the context of both issuing vehicle permits and determining the restrictions on the type of vehicle a licence holder can drive on the highway. Permits are either limited and restricted—in circumstances where a vehicle is being transferred to a new owner—or non-restricted and permanent. The class of permit required depends on the type of vehicle, and permit classes are categorized in terms of passenger capacity, purpose or weight, in the case of buses, and weight, in the case of other commercial vehicles. The purpose of a commercial vehicle, however, sometimes alters the class into which a vehicle falls. After establishing the vehicle classes, we identify the classes of driver's licence available, noting which class of driver's licence is required for each class of vehicle. Special attention was paid to the requirements of the graduated licensing system for class G licences and vehicles. The chapter then sets out the "Big Eddie" technique for determining which vehicles a particular licence holder is permitted to drive, and discusses offences related to driver's licences.

KEY TERMS

valtag

towed weight

gross weight

total weight

registered gross weight

REVIEW QUESTIONS

■ TRUE OR FALSE

Place a "T" in the space provided if the statement is true, and an "F" if the statement is false.

_T_ 1. A 10-day permit is valid throughout the province of Ontario.

_T_ 2. A mechanic, who has been issued a dealer and service plate, is permitted to use the plate on any motor vehicle that the mechanic is repairing.

_T_ 3. Everyone who drives a motor vehicle on a highway in Ontario must have a permit for the motor vehicle and surrender the permit or a true copy at a police officer's request.

_T_ 4. The buyer of a motor vehicle must apply to the Ministry of Transportation for a new permit within six days of becoming the owner, even if the new owner does not plan to operate the motor vehicle on the highway.

_T_ 5. It is lawful to take the plates off a motor vehicle that you own and affix them to another motor vehicle of the same class that you have just purchased within six days and drive that motor vehicle on the highway as long as you carry the prescribed documents and surrender them at a police officer's request.

_F_ 6. An "in transit" permit is only issued to motor vehicle dealers.

_T_ 7. If any of the requirements for the six-day temporary use of plates are violated, the plates are not lawfully authorized for use on the vehicle and the plates can be seized and the driver arrested.

_T_ 8. It is an arrestable offence to alter both a permit and a number plate.

_T_ 9. A dealer in motor vehicles, who wishes to transport a brand-new motor vehicle to any other location in Ontario, can lawfully use a dealer and service plate or an in-transit permit.

_T_ 10. A driver with a class B driver's licence can lawfully drive any bus on a highway.

_F_ 11. The holder of a class M2 driver's licence cannot drive at night or on any road with a speed limit above 80 km/h.

_F_ 12. A driver with a class F driver's licence can lawfully drive class D and G vehicles on a highway.

_F_ 13. A school bus with a weight of 10 000 kg when empty can be lawfully driven on a highway by a driver with a class G licence if the 20-seat bus has no passengers.

F **14.** A driver with a class B driver's licence could lawfully drive a tractor-trailer combination on a highway because a class B driver's licence is the "top" licence.

F **15.** Ambulances are considered to be class F vehicles.

T **16.** Class B and E vehicles are school-purposes buses and applicants for these classes of driver's licence are criminally screened.

T **17.** A person with any class of driver's licence that is determined by weight cannot lawfully drive any bus that is transporting passengers on a highway.

F **18.** To pull a trailer lawfully on a highway with a weight of 2000 kg, a driver of a 5000 kg motor vehicle would lawfully require at least a class D driver's licence.

F **19.** The holder of a class G1 driver's licence must be accompanied by a driver with at least four years of driving experience and hold at least a G2 driver's licence.

T **20.** An M1 driver's licence is only valid for 90 days.

F **21.** The holder of an M2 driver's licence can drive any motor vehicle on any highway.

T **22.** The holder of a class M driver's licence can lawfully drive a class G vehicle under the conditions that apply to a class G1 driver's licence.

■ SHORT ANSWER

Briefly answer the following questions.

1. What are you required to do with the plates and permit of a vehicle that you are selling?

2. Where would you expect to find the valtag on a passenger vehicle? On a commercial vehicle?

3. If you are taking advantage of the six-day temporary use of plates provision, what documents must you have in your possession while driving the vehicle on the highway in the following circumstances?

   a. The car is a new car and you are the first owner.

   b. The car is a used car.

4. What are the conditions precedent that must be met to acquire the following?

   a. A 10-day permit.

   b. An "in transit" permit.

c. A dealer and service plate.

5. Explain what class of driver's licence would be required in the
following situations:

a. A Greyhound bus (seating capacity is 48) that has been hired by
a school board for a high school ski trip on a weekend.

b. A motor vehicle pulling a trailer with a weight of 5000 kg, where
the total weight of the motor vehicle and trailer is 15 000 kg.

6. Explain the circumstances in which vehicles in one class are treated
as class G vehicles for the following situations. Explain the reasons
for this reclassification.

a. The classification of a class D farm truck as a class G vehicle.

b. The classification of a class D and G tow truck as a class G
vehicle when towing a disabled vehicle.

c. The classification of a class F bus as a class G vehicle.

■ DISCUSSION QUESTIONS

1. Orestes Smith has plates that were first issued in 1978. Each time he purchased a new car, he elected to transfer the plates from the old car he sold to the new car. It is now 2000. The plates were rusting, and most of the paint had worn out. Too cheap to buy new plates, Orestes bought a can of white paint, and a can of dark blue paint. He repainted both plates, with a white background and blue numbers and letters. The blue letters are very slightly different in tone. The plates are more legible than they were prior to being repainted, although it is obvious on close inspection that they are old plates that have been repainted. A police officer sees the painted plates, and charges Orestes under s. 12(1)(a) of the HTA. Discuss the arguments in favour of, and opposed to, conviction.

2. What were the reasons for the introduction of a graduated licence system for G and M class drivers? Contrast the graduated licence system with the old L and R system. How effective is the graduated licence system in dealing with the problems that gave rise to the graduated system? (To answer this question, you may wish to examine collision statistics covering the period in which the graduated system and its predecessor operated, and do a microfilm or Internet search of a newspaper database from 1990 to the present. (Try, for example, www.theglobeandmail.com.)

NOTES

1 The regulations (O. reg. 304/94, s. 2(1), table) still describe the L, which has been replaced by the graduated G licence, and the R, which has been replaced by the graduated M licence. As the L and R licences are no longer issued, they are not discussed in this text.

CHAPTER 4

Rules of the Road

CHAPTER OBJECTIVES

After completing this chapter, you should be able to:

◆ Determine what speed limits may apply to a highway, depending on location, type or class of roadway, use of roadway, or other relevant factors.

◆ Determine the appropriate fine for a speeding offence under the HTA.

◆ Know the essential elements of speeding-related offences.

◆ Identify and understand the basic rules of the road.

◆ Identify exemptions, exclusions, and exceptions to the basic rules of the road.

◆ Understand the basis for the exemptions, exclusions, or exceptions to the basic rules of the road.

◆ Apply the rules of the road to given situations and determine whether any laws have been violated.

◆ Identify what equipment is mandatory on different classes of vehicles.

INTRODUCTION

This chapter covers the rules of the road as set out in part X of the *Highway Traffic Act* (HTA), ss. 133-191. We will also discuss the rules regulating speed that are set out in part IX, ss. 128-132, and key equipment requirements set out in part VI, ss. 61-107. Some of the statutory rules of the road also outline specific offences and their penalties.

RULES OF THE ROAD: SPEED

Speed

The standard speed on highways in less-developed areas is 80 km/h (HTA, s. 128(1)(a)(i)); in built-up areas, the limit may be 80 km/h if the highway is a controlled access highway (for example, highway 401)

(HTA, s. 128(1)(a)(ii)). However, in most built-up areas, the standard speed is reduced to 50 km/h (HTA, s. 128(1)(b)). The Ministry of Transportation may also designate part of a highway as a construction zone, and set a suitable speed for that zone. It may also set speed limits in provincial parks that are different from the standard speed limits set out in ss. 128(1)(a)-(b) (HTA, ss. 128(8), 128(7)(a)). However, local municipalities[1] may pass bylaws that take precedence over the provincially set speeds in order to set different speed limits for highways in four situations:

1. On a highway that passes through the territorial jurisdiction of the municipality (HTA, s. 128(2)), although the municipality must pick the speed limit from an array offered in HTA, s. 128(3) (40, 50, 60, 70, 80, 90, and 100 km/h).

2. Where vehicles are driven in public parks or exhibition grounds within the municipality's jurisdiction, the speed may be set by the municipality, but shall not be below 20 km/h (s. 128(4)).

3. On highways within the municipality's jurisdiction that adjoin a school entrance, the speed may be reduced to 40 km/h for 150 m on either side of the entrance between 8 a.m. and 5 p.m. when school is in session (s. 128(5)).

4. On bridges within a municipality's jurisdiction, provided that the speed shall not be less than 10 km/h.

In addition to prescribing maximum speeds on highways, the ministry may, by regulation, also prescribe speeds for different types of motor vehicles. When a municipality, under a bylaw, or the ministry, by regulation, has posted a speed for the highway, it is not valid and enforceable until the bylaw or regulation is posted and made public. But, the validity of the speed limit does not depend on the presence of, or the erection of, speed limit signs. If the bylaw or regulation is properly proclaimed and valid, the speed limit it prescribes takes precedence over the limits set out in s. 128(1)(a), and it is enforceable from that time whether or not speed limit signs have been erected.

Whatever the limit, the HTA exempts fire trucks, police vehicles, and ambulances from posted speed limits in the following circumstances (s. 128(13)):

◆ Fire trucks are only exempt when responding to a fire or emergency, not when returning from one.

◆ Police vehicles are only exempt when carrying out police duties.

◆ Ambulances are exempt only when responding to an emergency or transporting a patient in an emergency.

Remember that the exemption attaches to the *use* of the vehicle, and not merely to the vehicle itself.

Speeding Offences

Violations of s. 128, or regulations or bylaws made under its authority, may result in fines that increase progressively, depending on how much beyond the speed limit the person was driving (ss. 128(14)-(15)).

Speeding Fines

Less than 20 km over the limit	$3.00 for each km over the speed limit
Between 20 and 34 km over the limit	$4.50 for each km over the speed limit
Between 35 and 49 km over the limit	$7.00 for each km over the speed limit
50 or more km over the limit	$9.75 for each km over the speed limit and the court may also suspend the person's driver's licence for a period of up to 30 days.

These fines can be doubled if the offence occurs on a part of a highway designated as a "community safety zone" by the province or by a municipality (where the highway is under municipal jurisdiction). A community safety zone can be created under s. 214.1, where "public safety is of special concern on that part of the highway." For example, a stretch of highway where there have been frequent serious collisions due to excessive speed might attract this designation, as could a stretch of highway near a senior's residence, where risks to residents are high.

Breach of other provisions of the HTA, including most of the rules of the road in part X, will also attract doubled fines in a community safety zone (s. 214.1(1)).

Although the law is usually concerned about excessive speed, the HTA also prohibits driving a motor vehicle at "such a slow rate of speed as to impede or block the normal and reasonable movement of traffic," except where a slow rate of speed is necessary for safe operation (for example because of the weather, or where the vehicle is involved in road maintenance). How slow is slow? There is no minimum limit set, and reference should be made to the maximum speed posted and the test set out in the section (s. 132(1)): Is the driver impeding or blocking normal or reasonable traffic flow?

In addition to speeding, another broadly described offence in part IX is careless driving, which is defined as driving on a highway without "due care and attention" or "without reasonable consideration for other persons using the highway." On conviction, the driver can be liable to a fine of between $200 and $1,000 or to imprisonment for a term of up to six months or to both a fine and imprisonment. In addition, the person's licence may be suspended for up to two years. Note that there are no specific acts that constitute this offence and that it is subjectively defined. What would a reasonable person consider an act of "driving without due care and attention" or driving "without reasonable regard for other users of the highway"? A person may be charged with careless driving when the commission of another HTA offence, such as speeding, results in a collision, or in circumstances where a situation of great danger is created (s. 130).

RULES OF THE ROAD

For each section of the HTA discussed in this chapter, reference should be made to the short-form set wordings and fines in the *Provincial Offences Act* (POA) (see appendix A). The different wordings used in each section will help you understand the complexity of what is included in the section.

Direction of Traffic by Police Officer, Section 134

A police officer who is required to maintain orderly movement of traffic, to prevent injury or damage, or to deal with an emergency may direct traffic, and in the event that his or her directions conflict with the rules of the road, the officer's exercise of discretion to direct traffic takes precedence over the rules of the road. As part of the power to direct traffic, an officer may also close a portion of a highway by posting signs or traffic signalling devices, in which case no one may drive on the closed roadway except emergency vehicles. Refer to the POA wordings to appreciate all the charges within this section.

Right of Way: Uncontrolled Intersection, Section 135

Where two roads intersect and there is no traffic control sign or device, a driver approaching an intersection shall yield to a vehicle that has already entered the intersection from an adjacent highway. If both vehicles enter the intersection from adjacent highways at the same time, the vehicle on the right has the right of way over the vehicle on the left. Note that this section uses a broad definition of vehicle, but explicitly includes streetcars. See figure 4.1.

Stop-Sign Controlled Intersections, Section 136

When approaching a stop sign at an intersection, a driver is required to come to a full stop

◆ at the stop line or, if none,

◆ at a crosswalk or, if there is neither a stop line nor crosswalk, then

◆ immediately before entering the intersection.

If a driver stops on top of the stop line or crosswalk, he or she could be charged with "disobey stop sign—stop wrong place." If a driver proceeded all the way into the intersection (past the extension of the edges of the adjoining roadway), he or she should be charged with "disobey stop sign—fail to stop." The driver shall yield the right of way to traffic on the adjacent cross road that is in the intersection or so close to the intersection that to proceed would create an immediate hazard (for example, if the driver pulled out from the stop line, causing a vehicle with the right of way to brake sharply). Again, refer to the POA wordings to appreciate all the charges within this section.

■ **Figure 4.1   Right of Way—Uncontrolled Intersection**

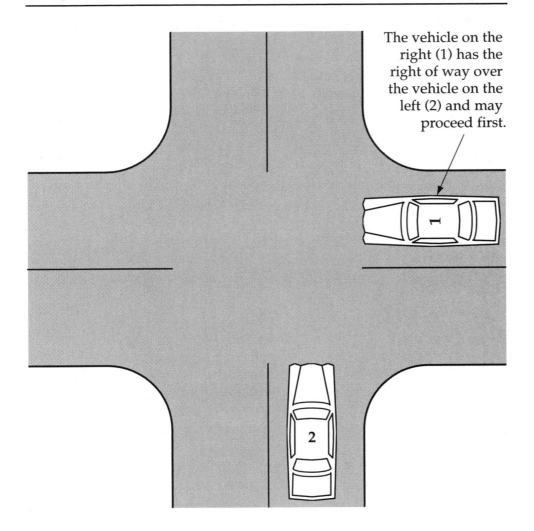

The vehicle on the right (1) has the right of way over the vehicle on the left (2) and may proceed first.

Yield Sign—Controlled Intersections, Section 138

A driver approaching an intersection controlled by a yield right-of-way sign shall slow down or stop, if necessary, in order to yield the right of way to traffic already in the intersection or so close to the intersection that failure to yield would create an immediate hazard. When entering a highway from a private road, the driver is required to yield to highway traffic whether or not the private road is controlled by a yield sign (s. 139).

Pedestrian Crossovers, Section 140

A driver shall yield to a pedestrian or person in a wheelchair if the person is proceeding in the crossover on the part of the roadway that the driver is approaching or, if the person is proceeding on the other side of the roadway, the driver must still yield and wait until the pedestrian has safely crossed the roadway.

If one vehicle is overtaking another vehicle stopped at a crossover, the driver of the overtaking vehicle shall stop before entering the crossover and yield the right of way to any pedestrian in the crossover or approaching the part of the crossover that the vehicle is about to cross, unless proceeding would not endanger the pedestrian. See figure 4.2.

If a vehicle is overtaking another vehicle that is moving within 30 m of a crossover, the overtaking vehicle shall not allow the front of the vehicle to pass beyond the front of the vehicle that is being overtaken. Because the overtaking driver's view of a pedestrian to his or her right would be obstructed both while approaching the intersection or while stopped, this rule is intended to prevent the overtaking driver from hitting a pedestrian whom he or she cannot see until it is too late to stop. On the other hand, a pedestrian or person in a wheelchair is obliged not to enter an intersection where a vehicle is so close that it is impractical or impossible for the driver to yield the right of way. Also, cyclists who wish to use a crossover must become pedestrians by dismounting and walking their bikes across the highway. See figure 4.3.

Right Turns

A driver intending to turn right must use the right-hand lane or, if there is only one lane, must move to the right of the through lane as close to the curb as possible and enter the right-hand lane of the intersecting highway as close to the right of the roadway as possible. If there is more than one lane designated as a right-hand turn lane, a driver shall approach the intersection in one of the lanes, and turn from that lane into the corresponding adjacent lane. See figure 4.4.

Left-Hand Turns, Section 141

A driver intending to turn left on a roadway—for example, to enter a private driveway—shall cross the path of vehicles approaching from the opposite direction only when it is safe to do so. It is safe as long as you do not cause an accident or an abrupt, panic reaction by drivers of approaching vehicles.

Where a driver intends to turn left at an intersection, he or she shall do so by approaching the intersection in the left-hand lane or, if there is only one lane, as close to the centre line as possible. A driver shall enter the intersection to the right of the centre line and leave the intersection in the left-hand lane marked for that use. Where the left-turn lane is not marked, the driver shall pass immediately to the right of the centre line of the intersecting highway. If there is more than one left-turn lane, the driver shall approach the intersection in one of the lanes, leave the intersection in that lane, and enter the corresponding lane of the intersecting highway. See figure 4.5.

Exception to these rules can be made for long vehicles, such as tractor trailers, that cannot make a right or left turn in the confines of the turn lanes provided. Such vehicles are deemed to be in compliance with

■ **Figure 4.2   Overtaking Stopped Vehicle at Crossover**

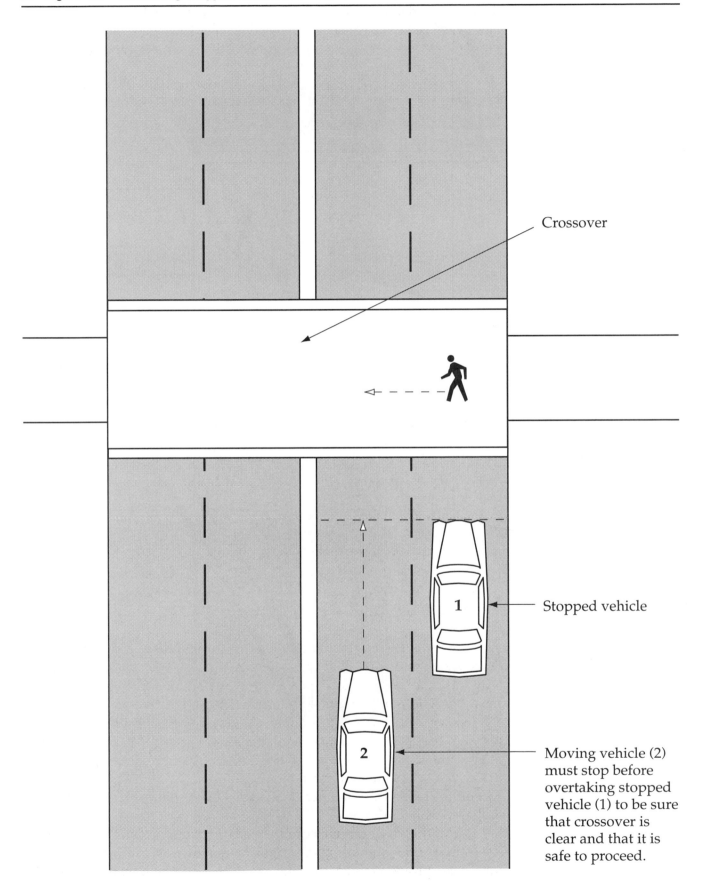

Crossover

Stopped vehicle

Moving vehicle (2) must stop before overtaking stopped vehicle (1) to be sure that crossover is clear and that it is safe to proceed.

■ **Figure 4.3   Overtaking Moving Vehicle Near Crossover**

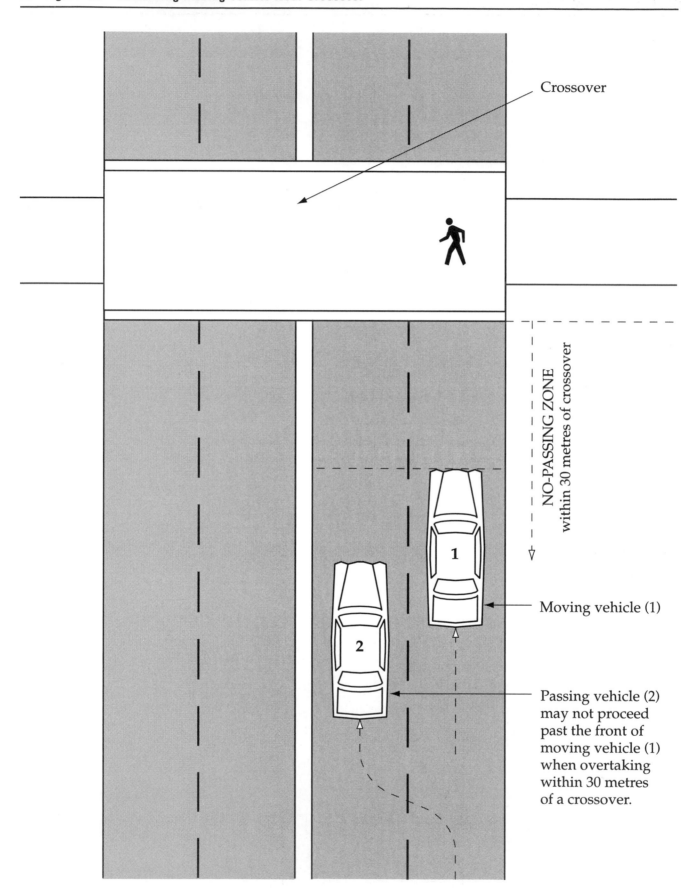

Crossover

NO-PASSING ZONE
within 30 metres of crossover

Moving vehicle (1)

Passing vehicle (2) may not proceed past the front of moving vehicle (1) when overtaking within 30 metres of a crossover.

■ **Figure 4.4 Right-Hand Turn**

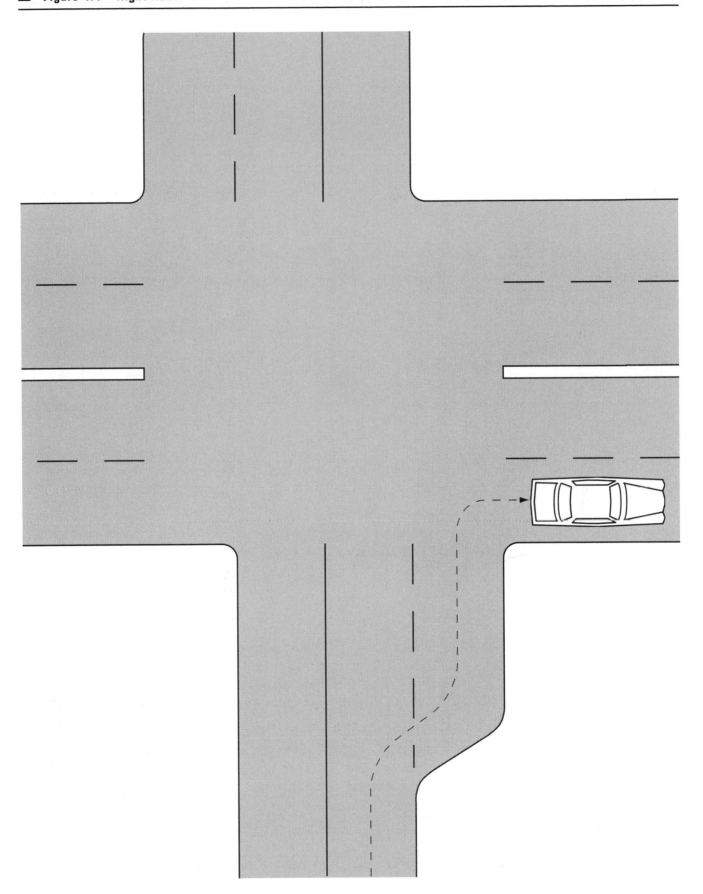

■ **Figure 4.5 Left-Hand Turn**

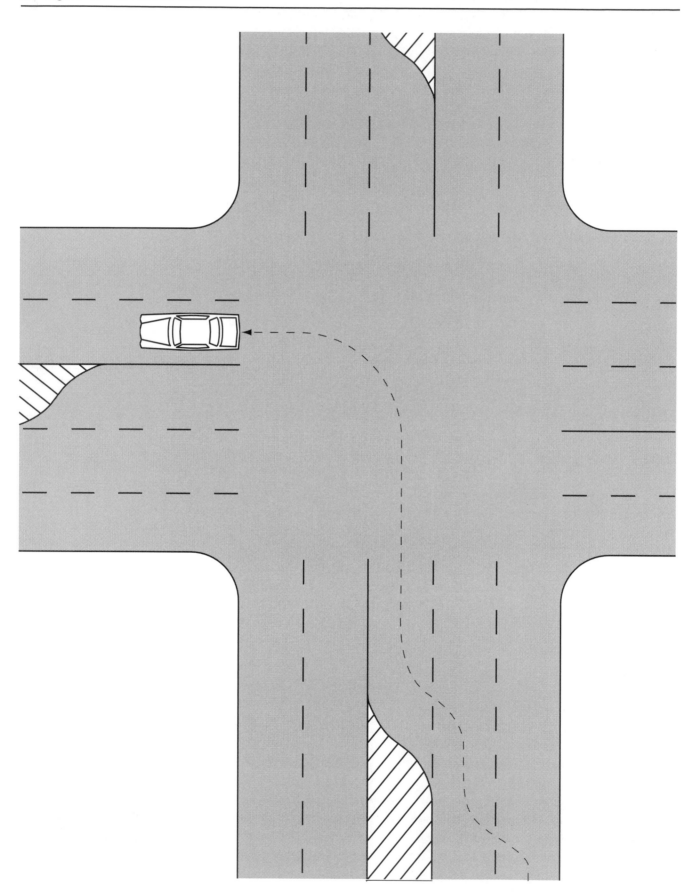

s. 141 if they comply as closely as is practicable. In reality, a long vehicle may need to make a wide right turn, moving quite far out from the curb or the right-turn lane, in order to complete the turn without running over the curb or the sidewalk. Similarly, a long vehicle may need to make a wide left turn in order to avoid sideswiping a centre-line road divider or traffic signal. See figure 4.6.

The turn rules are also relaxed for road-service vehicles, which may make right and left turns without complying with the rules if the turns can be made safely. A road-service vehicle may also proceed straight ahead through a left-turn lane, if it is safe to do so.

Signalling, Section 142

Drivers are obliged to signal right and left turns, lane changes, and exits from highways to private roads or drives, if any other vehicle might be affected by the turn or manoeuvre. In other words, drivers are not obligated to signal if no vehicle is near them. Drivers are also obliged to signal when moving onto the roadway from a parked position. Signals may be given by mechanical/electrical means or by hand signals. The hand signals for each turn are as follows:

◆   Left Turn: Extend the arm horizontally out the left side of the vehicle.

◆   Right Turn: Extend the arm upward out the left side of the vehicle.

Drivers are also obliged to indicate stops. Usually, applying the brakes activates a red or amber light on the rear of the vehicle to indicate a stop. To signal a stop using hand signals, extend the arm downward out the left side of the vehicle. The cyclist's hand signals are the same as those for motor vehicle drivers, although a cyclist may also signal a right turn by extending the right arm horizontally on the right side of the bicycle. See figure 4.7.

Yielding to Buses in Bus Bays, Section 142.1 (not yet proclaimed in force)

Drivers in a lane adjacent to a bus bay shall yield right of way to a bus leaving the bus bay and re-entering traffic when the driver of the bus has signalled his or her intention to do so. A bus driver shall not signal an intention to re-enter traffic until he or she is ready to do so, and the driver shall not re-enter the stream of traffic if a vehicle in the adjacent lane is so close that it is impractical for the driver of that vehicle to yield the right of way. At publication, this provision has not been proclaimed into force, and regulations defining "bus bay" and appropriate signs and signals have not been **gazetted** or proclaimed. Some municipal transit systems have placed signs on the rear of buses, requesting drivers in lanes adjacent to bus stops to yield the right of way to a bus signalling re-entry to the stream of traffic. These signs do not constitute a legal requirement to yield, but act as a request. See figure 4.8.

gazetted
refers to the printing of regulations in the Ontario Gazette, *at which time the regulation is presumed to be in force*

■ **Figure 4.6 Wide Turns**

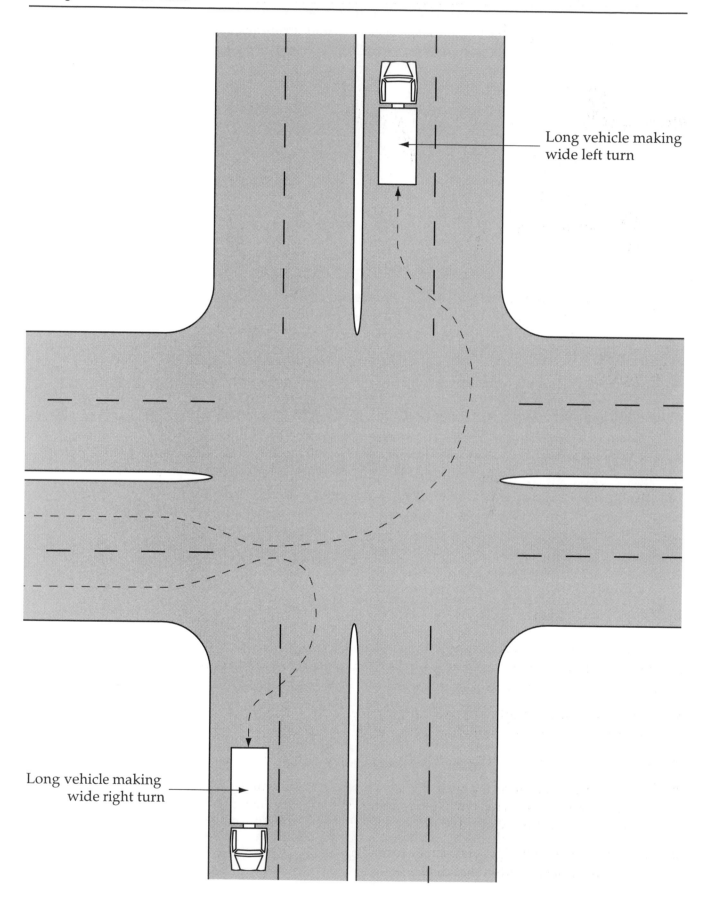

Long vehicle making
wide left turn

Long vehicle making
wide right turn

■ **Figure 4.7   Hand Signals**

Left-hand turn: Left arm straight

Stop: Left arm bent down

Right-hand turn: Left arm bent up

Right-hand turn on bicycle: Right arm straight

U-Turns, Section 143

In general, drivers may make u-turns provided that it is safe to do so and that they signal their intention to do so. However, u-turns are prohibited in the following circumstances:

◆ On a curve, where traffic approaching from either direction cannot be seen by the driver making the u-turn within a distance of 150 m.

◆ On or within 30 m of a railroad crossing (absolute prohibition).

◆ On an approach or near the crest of a grade, where the turning vehicle cannot be seen by a driver of another vehicle approaching from either direction within 150 m.

◆ Within 150 m of a bridge, viaduct, or tunnel, where the driver's view is obstructed within that distance.

■ **Figure 4.8   Yielding to Bus**

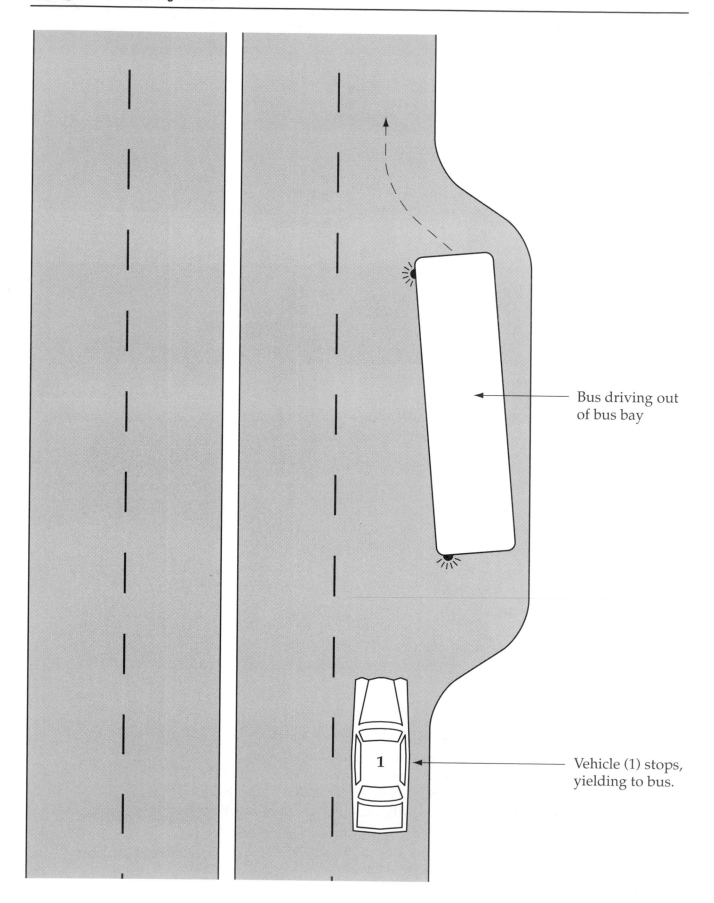

Bus driving out
of bus bay

Vehicle (1) stops,
yielding to bus.

Traffic Signals, Section 144

Where there is a traffic signal at an intersection, a driver must stop at the stop line or, if there is no stop line, before entering a crosswalk or, if there is no sign or crosswalk, immediately before entering the intersection. If there is a traffic signal that is not at an intersection, the same rules apply, except that if there is neither a sign or crosswalk, the vehicle will stop at least 5 m back from the traffic signal. See figure 4.9.

Subsections 144(2) and (3) provide that where a highway includes two roadways that are 15 m or more apart (whether or not the 15 m includes left-turn lanes), and it is crossed by an intersecting roadway, each crossing shall be considered a separate intersection. However, at publication, these subsections were not yet proclaimed in force. See figure 4.10.

When a driver is permitted to proceed, but there is a pedestrian lawfully in a crosswalk, the driver shall yield to the pedestrian in the crosswalk. For example, where the driver wishes to make a right turn on a green light and pass through a crosswalk, he or she must yield to any pedestrian lawfully walking through a crosswalk on a green signal. A driver who may turn right on a red signal must also yield to oncoming traffic in the lane he or she seeks to enter because the traffic facing a green signal has the right of way. This rule also applies to vehicles in private driveways and roadways controlled by a traffic signal where the driver faces a red signal and wishes to turn right.

Where there is a traffic signal system with different light or arrow signals for different lanes, the driver shall obey the signal for the lane he or she is in.

Green Signals

A driver approaching a green circular signal may proceed or turn left or right, unless otherwise indicated. A driver approaching a flashing green light or a solid or flashing green arrow together with a circular solid green light may proceed forward or turn left or right. If a driver is approaching a green arrow, or arrows in combination with a red or amber circular signal, the driver may proceed only in the direction indicated by the green arrows.

Amber Signals

A driver approaching an amber light shall stop his or her vehicle if he or she can safely do so; otherwise, he or she may proceed through the light with caution. Similarly, if a driver is approaching an amber arrow, he or she shall stop if it is safe to do so; otherwise, he or she may proceed with caution in the direction indicated by the amber arrow. A driver approaching a flashing amber light may proceed with caution; this light functions much like a yield sign.

■ **Figure 4.9   Traffic Signals**

Traffic signals where there is no intersection: Where to stop

1. Stop at the stop line if there is one.
2. If there is no stop line, stop at the crosswalk.
3. If there is no stop line or crosswalk, stop 5 metres back from the traffic signal.

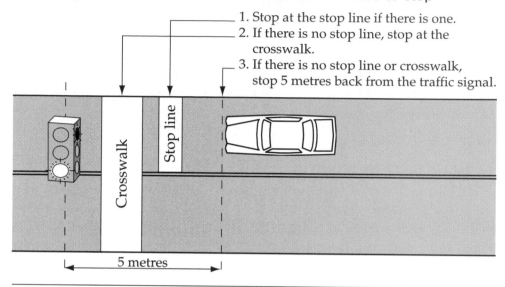

5 metres

Traffic signals at intersection: Where to stop

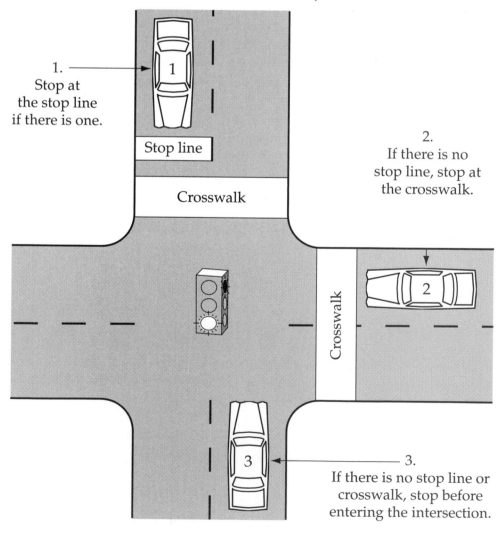

1.
Stop at
the stop line
if there is one.

Stop line

Crosswalk

2.
If there is no
stop line, stop at
the crosswalk.

Crosswalk

3.
If there is no stop line or
crosswalk, stop before
entering the intersection.

■ **Figure 4.10   Left Turn at Intersection with a Median Wider than 15 Metres**

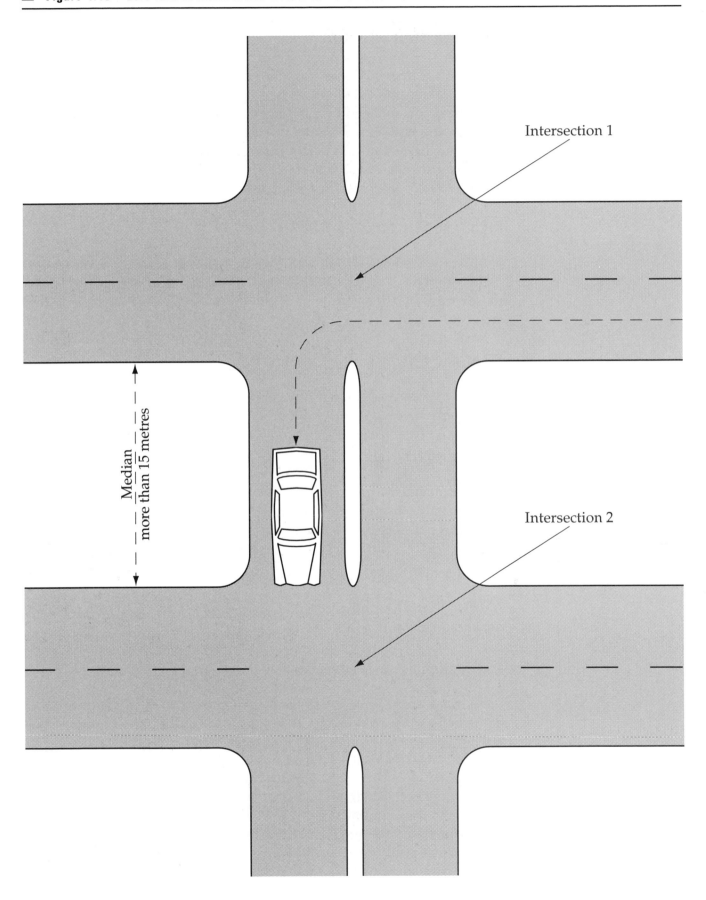

Red Signals

A driver approaching a red signal shall stop and not proceed until a green signal is shown. Anyone who violates the rule with respect to a red or amber signal is guilty of an offence under s. 144(31.2) and is liable to a fine not less than $150 and not more than $500. Sections 144(18.1)-(18.6) deal with a charge of running a red light where the evidence for the offence has been obtained by a red-light camera. In this case, a charge is issued on the basis of the camera evidence and may be laid against the owner of the offending vehicle if the driver cannot be identified. The charge must be laid under s. 144(18.1) if it is against the owner, or under s. 144(18.2) if it is against the driver.

Right and Left Turns on Red Signals

Despite the stop-on-red rule, a driver facing a red signal, who stops and yields the right of way to approaching traffic, may turn right on a red signal or turn left on a red signal from a one-way street into a one-way street. See figure 4.11.

Right and Left Turns for Transit Authority Buses

A bus driver on a scheduled route approaching a traffic signal showing a white vertical bar may turn right or left with caution.

Emergency Vehicles

A driver of an emergency vehicle as defined in the HTA—that is, the vehicle is being used in an emergency—may, after stopping, proceed through a red signal if it is safe to do so.

Flashing Red Signal

A driver shall stop and proceed with caution, treating a flashing red signal in the same way as a stop sign.

Traffic Signals and Pedestrians

Pedestrians are not free to step out on the roadway at any time or place of their choosing, even though they generally have the right of way when lawfully crossing the roadway. First, where there is a crosswalk, a pedestrian must use the crosswalk and not simply cross the road at a location of his or her own choosing. A pedestrian facing a circular green signal, a green arrow pointed straight ahead, or a "walk" sign may cross the roadway in the direction indicated. However, a pedestrian facing a flashing green signal or flashing green left-turn arrow in conjunction with a solid green signal shall not enter and cross the roadway. Nor shall a pedestrian, facing an amber or red signal or a "don't walk" signal, cross the

■ **Figure 4.11   Right and Left Turns on Red Signals**

Right turn
on red signal

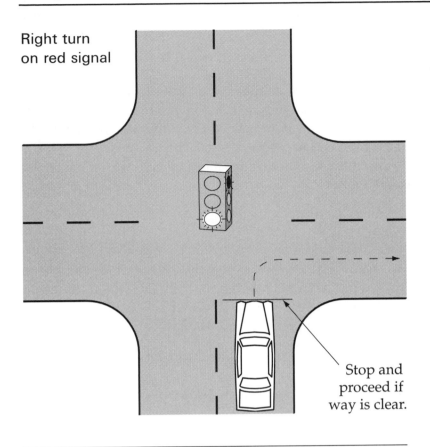

Stop and
proceed if
way is clear.

Left turn on
red signal from
one-way street
into one-way
street

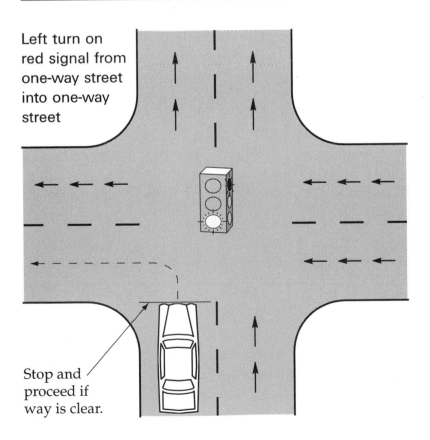

Stop and
proceed if
way is clear.

roadway. Bicyclists are prohibited from riding in a crosswalk, and must dismount and walk if they intend to use a crosswalk.

Blocking Intersections, Section 145

Municipalities may pass bylaws prohibiting drivers from entering an intersection unless "traffic in front of him or her is moving in a manner that would reasonably lead him or her to believe he or she can clear the intersection before the signal … changes to … red." The bylaw does not apply to drivers entering an intersection to make a left or right turn if the driver has signalled an intention to do that.

Slow Vehicles, Section 147

A vehicle that is travelling at a slower speed than other traffic shall keep to the right-hand lane or, if there is only one lane, as close to the right curb as possible, except where a vehicle is slowing to make a left-hand turn or overtaking another vehicle. Road-service vehicles are exempt from this rule.

Passing (Overtaking), Section 148

The HTA considers two situations involving passing vehicles: vehicles meeting head on and vehicles travelling in the same direction. In the "head on" case, each driver is expected to turn to the right of the roadway to allow each other room to pass, assuming that the road does not have well-marked lanes of adequate width. Similarly, a motor vehicle meeting a bicycle is expected to give the cyclist sufficient room to pass. If one vehicle, because of weight or load, cannot turn to the right to make room for another to pass, the driver of the first vehicle shall stop and, if necessary, assist the other vehicle to pass. This scenario might arise with an oversized or long vehicle on a narrow highway with narrow lanes and/or no hard shoulder.

equestrian
a person riding on a horse

In the case of a vehicle or **equestrian** overtaking another vehicle or equestrian, the one being overtaken is required to pull to the right in order to permit the other driver to overtake him or her. Similarly, the overtaking vehicle is obliged to pull out to the left as far as necessary to avoid collision with the other vehicle or equestrian. The vehicle being overtaken is not expected to pull off the road, but is expected to leave one-half of the roadway free, if possible. Where a vehicle is passing a bicycle, the cyclist is expected to pull to the right to let the faster vehicle pass; at the same time, the driver or equestrian overtaking is expected to pull to the left to pass safely without running the cyclist off the road.

Whenever passing, it is the responsibility of the overtaking driver to ensure that the left lane is free of traffic to permit passing and that no one is overtaking him or her.

In general, no vehicle is to be driven or operated to the left of the centre of a highway designed for two-way traffic, when passing or otherwise, in the following cases (HTA, s. 149(1)):

◆ when approaching the crest of a hill, where the driver's view is obstructed;

◆ on a curve in a roadway, where the driver's view is obstructed;

◆ within 30 m of a bridge, viaduct, or tunnel, where the driver's view is obstructed so that an approaching vehicle cannot be seen within that distance;

◆ within 30 m of a railway crossing, whether or not the view is obstructed.

There are some exceptions: highways divided into lanes, where there are more lanes in one direction than another, and one-way roads. Road-service vehicles also may be driven to the left of the centre line, provided that appropriate precautions are taken (s. 149(2)).

Passing on the Right and the Use of Shoulders, Section 150

Although passing on the right is usually prohibited, there are some circumstances where it is permitted:

◆ where the vehicle being overtaken is about to make a left turn and has signalled a left turn, and the pavement of the lane is wide enough to safely permit the manoeuvre;

◆ where a highway is designated for the use of one-way traffic.

However, no vehicle shall pull off the roadway to pass another vehicle. Remember that the roadway includes the travelled part of the pavement, but not the shoulder. There are exceptions to this rule—if the shoulder is paved, and the vehicle being overtaken has signalled and is making a left turn, passing on the right is permitted. Tow trucks responding to a police request for assistance, road-service vehicles, and emergency vehicles may also pass on the right. There is also a provision, which has not yet been proclaimed in force, that permits a person with authority, employed on a road-building machine or a road-service vehicle, to direct traffic to pass that vehicle on the right.[2]

The ministry may also designate, through a regulation and appropriate signs, any paved shoulder on a King's Highway for the use of traffic (HTA, ss. 151-152).

One-Way Traffic, Section 153

A one-way traffic lane is created by designation and by the posting of official one-way signs.

Multilane Highways, Section 154

A highway may be divided into several clearly marked lanes. A vehicle must be driven within a lane, and shall not change lanes until the driver determines that the lane change can be made safely. Where a highway is divided into three lanes, no vehicle shall be driven in the centre lane, unless the vehicle is overtaking, making a left turn, or the lane is designated and signed for the use of vehicles to travel in a particular direction. Before using the lane, a driver must be sure that the roadway is visible and clear of other traffic for a safe distance.

Any lane may be designated for a particular class of vehicles, for slowly moving traffic, or for traffic travelling in a particular direction where the lane has official signs posted (ss. 154-155).

Divided Highways, Sections 156-157

Traffic on a divided highway must stay on the roadway, and move in the direction indicated. Vehicles may not drive on the median, or cross the median to another roadway, unless a crossing has been provided. A road-service vehicle may operate off the roadway, but must stay on its side of the separation between roadways. Reversing is also prohibited on divided highways, on either the roadway or shoulder, where the maximum speed is more than 80 km/h. Emergency vehicles, road-service vehicles, and drivers reversing to render assistance to another driver are exempt from this rule.

Maintaining a Safe Distance, Sections 158-159

headway
the distance between one vehicle and another behind it

A driver of a vehicle following another vehicle is expected to maintain a safe **headway** between his or her vehicle and the vehicle in front. There is no specific rule setting out a distance in metres; rather, a driver shall have regard to speed, amount of traffic, and highway conditions. However, if the vehicle following is a commercial vehicle travelling more than 60 km/h, it must keep at least 60 m back from the vehicle in front. This rule should not to be interpreted to prevent a following vehicle from drawing closer if it is overtaking and passing another vehicle.

When an emergency vehicle approaches a vehicle from any direction, with emergency signals on, the driver is obliged to pull to the right-hand curb and stop, provided that the vehicle does not stop in an intersection. Where there is more than one lane in the same direction, the vehicle may pull to the nearest curb or side of the road and stop; this means that traffic in the left lane of a one-way highway with two lanes in the same direction, should pull to the left-hand curb. See figure 4.12.

If a driver is following a fire truck that is responding to an alarm (with its emergency signals flashing), the driver must keep back 150 m.

■ **Figure 4.12   Giving Way to Emergency Vehicle**

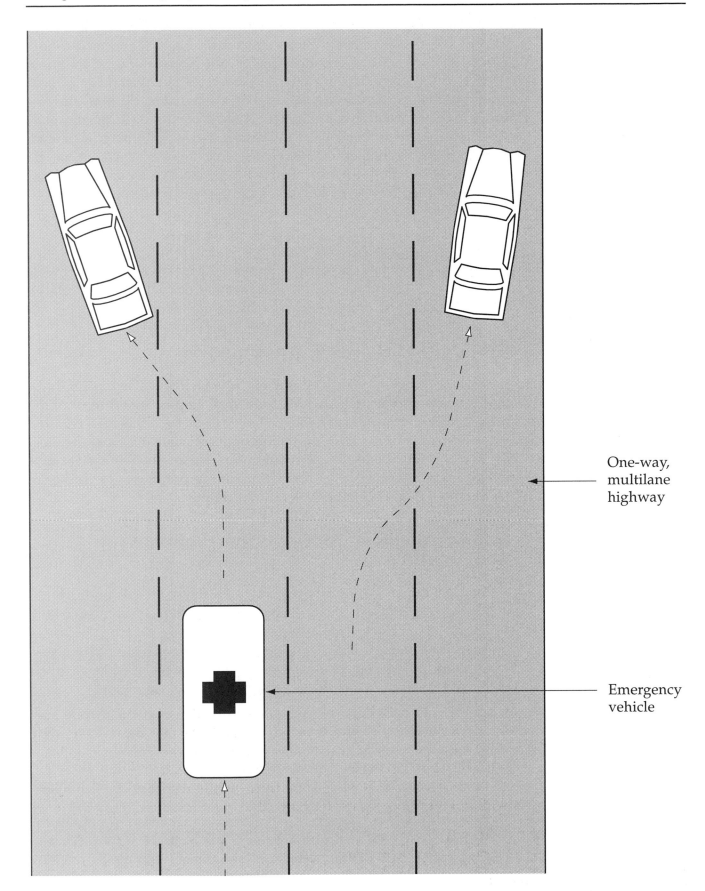

One-way, multilane highway

Emergency vehicle

Towing Other Vehicles, Sections 160-161 and 178

A vehicle may only tow one vehicle unless the towing vehicle is a commercial vehicle. This means that a sport utility vehicle, no matter how powerful, may not tow a camper trailer and a boat trailer at the same time. Nor shall any person ride as a passenger in any camper or boat trailer in tow (s. 188). Towing a person on skates, a bicycle, skis, sled, toboggan, or toy vehicle is prohibited. Also, a person on a bicycle, skis, sled, toboggan, toy vehicle, or motor-assisted bicycle may not attach themselves to, or cling to, a motor vehicle on a highway (s. 178). A bicycle that is designed for one person shall not carry more than one person, and a motor-assisted bicycle, by definition, can carry only one person.

Crowding the Driver's Seat, Section 162

A driver shall not have persons or property in the front (if a bench seat) or driver's seat that impedes the management or control of the vehicle. Note that there is no precise or explicit list of prohibitions.

Stopping at Railway Crossings, Sections 163-164

A driver approaching a railway crossing when a flagperson or signal system is warning of an approaching train shall stop at least 5 m from the nearest rail and proceed only when it is safe to do so. If there is a crossing gate or other barrier, driving around or under it while it is closed or closing is prohibited. Remember that public buses and school buses are subject to special rules regarding precautions at railroad crossings. These are set out in s. 174 and discussed later in this chapter.

Opening Vehicle Doors on the Highway, Section 165

No one shall open a door on either side of a motor vehicle on the highway before ensuring that this will not interfere with the movement of any other person or vehicle. Similarly, no one shall open a door on the side of the vehicle available to moving traffic, or keep it open longer than necessary to pick up or drop off passengers. In urban areas, it is the violation of this section that often leads to cyclists getting the "door prize."

Approaching and Passing Streetcars, Section 166

No vehicle or equestrian shall overtake a streetcar standing in the roadway for the purpose of taking on or discharging passengers. All vehicles must stop at least 2 m back from the front or rear entrance of the streetcar on the side on which passengers are disembarking, and may not resume until all passengers have boarded the streetcar or are clear of it. Where a safety zone for loading and disembarking passengers has been created by municipal bylaw, other vehicles are not required to stop. As well, no vehicle shall pass on the left any streetcar that is operating in the centre of the roadway, whether it is standing or moving, except where the streetcar is operating on a one-way street.[3] Municipal fire trucks may pass a streetcar on the left in the course of responding to an emergency.

Approaching Horses Ridden or Driven on the Highway, Section 167

The driver of a motor vehicle or motor-assisted bicycle is obliged to approach with caution an equestrian, a vehicle being drawn by a horse or other animal, or a horse being led, so as not to frighten the animal or cause injury to persons riding on the animal or in a vehicle drawn by the animal. This section is of little significance in urban areas, but is of some importance where members of some Mennonite and other Anabaptist religious communities use horses and horse-drawn wagons and carriages on highways.

Use of Headlights, Sections 168-169

When vehicle lamps are required to be lit, the driver shall use the lower beam when approaching within 150 m of an oncoming vehicle and when following within 60 m of another vehicle, except when in the act of overtaking that vehicle. Emergency vehicles and public-utility vehicles may be equipped with high beam lamps that produce alternate flashes of white light to be used when responding to an emergency.

Parking, Standing, or Stopping, Section 170

The general rule is that no vehicle shall stand, stop, or park on the roadway where it is possible to park off the roadway. If it is not possible to park off the roadway, there must be a clear view of the vehicle for 125 m in either direction. There are some exceptions to this rule:

◆   Roadways in a city, town or village, township, county, or police village that have bylaws regulating parking, standing, and stopping.

◆   Road-service vehicles, if they have parked safely.

◆   Vehicles that are so disabled that it is impossible to avoid temporarily contravening these provisions.

Parking on many highways is controlled by regulations or, in built-up areas, by municipal bylaws, so that the basic rule often does not apply. If there is a conflict between a municipal bylaw and a ministry regulation governing a stretch of roadway, the regulation will prevail. If a police officer or municipal bylaw enforcement officer with duties under the HTA finds a vehicle on the highway contravening these provisions, he or she may move the vehicle or have it towed.

A vehicle parked or standing on the highway must be secured to prevent the vehicle from being set in motion. This means that the parking brake or hand brake should be set and, if on a grade, the wheels should be blocked.

There are special safety rules for parking or standing commercial vehicles. If the highway permits a speed in excess of 60 km/h during a time when lights are required, the vehicle shall have a sufficient number of flares, lamps, or lanterns, approved by the ministry, that will display warning lights visible for 150 m for a period of eight hours. Alternatively, the vehicle may be equipped with ministry approved reflectors. If the commercial vehicle becomes disabled and is parked on the roadway where the speed is in excess of 60 km/h at a time when lights are required, the driver is required to light the lamps or lanterns or set out flares and reflectors, which shall be placed 30 m in advance of the vehicle and 30 m behind the vehicle.

In no case shall a vehicle be parked to interfere with the movement of traffic or the clearing of snow. A violation may result in a fine of between $20 and $100. However, if there is a municipal bylaw that deals with impeding traffic or clearing snow, it shall prevail over the rule in the HTA. In either case, a police officer or bylaw enforcement officer may remove the vehicle and store it in a suitable place, and the costs of doing this shall be a lien on the vehicle, enforceable like a civil debt. An unpaid lien may result in the vehicle being sold and the sale proceeds applied to pay off the debt.

Control of Tow Trucks, Section 171

As tow-truck operators can monitor police and emergency communications, several may arrive at the scene of a collision, sometimes before police and ambulances. It is not hard to imagine a collision scene, with several competing tow-truck operators attempting to sell their services. In order to make it easier for emergency crews and police to do their jobs at a collision scene, the HTA sets out some rules governing what tow-truck operators may and may not do at a collision scene on a King's Highway:

◆   No operator may make or convey an offer of towing services while the operator is within 200 m of the scene of a collision or a vehicle involved in a collision.

◆   No tow truck may park or stop within 200 m of a collision scene or a vehicle involved in a collision, if there are already enough tow trucks at the scene to tow vehicles damaged in the collision.

If the police, highway maintenance staff, a person involved in a collision, or other authorized person request the services of a tow truck, the restrictions in s. 171 do not apply. Note that s. 171 applies to King's Highways (numbered provincial highways), but not to other provincial roads or county or municipal roads. However, counties, regional governments, and municipalities may regulate the activities of tow-truck operators through licensing and bylaws. Contravention of s. 171, where it does apply, may result in fines of between $200 and $1,000 for a first offence. A subsequent offence, within five years less a day of a previous conviction, may result in a fine of between $400 and $2,000.

Racing on Highways, Sections 172-173

Drag racing and other types of motor-vehicle racing on a highway is prohibited, as is "driving … on a bet or wager." With respect to betting on a driving activity, the language is broad, and includes betting on a race and other driving activities that might draw bets, such as driving headlong at another vehicle to see which driver will "chicken out" first. A conviction for this offence carries a fine of between $200 and $1,000, and/or imprisonment for up to six months. In addition, the driver's licence may be suspended for up to two years. Note that racing bicycles does not appear to be prohibited, as the more explicit term of motor vehicles is used in defining the offence.

Racing animals by riding or driving a horse or other animal "furiously" is also explicitly prohibited. Because a horse or other animal may very well not exceed a posted speed limit, evidence of racing would consist of driving or riding the animal "furiously" at or near its apparent top speed.

Public Vehicles and School Buses at Railway Crossings, Section 174

A public vehicle is required to stop at a railway crossing that does not have gates or signal lights. The driver must look both ways, open the door to listen for a train, put the vehicle in gear, and cross the tracks without changing gears. A driver of a school bus must do the same at a railway crossing, even if the crossing is equipped with gates and signal lights.

School Bus Safe Operation, Section 175

A school bus driver who is about to stop to drop off or pick up children or developmentally delayed adults must switch on the overhead red signal lights on the bus, and, as soon as the bus is stopped, the driver must activate the school bus stop arm. These devices must remain on until all passengers who have to cross the highway to the other side or to a median strip have done so.

However, the signalling system is not to be used by the driver

◆   at an intersection controlled by traffic signals or within 60 m of it; or

◆   where there is a traffic signal, other than at an intersection, at a sign or roadway marking, indicating where a bus should stop, just before a crosswalk, within 5 m of a traffic signal, or within 60 m of the locations identified here.

Where there is a school bus loading zone, a driver must pull the bus as close to the right-hand curb of the loading zone as possible. The school bus driver need not use the stop signalling system if loading or unloading in a school bus loading zone.

Where a driver of a vehicle approaches a stopped school bus from either direction (other than at a highway separated by a median strip) with its stop signalling system on, the driver must stop before reaching the bus until the signal system is switched off or the bus moves. If a driver approaches the rear of a stopped school bus, he or she must stop at least 20 m behind the school bus. Failure to stop when required, on conviction, can result in a fine of between $400 and $2,000. For a subsequent offence committed within five years less a day of a previous conviction, a fine of between $1,000 and $4,000 may be levied.

School Crossing Guards, Section 176

A school crossing guard, about to direct children across a highway with a speed limit of not more than 40 km/h, shall display a school crossing stop sign, and a driver must stop before reaching the crossing.

Hitchhiking, Section 177

Hitchhiking is prohibited on all highways, as is stopping or attempting to stop vehicles to sell the drivers or occupants goods or services. However, if a vehicle is stopped, offering goods and services to the driver or occupants does not appear to be prohibited under the HTA, although it may be prohibited under muncipal bylaw or other legislation.

Pedestrians Walk on the Left, Section 179

Where there is no sidewalk, a pedestrian walking on the highway shall walk on the left, keeping as close to the curb as possible. This does not apply to someone walking a bicycle, if crossing to the left side of the road is impracticable. Pedestrians may also be prohibited from walking on a highway, and a police officer may require a pedestrian in a prohibited area to accompany the officer to an intersection with the nearest highway where a pedestrian is permitted (s. 185(3)).

Littering or Depositing Snow or Ice on the Highway, Sections 180-181

Anyone who litters or deposits any kind of rubbish on the highway is guilty of littering; litter is broadly defined. Similarly, no one may deposit snow or ice on the roadway without the permission of the ministry or authority responsible for maintaining the road.

Logs To Be Kept by Drivers of Commercial Vehicles, Section 190

There is a blanket requirement that drivers of commercial vehicles maintain a daily log and carry it when in charge of a commercial vehicle. The log is used to record hours of work and other working-condition matters, as prescribed by the regulations. Similarly, the regulations may exempt various types of commercial vehicle drivers from keeping a log. A log must be surrendered to a police officer on request. Violation of s. 190 or regulations made under it can lead to a fine of between $250 and $20,000 and/or to a term of imprisonment of up to six months.

VEHICLE EQUIPMENT REQUIREMENTS

Although many requirements with regard to the design and structure of a vehicle are the responsibility of manufacturers, there are some requirements that are the responsibility of the owner or driver of a vehicle. Often, when a police officer stops a motor vehicle, it is apparent that the vehicle does not meet equipment requirements or standards. In such cases, a police officer has some broad powers under HTA s. 82 to require the driver or owner of a motor vehicle, including a motor-assisted bicycle, to subject the vehicle to examination and tests as the officer sees fit (s. 82(2)). If the vehicle is found to be unsafe, it can be ordered off the highway until it is fixed. A written notice to that effect must be issued by the police officer, who also has the power to remove the plates from the vehicle (ss. 82(4)-(5)). There are similar provisions for commercial vehicles (s. 82.1). Some of the more frequently encountered equipment requirements are set out below.

Lighting Requirements, Section 62

The basic requirement is two white or amber lights in front, and one red lamp in back, to be switched on one half-hour before sunset to one half-hour after sunrise, or when fog or adverse weather reduces visibility. Lights must be visible at a distance of 150 m. In addition, front lights must be powerful enough for a driver to see a person clearly at a distance of 110 m. However, for those who would like to install banks of fog or flood lights on the front of a vehicle, the limit is four bright lights in total, including the headlights that are part of the vehicle. There are slightly different requirements for motorcycles, which must have two lamps: one white, in front, and one red, at the back. If the motorcycle has a side car, there must be two white lights in front on either side of the vehicle and one red light at the rear. The rear light on motorcycles and other motor vehicles must illuminate the number plate.

For long and wide vehicles, there are further requirements of marker lights on the side of the vehicle.

Bicycles are required to have a white or amber front light and a red tail light or reflector, visible for 150 m. The headlight does not have to cast as powerful a light as other motor vehicles do. Its primary purpose is to make the bicycle visible from the front to other road users, rather than to illuminate the roadway for the cyclist. As well, the front fork must have white reflector tape, and the rear must have red reflector tape on the rear forks.

Windshield Wipers and Mirrors, Sections 66 and 73

All motor vehicles, except motorcycles, are required to have windshield wipers. All motor vehicles must have mirrors that allow the driver to see vehicles behind him or her. Mirrors must allow a view through the rear of the vehicle, unless the driver can see behind his or her vehicle with side-view mirrors on either side of the vehicle. Windshields must be free of sight-line obstructions, such as stickers, and windshields and windows to the right or left of the driver may not be colour coated to obstruct the view of road or to conceal a view of the interior of the vehicle.

Mufflers, Section 75

All motor vehicles, including motor-assisted bicycles with internal combustion engines, must have mufflers, and the use of "cut-outs" and hollywood mufflers is expressly prohibited. Excessive noise from horns or bells on a vehicle is also prohibited.

Radar Warning Devices, Section 79

Radar warning devices are illegal and may be seized from a vehicle. No compensation is paid.

Commercial Vehicles—Wheels Becoming Detached, Section 84.1

In response to a public concern about unsafe commercial vehicles on highways, it is an offence if a wheel becomes detached from a commercial vehicle, or from a vehicle being towed by a commercial vehicle. This is a strict or absolute liability offence; an occurrence will result in a conviction, no matter how careful or diligent the accused was in checking and maintaining the wheels.

Helmets, Section 104

Motorcyclists and bicyclists must wear approved helmets while driving on a public highway, as must passengers on motorcycles under the age of 16. Parents of children under 16 shall not knowingly permit or authorize the child to ride a bicycle without a helmet.

CHAPTER SUMMARY

This chapter is designed to give the reader an overview of the rules of the road created under the HTA in part IX (speed) and part X (rules of the road), and makes further reference to some of the basic equipment requirements in part VI. Each rule is described in general terms, its exceptions and exemptions are noted, and the penalties for offences are noted where that information is provided in the HTA. For the specific elements of a charge, the reader should read the relevant section of the HTA that has been identified in the chapter and the relevant regulations.

KEY TERMS

gazetted

equestrian

headway

REVIEW QUESTIONS

■ SHORT ANSWER

1. A police officer may direct traffic when he or she considers it reasonably necessary to do so.

   a. Describe three situations in which he or she may consider it necessary to direct traffic.

   b. Could a pedestrian be prosecuted for disobeying a police officer's manual signal for traffic direction? Explain your answer.

   c. May a police officer legally direct a motorist through an intersection against a red traffic light? Explain your answer.

   d. Give the statutory references for a, b, and c.

2. a. Under what section of the HTA do the police have the authority to close a highway?

    b. What procedure should a police officer follow to close a highway lawfully?

    c. Identify the person or persons who are exempt from the prohibition of operating a vehicle on a closed highway.

3. a. Certain rules govern traffic at uncontrolled intersections (where there are no signs or signals). Describe the two rules that have to do with right of way that are imposed on drivers of vehicles approaching uncontrolled intersections.

    b. Give the statutory reference.

4. a. The driver of any vehicle or streetcar, on approaching a stop sign at an intersection, is required to stop in one of three places. Identify these places and list them in the proper order.

    b. Give the statutory reference.

5. After a driver has lawfully stopped at a stop sign, there is a lawful requirement for both the stopped driver and the traffic on the through highway.

    a. Describe the requirements for the stopped driver.

    b. Describe the requirements for traffic on the through highway.

    c. Give the statutory reference.

6. Section 144 of the HTA describes the rules regarding traffic signals.

    a. This section expands the definition of "intersection" to include an area beyond the area that is enclosed within the extension of the curb lines. What extra area is now included in this definition?

    b. Where must a driver of a vehicle stop when approaching an intersection, facing a red light?

c. Where must the driver of a vehicle stop when approaching a red traffic signal at a location other than at an intersection?

d. Section 144 describes the rules with regard to traffic signals other than red lights. List these other traffic signals and what they require or permit a driver to do.

7. a. What responsibility is placed on the driver of a vehicle who is approaching an intersection and facing a yield sign?

b. Give the statutory reference.

8. a. What responsibility is placed on the driver of a vehicle intending to enter a highway from a private road or driveway?

b. Give the statutory reference.

9. **a.** List and describe the three duties imposed on a driver of a vehicle at a pedestrian crossover.

   b. Give the statutory reference.

10. Section 141 sets out the correct method for making turns at an intersection.

    a. Describe the term "centre line," as it is used in this section.

    b. Describe the lawful requirements with regard to the position of a vehicle making a right turn at an intersection, including multiple-lane situations.

    c. Describe the lawful requirements with regard to the position of a vehicle making a left turn at an intersection, including multiple-lane situations.

11. **a.** Two duties are imposed on the driver of a vehicle on a highway before turning left or right an at intersection, private drive, or from one lane to another. What are those two duties?

    b. Give the statutory reference.

    c. Is the driver of a vehicle that is parked or stopped on the highway always required to signal before setting the vehicle in motion? Explain.

    d. How may a driver commit an offence with regard to the use of directional signals for an improper purpose?

12. **a.** Under certain conditions, the driver of a vehicle on a highway is prohibited from turning his or her vehicle so that it proceeds in the opposite direction—that is, making a u-turn. List the conditions that prohibit u-turns.

b. Under what conditions is a driver prohibited from making a u-turn, regardless of the view?

c. Give the statutory references for a and b.

13. **a.** Driving to the left of the centre of a roadway is prohibited under certain conditions. List these conditions.

b. When is a driver prohibited from driving left of the centre of a roadway, regardless of the view?

c. Name the exceptions listed when it is not an offence to drive left of the centre of a roadway.

d. Give the statutory references for a, b, and c.

14. Certain duties are imposed on persons driving vehicles on highways when being met or overtaken by other vehicles.

   a. Give the statutory reference.

   b. What must a driver do when meeting an oncoming vehicle?

   c. What two duties are imposed on the driver of a vehicle intending to overtake and pass another vehicle going in the same direction?

15. a. What duty is imposed on the driver of a vehicle that is being overtaken by a faster vehicle?

   b. Give the statutory reference.

16. **a.** The driver of a motor vehicle on a highway may overtake and pass to the right of another vehicle only where the movement can be made in safety and under certain circumstances. What are these circumstances?

b. Give the statutory reference.

c. Name two circumstances where it is permissible to pass on the right while going off the roadway.

17. **a.** Certain duties are imposed on drivers of vehicles using highways that have been divided into clearly marked lanes. This means a highway with three or more clearly marked lanes, not a highway divided only by a centre line. What must the driver do before moving from one clearly marked lane to another?

b. Give the statutory reference.

c. Is it permissible to drive straddling the lane markings? Explain.

d. Give two examples of how lanes may be designated for use of
certain traffic by erecting official signs for a particular movement
of traffic.

e. When may the driver of a vehicle lawfully use the centre lane of
a highway divided into three lanes?

18. There are six instances in the HTA where the driver of a vehicle
must stay on the right-hand side of the road, having regard to the
direction in which the vehicle is being driven. Identify these six
instances.

a.

b.

c.

d.

e.

f.

19. a. What are the duties imposed on the driver of a vehicle on the approach of an emergency vehicle that is sounding a bell or siren or has a flashing red light on the roof?

b. Give the statutory reference.

c. Under law, what is the minimum distance that a vehicle must remain behind a fire department vehicle responding to an alarm?

20. What sections of the HTA prohibit a person from being towed on a bicycle, sled, or toboggan or from attaching himself or herself to the outside of a vehicle while riding a bicycle, sled, or toboggan or from clinging to a vehicle?

21. a. Crowding the driver's seat so as to interfere with the proper management or control of the vehicle is prohibited. Give two examples of how this offence could be committed.

b. Give the statutory reference.

22. **a.** The driver of a vehicle approaching a railway crossing must stop when an electrical or mechanical signal device or a flagman is giving warning of an approaching train. Give the statutory reference.

    b. Where must the driver stop?

    c. When may the driver proceed?

23. **a.** Two duties are imposed on a person who opens the door of a motor vehicle on a highway. What are these two duties?

    b. Give the statutory reference.

24. The driver of a motor vehicle on a highway is required to use the lower beam of a multiple-beam headlamp when lighted lamps are required under certain circumstances. Within what distance must the lower beams be used in the following instances?

   a. When approaching another vehicle.

   b. When following another vehicle.

   c. Give the statutory references for a and b.

25. a. Three duties are imposed on the driver of a school bus when picking up or dropping off children or developmentally handicapped adults. What are these duties?

   b. In what two locations on a roadway should the driver of a school bus not activate the flashing red lights when picking up or dropping off children or developmentally handicapped adults?

c. Describe where the driver of a vehicle or street car must stop in relation to a school bus when encountering a school bus that is stopped for the purpose of picking up or discharging children or developmentally handicapped adults in the following instances.

    i. When facing the bus.

    ii. When following the bus.

d. Give the statutory references for a, b, and c.

26. a. What are the minimum exterior lamp requirements for a passenger motor vehicle other than motorcycles?

    b. Are you permitted to take your car to have the windows tinted?

c. Must all passengers on motorcycles wear helmets?

d. Give the statutory references for a, b, and c.

27. Create a chart that lists distances (30 m, 150 m, and so on) set out in sections of the HTA that you have studied in this chapter. For each distance listed, summarize the various statutory requirements. (For example, under 30 m, you could describe various requirements governing u-turns and passing other vehicles.)

∎ DISCUSSION QUESTIONS

1. Anna is driving on a highway where the posted speed is 80 km/h. The roadway is clear, dry, and level. Anna hears a grinding sound whenever she puts her car into fourth gear, so she decides to leave it in third gear, which allows her to travel at about 55 km/h and no faster. Traffic is beginning to build up behind her, and some drivers are growing impatient, passing in relatively risky places (on curves and hills with limited visibility). Can Anna be charged with any offence? Should she be, in these circumstances? Discuss the pros and cons of charging her.

2. Describe how red-light camera systems and photo-radar systems work. What are the arguments in favour of these kinds of systems, and what are the arguments against using them? Is there any evidence to show how effective these kinds of systems are? (This may require some research. You may wish to use a web browser's search engine, such as Yahoo, to search for "photo radar" and "red light camera." You can also search newspaper indices, which you may also do online, for example, at www.theglobeandmail.com.)

3. You have been asked to write a code of road rules for bicyclists and users of motor-assisted bicycles. Use the rules of the road as the basis for providing practical guidelines for bicycle and motor-assisted bicycle riders, noting where the rules require drivers of these vehicles to act in certain ways and where these drivers need to adapt to some of the rules of the road that cannot easily be applied to bicycles (making left turns at a multilane intersection, for example).

4. You are assigned the job of writing a guide for the drivers of certain classes of vehicles, alerting them to the exemptions and exceptions to the rules of the road that apply to them and their vehicles. Examining the rules of the road, prepare a guide for drivers of the following vehicles:

   a. road-service vehicles, including self-propelled road-building machinery;

   b. school buses;

   c. ambulances; and

   d. fire trucks.

NOTES

1 "Municipality," as used here, includes cities, towns, incorporated and unincorporated villages, and police villages.

2 SO 1994, c. 27, s. 138(14), amending HTA s. 150, by adding clause (f) to subsection (3).

3 Section 166 also refers to electric railways. This reference is to a form of streetcar referred to as an interurban car or radial railway. These were relatively high-speed streetcars, often on their own rights of way, that provided service to suburban areas in the first two decades of the twentieth century. The fact that the reference is still there long after the last of the railways had disappeared, and after many statutory revisions, indicates that the HTA is a relatively old statute that has not been thoroughly revised in terms of language and content.

CHAPTER 5
Motor Vehicle Offences

CHAPTER OBJECTIVES

After completing this chapter, you should be able to:

Distinguish between a charge and an arrest, and know the circumstances where a police officer should either arrest and charge, or simply charge, an offender.

◆ Understand and be able to apply the ticketing procedure in the POA.

Identify arrestable offences under the HTA.

Recognize the circumstances that entitle an officer to seize permits, licences, equipment, and vehicles under the HTA.

Determine the appropriate charge for failing to have automobile insurance and for failing to produce evidence of insurance, as required by the *Compulsory Motor Vehicle Insurance Act*.

Understand and appreciate the difference between the definitions of "motor vehicle" in the HTA and the CCC.

Understand the difference between, and importance of, "reasonable suspicion" and "reasonable grounds" in connection with alcohol-related driving offences.

Identify and understand the essential elements of the offences of being "impaired" and being "over 80" that must be proved to obtain a conviction.

Know the function and purpose of a roadside screening device and a breathalyzer and the relationship between these two instruments in providing evidence of alcohol-related driving offences.

◆ Understand and appreciate the kind of evidence needed to support "reasonable suspicion" and "reasonable grounds" that a driver is either "impaired" or "over 80."

Know when a lawful demand may be made for a breath sample for a screening device or breathalyzer or for a blood sample in connection with alcohol-related driving offences.

◆ Know when the grounds exist for a blood warrant, and what facts must be proved to satisfy a Justice of the Peace that a warrant should be issued.

◆ Understand the significance and application of the "two-hour rule," in connection with blood and breath samples, and the "four-hour rule" in connection with blood warrants.

◆ On assessing evidence, determine whether an "impaired" or "over 80" charge can be laid.

◆ Identify when an arrest for an alcohol-related offence can be made, and at what point the offender must be advised of the right to counsel.

◆ Know under what circumstances a 12-hour or 90-day suspension can be made under the HTA.

◆ Understand the essential elements of the offence of driving while disqualified and be able to apply that understanding to determine the various circumstances in which that charge can be laid.

◆ Understand the difference between an HTA suspension and a CCC prohibition and the importance of that distinction.

◆ Understand what limits are placed on drivers as a result of various types of suspension and prohibition orders.

INTRODUCTION

This chapter introduces the reader to safe stop and pursuit procedures, some of the more common offences under the *Highway Traffic Act* (HTA), and a variety of offences in the Canadian *Criminal Code* (CCC) that involve motor vehicles. Particular attention is paid to identifying the essential elements of offences and the circumstances required in order to proceed with a charge or an arrest. In reading this chapter, you may wish to refer to a copy of the HTA or CCC for the specific language used in creating an offence and as a reference to defences, procedures, and penalties.

MOTOR VEHICLE STOPS

The general public comes into contact with police officers during motor vehicle stops. Public support for the police can be greatly enhanced if this contact is conducted professionally. Make all your ~~vehicle stops~~ **GREAT** ~~stops.~~

The procedure outlined here provides a guide on how to handle the verbal interaction between the officer and the motorist in situations where there is no risk to the officer.

~~Greeting~~

◆ Greet the driver courteously.

◆ "Good morning, sir/ma'am" is sufficient.

◆ Do not make this greeting in the form of a question. "How are you this morning?" invites a sarcastic response.

◆ Do not ask the driver if he or she knows why he or she was stopped—this is asking the driver to incriminate himself or herself, and you should have the evidence needed for the moving violation or you would not have stopped the vehicle. This is not an investigative situation where you have no suspect.

Reason for the stop
◆ Immediately after the greeting, inform the driver of the reason for the stop: "The reason I stopped you was _____."

◆ The driver is going to ask you what the problem is anyway, so tell him or her promptly.

Explanation
◆ Pause *briefly* after telling the driver why you have stopped him or her.

◆ The pause permits the driver to offer an explanation if there is one.

◆ Sometimes the driver has a valid explanation and a police officer will look foolish in court if the officer showed no interest in an explanation that could have saved everyone concerned a lot of time and effort.

Accreditation
◆ After pausing briefly for an explanation, ask the driver to produce his or her driver's licence, permit, and evidence of insurance.

◆ If the driver takes the pause as an opportunity for verbal abuse, cut him or her off with your demand for accreditation that he or she must lawfully provide.

◆ If the driver continues the verbal abuse, sternly repeat your demand for the documents and *do not engage in an argument*.

Tell the driver what you are going to do and what he or she must do

◆ Tell the driver if you are going to give him or her a ticket.

◆ If you do not tell the driver what you are going to do, he or she is likely to get out of the car and walk back to the cruiser to ask if he or she is going to be given a ticket—this makes the stop much more dangerous.

◆ Tell the driver to stay in his or her car and that you will be approximately five minutes if there are no interruptions.

◆ When you return to the driver's window, courteously explain the driver's responsibilities with regard to the "ticket."

If the above procedure is followed, the motorist often responds with "thank you." The motorist is obviously not thanking you for the ticket, but for the courteous and professional way that you treated him or her. This positive experience is stimulating and much more beneficial than a stressful experience where the officer is verbally abused. Remember, it is important to pause for an explanation, but cut the driver off quickly with the demand for the driver's licence, permit, and insurance if the driver becomes verbally abusive.

Recognizing Driver Behaviour

If the police officer does experience some verbal abuse, then it is valuable to recognize the driver's patterns of behaviour. Recognizing the behaviour enables the officer to understand the interaction and not personalize the comments. The cumulative effect of personal verbal attacks can be devastating for the officer's mental health. The motorist is usually attacking what the officer represents and not the officer personally.

Negative driver's responses can be grouped into six categories.

1. **Indignant Response**

   "Is this all you've got to do?"

   "Why aren't you catching the rapists and murderers instead of stopping me for _____?"

2. **Influencing Response**

   "I'm a good friend of the chief."

   "Is _____ working today?"

3. **Denial of Responsibility**

   "You're absolutely wrong!"

   "I did no such thing!"

4. **Assertion of Discrimination**

   "You stopped me just because I'm _____!"

5. **Insulting Response**

   "You're just a _____!"

   "All you cops are the same!"

6. Emotional Response

> "Officer, I can't afford a ticket, I have to feed my kids."

> "Officer, my husband will kill me if I get a ticket!"

Other emotional responses by a driver include excessive crying and attempts at flirtation with the police officer.

SUSPECT APPREHENSION PURSUITS

Rather than totally banning police pursuits or allowing pursuits for any infraction, the government of Ontario allows pursuits when specific criteria are met. On January 1, 2000, a regulation under the *Police Services Act*, "Suspect Apprehension Pursuits," O. reg. 546/99, came into force. Highlights of the regulation are set out below.

Highlights of the Suspect Apprehension Pursuits Regulation

◆ Pursuits may be carried out if a criminal offence is committed or is about to be committed, or if it is necessary to identify a vehicle or a person in it.

◆ Before launching a pursuit, the officer must determine there is no alternative method available to prevent an offence or identify a vehicle or person in it.

◆ An officer must determine that to protect public safety it is necessary to launch a pursuit and that this necessity outweighs risk to the public from the pursuit itself.

◆ This risk assessment is ongoing and continuous, and if the officer assesses that the risk to the public from continuing the pursuit outweighs the benefit of apprehending a person or vehicle, he or she is obliged to discontinue the pursuit.

◆ No pursuit should be continued for a non-criminal offence if the identity of the person is known and, once the motor vehicle or the fleeing person has been identified, the pursuit should cease.

◆ An officer is obliged to notify a dispatcher once a pursuit starts.

◆ The dispatcher is obliged to notify the communications supervisor and road supervisor, if there is one; either supervisor will further carry out the risk assessment to determine when and if to break off a pursuit.

◆ Every police service will establish its own pursuit rules that are consistent with this regulation and these rules must be in writing and describe the duties of the officers, dispatchers, and road and communications supervisors, and specify the equipment used in pursuits.

◆ Firearms should not be used for the sole purpose of stopping a fleeing vehicle.

◆ Where possible, pursuit in unmarked police vehicles should be avoided.

◆ A police vehicle may be used to physically stop a fleeing vehicle if the fleeing vehicle has lost control or collided and come to a stop, and is trying to escape after stopping.

◆ Police vehicles may be used to block a road on which a vehicle is escaping in order to block its escape.

◆ Police officers must undergo training in techniques of using police vehicles to physically stop fleeing vehicles.

◆ Where a pursuit involves more than one jurisdiction, the supervisor in the jurisdiction in which the pursuit begins is responsible for decisions about continuing the pursuit, but he or she may hand over responsibility to a supervisor in the other jurisdiction.

◆ An officer who decides not to initiate a pursuit, or who breaks one off, will not be deemed to have violated the code of conduct.

◆ All officers, dispatchers, and supervisors must receive pursuit training that is approved by the solicitor general, and all pursuits must be recorded on forms approved by the solicitor general.

The Suspect Apprehension Pursuit regulation, in force as of January 1, 2000, is set out in appendix C.

HTA OFFENCES

Charge Versus Arrest

arrest
results when a person's physical liberty is inhibited by conveying an intention to restrict the person's liberty; the actual restraint may involve physical force, although an arrest may occur without the use of force

Under the HTA, offenders are usually charged and given a ticket, which is more formally known as a Provincial Offence Notice. Because the offender usually produces a driver's licence and vehicle permit, there is no need to arrest a person to establish his or her identity, and a ticket can be used for most offences. The procedure for ticketing is described in the *Provincial Offences Act* (POA).

POA Ticketing Procedure

Reproduced in figure 5.1 are three pages of a multi-layered Provincial Offence Notice. The complete notice is reproduced as appendix B at the back of the book. You can photocopy it and practice completing a "ticket" with the appropriate information and wording for the charge for any scenario you create.

Instructions for Completing a Provincial Offence Ticket

Personal Service of Notice on Date of Offence

There are several pages to what is collectively called the Provincial Offence Ticket. The top page is the Certificate of Offence, which is the copy that is filed with the Provincial Offences Court. Printing firmly on this top page will mark all subsequent pages. A manipulation of the pages must occur so that original signatures of the issuing officer appear on both the page that is filed with the court and the page that is served on the defendant.

◆ Complete the Certificate of Offence (top page) down to and including the certification area (this is the area where the issuing officer certifies that he or she served the Offence Notice on the person charged). DO NOT sign the certification area yet.

◆ When describing the offence, make sure to use the short-form wordings for the offence as prescribed in the POA and reproduced in appendix A.

◆ Enter the set fine as prescribed in the POA.

◆ Remove the Offence Notice (second page) and the Payment Notice (last page). Now sign the certification area of this Offence Notice. This places an original signature on the Offence Notice that is served on the defendant. Serve both of these pages on the defendant.

◆ Return to the original Certificate of Offence (top page) and complete the Code Box (top left corner), if it is not preprinted.

◆ Sign the certification area on the Certificate of Offence. Now an original signature appears on the copy that is filed with the court and copies of the signature for other uses.

Personal Service of Summons on Date of Offence

When an offence has no set fine prescribed in the POA, an Offence Notice with an out-of-court settlement cannot be used. Instead, the defendant must be summoned to Provincial Offences Court and a justice of the peace will determine the fine at the conclusion of the trial.

In this case, a Summons will be served on the defendant instead of an Offence Notice and the Offence Notice will be discarded (see figure 5.2). A Summons can be found at the back of the ticket book. There are only three Summonses per book of 25 tickets because they are not used as often as tickets.

◆ Insert the Summons behind the Certificate of Offence (top page).

◆ Complete the Certificate of Offence down to and including the certification area. DO NOT sign the certification area yet.

■ Figure 5.1   Provincial Offence Ticket (Top Page)

ICON LOCATION CODE *CODE DE LOCALISATION RIII*	OFFENCE NUMBER *Nº D'INFRACTION*

FORM 1 PROVINCIAL OFFENCES ACT ONTARIO COURT OF JUSTICE
FORMULE 1 LOI SUR LES INFRACTIONS PROVINCIALES COUR DE JUSTICE DE L'ONTARIO

CERTIFICATE OF OFFENCE / *PROCÈS-VERBAL D'INFRACTION*

I/*JE SOUSSIGNÉ(E)*

BELIEVE AND CERTIFY THAT ON THE DAY OF
CROIS ET ATTESTE QUE LE JOUR DE

(PRINT NAME / *NOM EN LETTRES MOULÉES*)
Y/A   M/M   D/J   TIME/*À (HEURE)*   M

NAME
NOM _____
FAMILY/*NOM DE FAMILLE*

GIVEN/*PRÉNOM*   INITIALS/*INITIALES*

ADDRESS
ADRESSE _____
NUMBER AND STREET/*Nº ET RUE*

MUNICIPALITY/*MUNICIPALITÉ*   P.O./C.P.   PROVINCE   POSTAL CODE/*CODE POSTAL*

DRIVER'S LICENCE NO./*NUMÉRO DE PERMIS DE CONDUIRE*   PROV   ON

BIRTHDATE/*DATE DE NAISSANCE*   SEX   MOTOR VEHICLE INVOLVED
Y/A   M/M   D/J   *SEXE*   *VÉHICULE IMPLIQUÉ*
1 9   ☐ YES/*OUI*   ☐ NO/*NON*

AT/*À* _____

MUNICIPALITY/*MUNICIPALITÉ*

DID COMMIT THE OFFENCE OF:
A COMMIS L'INFRACTION SUIVANTE : _____

CONTRARY TO:
CONTRAIREMENT À : _____

SECT./*ART.*

PLATE NUMBER *Nº DE PLAQUE D'IMMATRICULATION*	YEAR/ *ANNÉE*	PROV	MAKE/ *MARQUE*	COLLISION INVOLVED *COLLISION IMPLIQUÉE*	WITNESSES *TÉMOINS*	CODE
		ON		☐Y/O ☐N	☐Y/O ☐N	

COMMERCIAL	CVOR / *CECVU*	C.V.O.R. NUMBER/*Nº DU CECVU*
☐ YES/*OUI*	☐ YES/*OUI*	

AND I FURTHER CERTIFY THAT I SERVED AN OFFENCE NOTICE PERSONALLY UPON THE PERSON CHARGED
JE CERTIFIE EN OUTRE QUE J'AI SIGNIFIÉ UN AVIS D'INFRACTION EN MAINS PROPRES À L'ACCUSÉ(E)
☐ ON THE OFFENCE DATE *LE JOUR DE L'INFRACTION.*
☐ OTHER *AUTRE*

SIGNATURE OF ISSUING PROVINCIAL OFFENCES OFFICER *SIGNATURE DE L'AGENT DES INFRACTIONS PROVINCIALES*	OFFICER NO. *Nº DE L'AGENT*	PLATOON *PELOTON*	UNIT *UNITÉ*

SET FINE OF *L'AMENDE FIXÉE DE* $ $	**TOTAL PAYABLE** $ $ **MONTANT TOTAL EXIGIBLE**	TOTAL PAYABLE INCLUDES COSTS AND APPLICABLE VICTIM FINE SURCHARGE. *LE MONTANT TOTAL EXIGIBLE COMPREND LES FRAIS ET LA SURAMENDE COMPENSATOIRE QUI S'APPLIQUE*

SUMMONS ISSUED. YOU ARE REQUIRED TO APPEAR IN COURT ON
ASSIGNATION DÉLIVRÉE. VOUS DEVEZ COMPARAÎTRE LE
Y/A   M/M   D/J   TIME/*À (HEURE)*   M

CT.ROOM / *SALLE D'AUDIENCE*   ONTARIO COURT OF JUSTICE P.O.A. OFFICE AT/ *COUR DE JUSTICE DE L'ONTARIO BUREAU - L.I.P. À* 279 WELLINGTON STREET, KINGSTON, ONTARIO / *279, RUE WELLINGTON, KINGSTON (ONTARIO)*

CONVICTION ENTERED. SET FINE (INCLUDING COSTS) IMPOSED.
CONDAMNATION INSCRITE. AMENDE FIXÉE (Y COMPRIS LES FRAIS) IMPOSÉE.
Y/A   M/M   D/J

JUSTICE/*JUGE DE PAIX*

Figure 5.1 Provincial Offence Ticket (Second Page)

Figure 5.1 Provincial Offence Ticket (Last Page)

PROVINCIAL OFFENCES ACT ONTARIO COURT OF JUSTICE
LOI SUR LES INFRACTIONS PROVINCIALES COUR DE JUSTICE DE L'ONTARIO

PAYMENT NOTICE / *AVIS DE PAIEMENT*

TO PAY THE TOTAL PAYABLE SHOWN, FORWARD YOUR PAYMENT WITH THIS NOTICE AND THE OFFENCE NOTICE TO THE ADDRESS SHOWN ON THIS NOTICE. SIGN THE PLEA OF GUILTY ON THE OFFENCE NOTICE (OPTION 1).

POUR ACQUITTER LE MONTANT TOTAL EXIGIBLE, FAITES PARVENIR VOTRE PAIEMENT, ACCOMPAGNÉ DE CET AVIS ET DE L'AVIS D'INFRACTION, À L'ADRESSE QUI FIGURE SUR LE PRÉSENT AVIS. N'OUBLIEZ PAS DE SIGNER LE PLAIDOYER DE CULPABILITÉ SUR L'AVIS D'INFRACTION (OPTION 1).

COMPLETE THE FOLLOWING INFORMATION / *VEUILLEZ DONNER LES RENSEIGNEMENTS SUIVANTS*

NAME / *NOM* ____________________

ADDRESS / *ADRESSE* ____________________

☐ CHEQUE/MONEY ORDER ENCLOSED *CHÈQUE/MANDAT JOINT* ☐ VISA ☐ MASTER CARD

CARD NUMBER *N° DE CARTE* |_|_|_|_|_|_|_|_|_|_|_|_|_|_|_|_|

CARD EXPIRY DATE (MONTH) *DATE D'EXPIRATION (MOIS)* |_|_| (YEAR) *(ANNÉE)* |_|_|_|_|

0960

SEE BACK FOR MAILING ADDRESS AND INSTRUCTIONS / *POUR CONNAÎTRE L'ADRESSE POSTALE ET LES INSTRUCTIONS, PRIÈRE DE VOIR AU VERSO*

OFFENCE NUMBER
N° D'INFRACTION

MAKE CHEQUE OR MONEY ORDER PAYABLE TO "CORPORATION OF THE CITY OF KINGSTON" AND WRITE THE NUMBER OF THE OFFENCE NOTICE ON THE FRONT OF THE CHEQUE/MONEY ORDER. DO NOT SEND CASH, CORRESPONDENCE OR POST-DATED CHEQUES WITH YOUR PAYMENT.

DISHONOURED CHEQUES WILL BE SUBJECT TO AN ADMINISTRATIVE CHARGE AND THE AMOUNT MAY BE REFERRED TO CENTRAL COLLECTION SERVICES.

FAIRE UN CHÈQUE OU MANDAT À L'ORDRE DU «CORPORATION OF THE CITY OF KINGSTON» ET ÉCRIRE LE NUMÉRO D'AVIS D'INFRACTION AU RECTO DU CHÈQUE/MANDAT. NE PAS ENVOYER D'ESPÈCES, NI DE LETTRE OU DE CHÈQUES POSTDATÉS AVEC VOTRE PAIEMENT.

LES CHÈQUES IMPAYÉS SONT ASSUJETTIS À DES FRAIS ADMINISTRATIFS ET LES RENSEIGNEMENTS CONCERNANT LE MONTANT IMPAYÉ PEUVENT ÊTRE TRANSMIS AU SERVICE CENTRAL DE RECOUVREMENT.

CARDHOLDER'S SIGNATURE
SIGNATURE DU DÉTENTEUR DE LA CARTE ____________________

TOTAL PAID
MONTANT TOTAL EXIGIBLE $ $

■ **Figure 5.2   Provincial Offence Summons**

ICON
LOCATION
CODE
CODE DE
LOCALISATION
RIII

FORM 6 PROVINCIAL OFFENCES ACT ONTARIO COURT OF JUSTICE
FORMULE 6 LOI SUR LES INFRACTIONS PROVINCIALES COUR DE JUSTICE DE L'ONTARIO

SUMMONS / *ASSIGNATION*

BELIEVES AND CERTIFIES
THAT ON THE DAY OF   Y/A   M/M   D/J   TIME/*À (HEURE)*
CROIS ET ATTESTE
QUE LE JOUR DE   **M**

NAME
NOM
                                                    FAMILY/*NOM DE FAMILLE*

                        GIVEN/*PRÉNOM*   INITIALS/*INITIALES*

ADDRESS
ADRESSE
                                                    NUMBER AND STREET/*Nº ET RUE*

MUNICIPALITY/*MUNICIPALITÉ*   P.O./*C.P.*   PROVINCE   POSTAL CODE/*CODE POSTAL*
DRIVER'S LICENCE NO./*NUMÉRO DE PERMIS DE CONDUIRE*   PROV

                                                                                                            ON

            BIRTHDATE/*DATE DE NAISSANCE*   SEX   MOTOR VEHICLE INVOLVED
            Y/A   M/M   D/J   *SEXE*   *VÉHICULE IMPLIQUÉ*

1 | 9   ☐ YES/*OUI*   ☐ NO/*NON*

AT/À

                                                                    MUNICIPALITY/*MUNICIPALITÉ*

DID COMMIT THE OFFENCE OF:
A COMMIS L'INFRACTION SUIVANTE :

CONTRARY TO:
CONTRAIREMENT À :

                                SECT./*ART.*
            PLATE NUMBER   PROV   CODE
Nº DE PLAQUE D'IMMATRICULATION

                                            ON

                    CVOR / *CECVU*
                    ☐ YES/*OUI*

THIS IS THEREFORE TO COMMAND YOU IN HER MAJESTY'S NAME TO   OFFICER NO.   PLATOON   UNIT
APPEAR BEFORE THE ONTARIO COURT OF JUSTICE   *Nº DE L'AGENT* *PELOTON* *UNITÉ*
POUR CES MOTIFS, ORDRE VOUS EST DONNÉ, AU NOM DE SA
MAJESTÉ, DE COMPARAÎTRE DEVANT LA COUR DE JUSTICE DE
L'ONTARIO

                    Y/A   M/M   D/J   TIME/*À (HEURE)*
                                                                                          M
            CT. ROOM / *SALLE D'AUDIENCE*   ONTARIO COURT OF JUSTICE P.O.A. OFFICE AT/
                                            COUR DE JUSTICE DE L'ONTARIO BUREAU - L.I.P. À
                                            279 WELLINGTON STREET, KINGSTON, ONTARIO /
                                            279, RUE WELLINGTON, KINGSTON (ONTARIO)

AND TO ATTEND THEREAFTER AS REQUIRED BY THE COURT IN ORDER TO BE DEALT WITH ACCORDING TO LAW. THIS
SUMMONS IS SERVED UNDER PART 1 OF THE PROVINCIAL OFFENCES ACT.
ET D'Y ÊTRE PRÉSENT(E) PAR LA SUITE LORSQUE LE TRIBUNAL L'EXIGERA, DE FAÇON À ÊTRE TRAITÉ(E) SELON LA LOI.
CETTE ASSIGNATION VOUS EST SIGNIFIÉE AUX TERMES DE LA PARTIE 1 DE LA LOI SUR LES INFRACTIONS PROVINCIALES.

SIGNATURE OF PROVINCIAL OFFENCES OFFICER
SIGNATURE DE L'AGENT DES INFRACTIONS PROVINCIALES

- ◆ Enter the next applicable Court Date.

- ◆ Remove the Summons copy. Enter the Certificate of Offence number in the top right corner of the Summons. Enter the location code in the Code Box in the upper left corner, if applicable.

- ◆ Sign the Summons and serve it on the defendant.

- ◆ In the certification area of the Certificate of Offence, strike out "Offence Notice / Avis d'infraction," initial the change, and print "Summons / Assignation."

- ◆ Enter the location code in the Code Box in the upper left corner, if applicable.

- ◆ Sign the certification area on the Certificate of Offence. Now an original signature appears on the copy that is filed with the court and copies of the signature for other uses.

- ◆ Discard the Offence Notice.

In this case, a Payment Notice (last page) did not have to be served on the defendant because there is no set fine for an out-of-court settlement.

Arrestable Offences Under the HTA

Some offences in the HTA are also arrestable. This means that the offender can be arrested as well as be charged with the offence. Not all offences in the HTA are cause for arrest. The HTA identifies those offences for which arrest is an option, and there is a list of those offences in this chapter. Usually, where a person is arrested for an HTA offence, he or she will be released once the offence has ceased and the proper identification has been obtained so that the offender can be ticketed.

It is important to note that an arrest and a charge are not the same thing, but are separate actions taken against an offender. A charge is a document that accuses the named person of committing an offence, sets out the offence, the location and time of the offence, and the requirement that the accused attend court at a named place and time to answer the charge. An arrest occurs when a person is taken into custody and is not released until certain conditions have been satisfied.

Under the HTA, a person can be charged without being arrested. If a person is arrested under the HTA, he or she is also likely to be charged.

Charge → court date to answer charge

Arrest → custody → release on condition and on being charged → court date to answer charge

---

HTA Arrest Authorities, Sections 217(2) and (3)

According to s. 217(2), power to arrest a person for violation of specific offences is granted to the following people under certain conditions:

◆ Any person finding someone committing an offence listed under s. 217(2) may, under s. 217(3), arrest that person without a warrant. This arrest power is sometimes referred to as a "citizen's arrest." The person making the arrest is obliged to use no more force than is necessary to make the arrest, and to turn the person over to the police as soon as possible.

◆ A police officer, under s. 217(2), may arrest a person without a warrant whom the officer, on reasonable grounds, believes has committed an offence listed in s. 217(2).

The s. 217(2) offences for which an offender may be arrested are as follows:

s. 9(1)	Making a false statement.
s. 12(1)(a)	Defacing or altering a permit, number plate, or evidence of validation.
s. 12(1)(b)	Using or permitting the use of a defaced or altered permit, number plate, or evidence of validation.
s. 12(1)(c)	Removing a number plate without the authority of the owner.
s. 12(1)(d)	Using or permitting the use of a number plate on a vehicle other than the number plate authorized for use on that vehicle.
s. 12(1)(e)	Using or permitting the use of evidence of validation on a number plate other than the evidence of validation furnished by the ministry for that vehicle.
s. 12(1)(f)	Using or permitting the use of a number plate or evidence of validation other than in accordance with the HTA or its regulations.
s. 13(1)	Confusing the identity of a number plate.
s. 33(3)	Failing to identify self on failing to surrender driver's licence.
s. 47(5)	Applying for, procuring, or having in his or her possession the plate portion of a permit issued to him or her while his or her permit is suspended or cancelled or while he or she is prohibited from owning a motor vehicle.
s. 47(6)	Applying for, procuring, or having in his or her possession a driver's licence while he or she is suspended or he or she is prohibited from operating a motor vehicle.
s. 47(7)	Applying for or procuring a Commercial Vehicle Operator's Registration (**CVOR**) while his or her CVOR is suspended.
s. 47(8)	Operating a commercial motor vehicle for which a CVOR is required without a CVOR in his or her possession or while his or her CVOR is suspended.

CVOR
the Commercial Vehicle Operator's Registration Certificate, which must be held by the operator of a commercial vehicle unless he or she is excluded or exempted under the HTA; requires commercial vehicle operators to comply with safety requirements under the HTA and other legislation

s. 51	Operating a motor vehicle for which the permit has been suspended or cancelled.
s. 53	Driving a motor vehicle while his or her driver's licence is suspended.
s. 106(8.1)	A passenger over 16 years of age who fails to wear a seat belt and fails to identify himself or herself when requested to do so by a police officer.
s. 130	Careless driving.
s. 172	Racing on a highway.
s. 184	Removing, defacing, or interfering with any notice or obstruction lawfully placed on a highway.
s. 185(3)	A pedestrian on a highway where prohibited.
s. 200(1)(a)	Failing to remain at the scene of a collision.
s. 216(1)	Failing to stop when signalled or requested by a police officer.

Seizure Authorities Under the HTA

The HTA authorizes the seizure of permits, validation tags, number plates, motor vehicles, driver licences, and radar warning devices in circumstances set out in the HTA.

Permits, Valtags, and Number Plates

Under s. 14(1), where a police officer has reason to believe that a permit, valtag, or number plate was obtained under false pretences, is not authorized for use on a particular vehicle or furnished for a particular vehicle, or is defaced or altered, the officer may seize the permit, valtag tag, or number plate, as the case may be (or all of them, if the facts warrant) and retain them until the facts as to the issue of improper use have been determined.

Radar Warning Device

Under ss. 79(3) and (4), a police officer who has reasonable grounds to believe that a motor vehicle is equipped with, or carries, a radar warning device may stop the vehicle, enter it, and search it. If he or she finds a radar warning device, it may be seized. If the person accused of having such a device is convicted, the seized radar warning device is **forfeited to the Crown**.

forfeited to the Crown
property belonging to a person, if possessed illegally, may under various statutes, be seized and become property of the government, which may then destroy it, sell it, or otherwise dispose of it without compensation to the person from whom it was seized

Driver's Licences

Under s. 48(5), a police officer may take possession of a person's driver's licence when he or she is given a 12-hour suspension.[1] If the person fails to deliver up the licence or is unable to deliver it, the licence is considered suspended and invalid. As well, if a court suspends a person's driving licence on conviction for an offence where suspension is a possible penalty, s. 212 authorizes a police officer to seize the licence. A police officer may also seize the licence under s. 212 when the licensee is notified of suspension by a police officer.

Motor Vehicles

A motor vehicle may be seized under s. 48(11) on a 12-hour suspension under s. 221(1) when it has been abandoned on or near a highway, and under s. 217(4), when the driver is arrested. The costs of the tow and subsequent storage charges are incurred by the owner of the vehicle.

COMPULSORY AUTOMOBILE INSURANCE ACT

Every owner of a motor vehicle registered in Ontario must maintain an insurance policy on the motor vehicle that conforms to the minimum insurance coverage requirements under the *Compulsory Automobile Insurance Act* (CAI).

Failure To Have Insurance

Under s. 2(1) of the CAI, no owner or lessee of a motor vehicle shall operate, or allow to be operated, a motor vehicle that is not insured. This section places the obligation to insure squarely on the owner or the lessee of the car (unless the lessor maintains the necessary insurance). Section 2(3) sets out stiff penalties for contravention of s. 2(1), and defines as a further offence the production of a false insurance card for inspection by the police that purports to show that the vehicle is insured when it is not. Fines of between $5,000 and $25,000 for a first offence, and between $10,000 and $50,000 for a subsequent offence, are steep enough that it is cheaper to maintain an insurance policy than to risk operating an uninsured vehicle. The offender, as defined in this section, is the owner of the vehicle. Charges would be laid under the penalty section, s. 2(3).

Failure To Surrender Insurance Card

Under s. 3(1), an operator of a motor vehicle shall have an insurance card for that motor vehicle in the vehicle, or an insurance card showing that the operator is insured on another contract of motor vehicle insurance, other than one for the car that is being driven. If the operator produces his own insurance card, rather than the one for the car he is driving, this does not alleviate the owner of the vehicle that has been stopped of the responsibility for insuring the motor vehicle. The operator is obliged to surrender either his or her own card, or the owner's insurance card, for inspection by the police on request. A person who fails to produce either insurance card is guilty of an offence and may be fined up to $400 under s. 3(3). The offender, according to this section, is the owner or the driver, if the driver is not the owner. Charges would be laid under the penalty subsection, s. 3(3).

If the driver produces an insurance card for a motor vehicle other than the one he or she is driving, the police should check with the owner to see if the vehicle is, in fact, insured. The police may ask the owner, even if the owner is at home, to surrender the insurance card. If the owner cannot or will not do this, the owner may be charged with permitting the operation of the vehicle without insurance, contrary to s. 2(1)(b) of the HTA. Case law is clear that, even if the owner is in his own home, the owner must produce the card or be charged with the offence.

Failure To Disclose Particulars of Insurance

Under s. 4(1), an operator of a motor vehicle on a highway who is directly or indirectly involved in a collision shall, on request of any other person involved, disclose to that person the particulars of the contract of motor vehicle insurance that insures the motor vehicle. The "particulars" are identified in s. 4(2) as follows:

(a) the name and address of the insured,

(b) the make, model and serial number (VIN) of the insured vehicle,

(c) the effective date and expiry date of the insurance contract,

(d) the name of the insurer,

(e) the name of insured's agent, if any (some insurance is sold directly without an agent),

(f) the policy number of the contract.

Failure to disclose particulars when requested can lead to a charge under s. 4(3) with a fine of up to $400, on conviction.

CRIMINAL CODE MOTOR VEHICLE OFFENCES

Laws about driving motor vehicles are within the jurisdiction of the province, under the division of powers set out in ss. 91 and 92 of the *Constitution Act, 1867*. All driving offences are provincial offences.

However, criminal offences involving drinking and driving or negligence causing serious injury or death using motor vehicles, vessels, aircraft, and railway equipment have been held to be constitutionally valid criminal law under the exercise of the federal power over criminal law and procedure as set out in s. 91(27) of the *Constitution Act, 1867*. This is because these offences are not merely about driving, but about behaviour deemed to be criminal. Furthermore, the offences in the CCC are different from and generally broader than the offences in the HTA.

The definition of motor vehicle in these "operation" and "care and control" offences (CCC, s. 253) is found in s. 2 of the CCC. It is much

---

DEFINITIONS OF "MOTOR VEHICLE"

CCC: A motor vehicle, as defined in the CCC, includes any land
             vehicle that is drawn, propelled, or driven by any means other
             than muscular power,

Except   railway equipment.

HTA: A motor vehicle, as defined in the HTA, includes automobiles,
             motorcycles, motor-assisted bicycles (unless otherwise
             indicated), and any other vehicle propelled or driven by power
             other than muscular power,

Except   motorized snow vehicles,
             farm tractors,
             self-propelled implements of husbandry,
             road-building machines,
             street cars or motor vehicles on rails, and
             traction engines.

---

broader than and quite different from the definition in the HTA. The CCC definition includes any land vehicle that is drawn, propelled, or driven by any means other than muscular power, except railway equipment. The CCC definition, therefore, includes snowmobiles, farm tractors, self-propelled implements of husbandry (that is, reapers and combines), road-building machines, and traction engines, whether operated on a highway or not.

This means that a person can be convicted of impaired operation of a farm tractor in his or her own back field, although such a charge would be unusual in the absence of a complaint related to danger to other persons or property.

"Impaired" Driving: Some Basic Terms and Concepts

The first of the CCC offences we will examine are those that are related to "impaired" driving. Before we examine the law associated with "impaired" operation of a motor vehicle, it is necessary to understand the following concepts.

Ability Impaired

Proof of impairment is established through a *description of a person's condition* due to the consumption of alcohol. The description must convince the court that the person so described does not have the ability to operate a motor vehicle safely because he or she has been drinking. Impairment is the result of a person's tolerance to alcohol. Some people are impaired after consuming just a few drinks, while others require many drinks before showing the effects of alcohol.

Over 80 mg

This is a *measure* of the amount of alcohol in 100 ml of a person's blood. It is unlawful to operate a motor vehicle with more than 80 mg of alcohol per 100 ml of blood. This measurement simply proves whether you are over the legal limit and should not be confused with proof of impairment. It is possible to be "over 80" and not be "impaired," or be "impaired," and not be "over 80."

Operating

Operating means that the person is *driving* a motor vehicle, steering a boat, or piloting an aircraft—that is, the vehicle is under way with the person directing its movement.

Care or Control

Care or control means that the person is not operating the motor vehicle, vessel, or aircraft, but is *using* the vehicle or its equipment, or is involved in some activity that risks putting the vehicle in motion. For example, a person who gets into the driver's seat of a car, puts the key in the ignition and turns the engine on, but does not drive it, would be considered to have the care and control of the vehicle.

Reasonable Suspicion

Reasonable suspicion refers to a hunch or suspicion for which there is some rational basis to suspect that someone has been consuming alcohol. Odour of an alcoholic beverage on someone's breath is sufficient evidence to form reasonable suspicion.

Reasonable Grounds To Believe

Reasonable grounds to believe refers to a set of circumstances that would satisfy an ordinary cautious and prudent person that there is reason to believe that certain facts are true, and which goes *beyond mere suspicion*. In other words, it requires much more evidence than the evidence that would establish reasonable suspicion. For example, in addition to smelling alcohol on a driver's breath, observations, such as the driver's difficulty keeping his or her balance when getting out of the car, provide reasonable grounds to believe that the driver is impaired. Observations of more than one of these behaviours or acts are usually required.

Belief Versus Suspicion

A police officer will often be challenged in court about his or her reasonable grounds to believe. The challenge will usually be about whether the officer had enough evidence to have "reasonable grounds for believing" or whether there was only enough evidence to support a "reasonable suspicion."

Reasonable suspicion is not usually enough to provide a lawful authority for police officers to take action. Reasonable suspicion is limited to the authority to demand a sample of breath into an approved roadside screening device. Police officers cannot arrest someone on reasonable suspicion that he or she committed an indictable offence.

"Reasonable grounds to believe" is a set of facts or circumstances that would satisfy an ordinary, cautious, and prudent person that there is reason to believe those facts are true, and which goes beyond mere suspicion. This definition indicates that belief is more than suspicion, and should be based on more information. Defence counsel will always question whether the police officer had enough evidence to convince an average person, other than himself or herself.

The second challenge to the officer will be the truthfulness of the evidence that supports reasonable grounds to believe. This evidence often consists of a police officer's subjective impressions (odour of alcohol or slurred speech) and is easiest to attack. The officer's testimony needs to include very specific and detailed examples of how the subject exhibited those characteristics. The more objective evidence gathered from the roadside screening device, breathalyzer, or blood test will corroborate the subjective impressions.[2]

Approved Screening Device, CCC, Section 254

An approved screening device is an instrument that indicates whether there are reasonable grounds to believe that a person is "over 80." In order to demand a sample of breath for the screening device, a police officer must have a reasonable suspicion that a person has been consuming alcohol. This instrument enables an officer to turn reasonable suspicion that a person has been drinking into reasonable grounds to believe that the person is "over 80," if the person fails the screening device test. This instrument does not indicate the exact amount of alcohol in the blood, but places the person in a "pass," "warn," or "fail" category.

Breathalyzer, CCC, Section 258

The breathalyzer is a more sophisticated instrument that accurately measures the amount of alcohol in a person's blood, rather than a device that merely identifies drivers who may be "over 80." In order for a police officer to demand samples of breath for a breathalyzer, he or she must have reasonable grounds to believe that a person is either "over 80" or the person's ability is "impaired." See figures 5.3 and 5.4.

Grounds for a Lawful Demand for an Approved Screening Device Test, CCC, Section 254(2)

Before a police officer[3] can demand that a breath sample be blown into a screening device, the officer must have "reasonable suspicion" that the operator or person who has care or control of a motor vehicle, vessel, aircraft, or railway equipment has alcohol in his or her body.

■ **Figure 5.3** **Measuring Reasonable Suspicion and Reasonable Grounds**

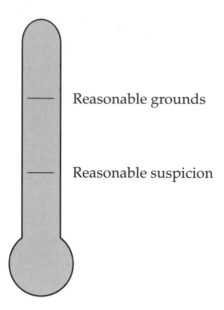

Reasonable grounds

Reasonable suspicion

Reasonable suspicion can arise when

◆ the officer smells the odour of an alcoholic beverage;

◆ the operator admits that he has consumed alcohol;

◆ the officer observes behaviour that indicates that alcohol has been consumed (glassy eyes, slurred or incoherent speech or movements); or

◆ the officer sees the driver consume an alcoholic beverage and climb into his or her car and drive away.

TURNING "REASONABLE SUSPICION" INTO "REASONABLE GROUNDS TO BELIEVE"

When an officer demands a breath sample for the roadside screening device and the person fails the screening-device test, the officer has "reasonable grounds to believe" that the person is "over 80." Failure of the screening device test is the only way for an officer to obtain the reasonable grounds to believe that the person is "over 80." It is unacceptable to the court that an officer could look at a person and reasonably determine with accuracy that a person is "over 80" because the officer does not know the person's tolerance for alcohol.

Grounds for a Lawful Demand for a Breathalyzer Test, CCC, Section 254(3)(a)

Before a police officer can lawfully demand that breath samples (2 samples at least 15 minutes apart) be provided by breathing into a breathalyzer

■ **Figure 5.4   Assessment of a Motorist with Regard to Alcohol Consumption**

The assessment of a motorist should fall
into one of these three categories:

This person has not consumed any alcohol
and is free to go.

There is **reasonable suspicion** that this person
has consumed alcohol.

There is **reasonable grounds** to believe that
this person's ability is impaired by alcohol.

device, the officer must have reasonable grounds to believe that the operator or person with care or control of a motor vehicle, vessel, aircraft, or railway equipment is "over 80" or that his or her ability is impaired by alcohol. Reasonable grounds arise under the following conditions:

◆ when, on reasonable suspicion, a person breathes into a roadside screening device and fails the test; or

◆ the person's behaviour and demeanour provides the officer with reasonable grounds to believe, going beyond reasonable suspicion, that the person's ability is impaired by alcohol.

Driver Evaluation

When a police officer approaches the driver of a motor vehicle that he or she has just stopped, there are three possible scenarios:

1. The officer quickly appreciates that the driver has not been drinking and the officer just continues with the driving offence for which the driver was stopped.

2. The officer forms reasonable suspicion that the driver has alcohol in his or her system. The officer can now lawfully make a demand that the driver provide a breath sample for a roadside screening device.

3. The officer forms reasonable grounds to believe that the driver's ability to operate a motor vehicle is impaired by alcohol. The officer can now arrest the driver on reasonable grounds to believe that he or she has committed an indictable offence. The officer will advise the suspect of the right to counsel and make the breathalyzer demand. The suspect is usually taken to the police station for the breathalyzer test.

Grounds for a Lawful Demand for Blood, CCC, Sections 254(3)(b) and (4)

In cases where a lawful breathalyzer demand could be made but the person is incapable of providing a breath sample or it is impractical to obtain a breath sample, a police officer can demand a blood sample (two test tubes). A person may be *incapable* of providing a breath sample because he or she has sustained an injury to the face, mouth, or lungs. It might be *impractical* to take a breath sample because the person has been injured and needs immediate medical attention; the safety of the person is more important than performing a breathalyzer test. However, before determining incapacity or impracticability, the officer must have reasonable grounds to believe a person is either "over 80" or "impaired."

Grounds for a Blood Warrant, CCC, Section 256

In some circumstances, instead of demanding a breath sample or blood sample, the police officer may apply to a justice of the peace (JP) for a warrant to obtain a blood sample, whether or not the person consents. However, there are some prerequisites that must be met before a blood warrant can be sought.

◆   There must have been a collision resulting in the death of another person or bodily harm to another person or to the alleged offender.

◆   The police officer has lawful grounds for a blood demand, but the person is unable to consent to the blood demand because of a mental or physical condition arising from the consumption of alcohol or from the collision.

An example of a mental condition that could prevent a person from consenting to a blood demand is shock. A person in shock would probably not hear the blood demand or understand it, and therefore could not properly consent to or refuse the demand. An example of a physical condition that could prevent a person from consenting to a blood demand is unconsciousness. Note that in charging a person with impaired operation causing bodily harm, the harm must be to a person other than the driver, although injury to the driver qualifies as grounds for a blood warrant. The person must be conscious and able to understand the blood demand made by a police officer. If the person refuses, he or she can be charged with "refusal" under s. 254(5). If the person consents, blood samples can be taken.

If the subject is unconscious or unable to understand the blood demand, the police officer must go before a JP to get permission to seize blood samples from the person. The JP acts as an independent adjudicator to determine if the police have sufficient grounds to justify issuing a warrant to seize blood from a person who cannot respond to a lawfully made blood demand. The JP's function is to protect the rights of the person, so that the police do not proceed at will to seize a blood sample without the subject's knowledge or consent. The officer has four hours from the time of the offence to obtain the warrant and a sample of blood. However, even though the officer has four hours to obtain the warrant and the blood samples, if the samples are not taken within two hours of the offence, the blood alcohol concentration (BAC) presumption is lost. In this case, whatever the blood alcohol reading, expert evidence will have to be given to show the rate at which the BAC is decreasing, and to give some idea of what the BAC was likely to have been at the time of the offence. If the officer is not sure when the person was driving the vehicle, he or she can always proceed with the arrest on the basis of having the care and control of the vehicle, because this can usually be established.

The reason for the blood warrant is often incorrectly presumed to be for situations where the person refuses a blood demand. This is not the case. If the person refuses a blood demand, he or she can simply be charged with refusal to supply a blood sample. The penalty is the same as for a conviction for being "impaired" or being "over 80."

Other reasons for obtaining a blood warrant rather than simply requesting a blood demand, besides the driver's inability to understand a

■ **Figure 5.5 Breath Demands**

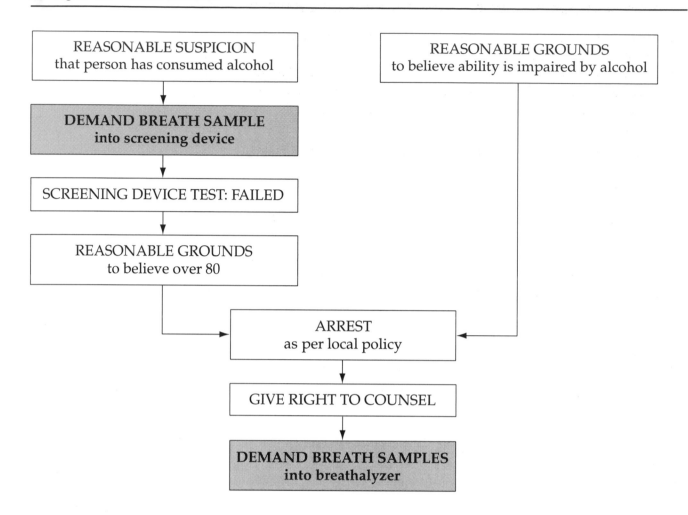

verbal demand by a police officer, is a collision that results in an injury. See figure 5.5.

| DEMAND: | Must be able to understand demand |
| WARRANT: | Incapable of understanding demand |

Two-Hour Limit on Obtaining Breath or Blood Samples, CCC, Sections 254 and 258

The demand for the breathalyzer or blood sample must be made within two hours of the commission of the offence of being impaired while operating or having the care and control of a motor vehicle, or being "over 80." In any case, the demand should be made immediately, or as soon as is practicable, once the officer has concluded that he or she has reasonable grounds to believe that the person's ability is impaired by alcohol or that the person has over 80 mg of alcohol per 100 ml of blood.

FOR A BREATHALYZER DEMAND TO BE LAWFUL

◆ The officer must have reasonable grounds to believe that the subject's ability is impaired by alcohol, or

◆ The officer must have reasonable grounds to believe that the subject has over 80 mg of alcohol per 100 ml of blood in his or her system, and

◆ The demand must be made within two hours of the offence (not the arrest).

FOR THE BAC PRESUMPTION TO BE LAWFUL

◆ The police officer must have had lawful grounds for a breathalyzer demand,

◆ The breathalyzer demand was made within two hours of the offence, and

◆ The first of two breathalyzer tests was within two hours of the offence, or both blood tests were within two hours of the offence.

The first of the two breath samples for breathalyzer analysis must be taken within two hours of the offence, or an important presumption in law is lost. The **legal presumption** is that the breathalyzer analysis indicates the BAC at the time of the offence, even though the test may be taken up to two hours after the offence. This can be important because as the body metabolizes alcohol, the BAC begins to drop.

The second breath sample, unlike the first, does not have to be taken within the two-hour limit for the presumption to hold. The second sample must be taken at least 15 minutes later, although 20 minutes is the usual practice (to make sure that it is more than 15 minutes after the first sample was taken). The breathalyzer technician reports the lower of the two readings to the court. Failure to justify to the court's satisfaction any delay in taking the breath or blood samples can lead to their exclusion as evidence. The court does not consider an inconvenience to police procedure a justifiable excuse.

legal presumption
the proof of one fact by the Crown means that another fact is presumed to be true without the Crown having to adduce evidence to prove the second fact; the accused may present evidence to disprove the fact presumed to be true, thereby rebutting the presumption

---

| BAC at time of test | = | BAC at time of offence |

Once a police officer believes that he or she has reasonable grounds to believe that a person has committed the indictable offences of operating or having care and control of a motor vehicle while impaired, or while being "over 80," the police officer can arrest the person immediately. The officer should then advise of the right to counsel and make a breathalyzer or blood demand. If the samples are obtained within two hours of the offence, the police have the benefit of the presumption that the blood alcohol concentration at the time of the offence is the same as at the time of the test. If the demand for breathalyzer or blood samples have been made within two hours of the offence, but the first of the two breath samples, or both blood samples, cannot be obtained within two hours of the offence, the person still has to provide the samples. However, the presumption that the BAC at the time of the offence is the same as at the time of the test, is lost.

Impairment by Drugs

The offence of being "impaired" refers to impairment by alcohol or drugs. However, a lawful demand for a breath sample for a roadside screening device or breathalyzer can only be made if alcohol is involved, not drugs.

A subject can be arrested for operating a motor vehicle while impaired by drugs. The police officer must obtain an admission as to the reason for the "impaired behaviour" or obtain a voluntary urine sample for analysis.

Double Barrelling

When a person fails the roadside screening device test and is arrested on the basis that there are reasonable grounds to believe that he or she has committed the offence of being "over 80," he or she can be charged only with being "over 80."

When a person's ability is assessed as being impaired by alcohol, the person may be arrested because there are reasonable grounds to believe that the person has committed the offence of being "impaired." If the subsequent breathalyzer tests prove that the person is "over 80," he or she can be charged with being both "impaired" and "over 80." Charging with both offences is often referred to as double barrelling, and is only possible when the subject is both "impaired" and "over 80." Remember that someone can be "over 80" and not show any signs of being "impaired." The Crown will use the double charges in the plea-bargaining process and usually only proceed with one of the charges against the accused.

12-Hour Suspensions in Alcohol-Related Driving Matters, HTA, Section 48

The 12-hour suspension is a useful tool for a police officer who encounters a driver who has enough alcohol in his or her system to cause concern, but not enough to charge the driver with being "impaired" or "over 80." It can also be used where a driver refuses to provide breath or blood samples. A 12-hour suspension involves taking the driver's licence from the driver of a motor vehicle and holding it for a 12-hour period. The province issues driver's licences under the HTA and authorizes their suspension. Because driving is a privilege and otherwise within the jurisdiction of the province, no court hearing is required when a licence is suspended. When a 12-hour suspension is in effect, the person may not drive a motor vehicle. A 12-hour suspension may be imposed when

◆ a driver blows "warn" on a roadside screening device,

- a driver blows 50 mg or more on a breathalyzer, or

- a driver refuses

    ◼ a roadside screening device breath sample demand,

    ◼ a breathalyzer breath sample demand, or

    ◼ a blood sample demand.

When the results of a breathalyzer test indicate a BAC *less* than 50 mg, no 12-hour suspension can be imposed lawfully, even if the person is charged with being "impaired" solely on the strength of the officer's subjective observations of the driver.

A police officer can have the motor vehicle seized and towed away at the expense of the owner if the officer believes that the car should be removed and that the owner cannot arrange for its removal.

90-Day Suspensions, HTA, Section 48.3

If a person blows "over 80" on both breathalyzer tests, or refuses to supply a breath sample for the breathalyzer, the police can immediately fax the Ministry of Transportation licensing office, which will fax back a 90-day suspension order. The driver must hand over the licence to the officer, who must forward the licence and other documents as required under the regulations to the registrar of motor vehicles. This will occur after an arrest but before trial, and is in addition to any penalty that the court might impose if the person is found guilty. If the person is found not guilty, there is no compensation for the suspension. As with the 12-hour suspension, the officer can have the vehicle towed away at the owner's expense, unless the owner can arrange for its removal.

The 90-day suspension has been strongly criticized because a person is punished before he or she is found guilty. And the punishment is severe; it can cause real hardship for an accused who may lose his or her job because he or she is unable to get to work. A similar provision has withstood a court challenge in Manitoba, in part because the suspension is seen as protection for the public, not punishment for the accused (HTA, s. 48.3(10)).

Operating a Motor Vehicle While Disqualified, CCC, Section 259(4)

This provision provides a penalty in some, but not all, cases where a person's licence has been suspended or he or she has been prohibited from driving. A person may be disqualified on conviction for:

- being "impaired,"

- being "over 80," or

- receiving an absolute or conditional discharge for either offence.

CASE ILLUSTRATION

In October 1995, a Fredericton, NB man was fined $300 for operating a motor vehicle while his ability was impaired by alcohol. The motor vehicle was an electric-powered wheelchair. The convicted man, Raymond MacDonald, suffers from muscular dystrophy and is unable to operate a manual wheelchair.

Any conviction for impaired operation of a motor vehicle carries a mandatory prohibition from operating any motor vehicle for a minimum of three months. This prohibition is imposed by the CCC and it applies throughout Canada on any road or areas where motor vehicles are permitted access. This conviction, therefore, prevented Mr. MacDonald from being able to move without assistance for three months on roads or other areas where motor vehicles are permitted access. He was effectively barred from those places by the prohibition order.

Although the criminal offence of operating a motor vehicle while ability is impaired by alcohol can occur anywhere, the resulting criminal prohibition usually applies to drivers of automobiles; the offender can usually find other ways of getting around. But Mr. MacDonald was unable even to move around his own community because his sole source of mobility was taken away from him. Although the prohibition is lawful on its face, it might not survive a challenge under the *Charter of Rights*, as it could be construed as a violation of the right not to be subjected to cruel or unusual punishment, under s. 12, or as discrimination on the basis of disability, prohibited by s. 15.

---

prohibition order
made on conviction for a CCC driving offence and disqualifies a person from driving a motor vehicle as defined in the CCC

suspension
may be made under the authority of the HTA for either a CCC offence or an HTA offence; disqualifies a driver from driving a motor vehicle as defined in the HTA on a highway as defined in the HTA

"Disqualified" means that either a judge has made a prohibition order or the province has suspended the licence, but only for a criminal conviction. There must be a criminal conviction to support a charge of driving while disqualified. A 12- or 90-day suspension under the HTA, or a suspension for unpaid parking tickets cannot be the basis for a charge of driving while disqualified. For these HTA violations, there is the s. 53(1) HTA offence of driving while suspended.

A **prohibition order** prohibits the operation of a motor vehicle as defined in the CCC on a street, road, highway, or other area where the public is permitted to operate a motor vehicle (for example, in a private parking lot). A prohibition order is imposed by a judge for a driving offence in the CCC.

A **suspension** of a driver's licence is done by the authority of a province under the HTA. In this case, the suspended driver cannot drive a motor vehicle (as defined in the HTA) on a highway (as defined in the HTA). A driver can be suspended for a CCC conviction or for an HTA offence.

The prohibition order is more extensive, as it covers all kinds of motor vehicles, except railway equipment. The HTA definition excludes several types of motor vehicles that would be included by the CCC. The prohibition order also covers practically any place that a motor vehicle could

■ **Figure 5.6   Drunk Driving Offence Procedure at a Glance**

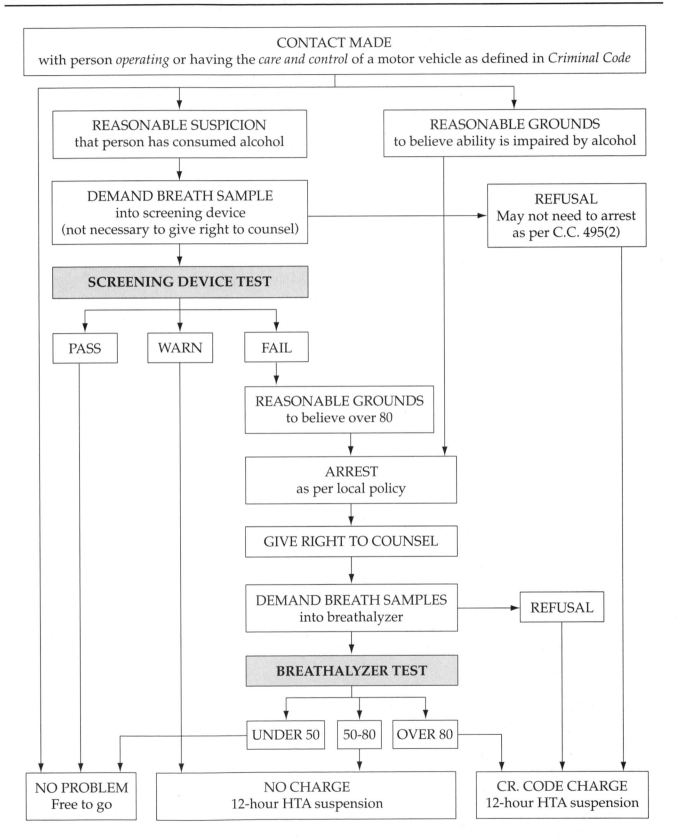

Note: This chart does not show the path for someone who may be charged with "ability impaired"—that is, who blew under 80 mg on the breathalyzer.

physically operate in or on. A suspension under the HTA only affects highways, which is a narrower definition. It is possible for a person to be both "prohibited" and "suspended" at the same time. When this situation arises, it is practical to think in terms of the prohibition order, as that is broader and more inclusive. Figure 5.6 indicates how different types of disqualifications give rise to different restrictions with regard to type of motor vehicle to be driven and place where it may be driven.

CHAPTER SUMMARY

This chapter identifies some of the more common motor-vehicle offences under federal and provincial law that a police officer is likely to encounter. The distinction between a charge and an arrest under the HTA is made, and the circumstances are identified where an officer can proceed with either a charge or an arrest. The procedures for both a charge and an arrest are explained. Particular attention is paid to HTA offences for which a person may be arrested, and where licences, vehicles, and equipment may be seized.

The *Compulsory Automobile Insurance Act* is examined in the context of the more common insurance-related offences of failing to have insurance and failing to have or produce evidence of insurance.

We examine driving-related criminal offences in the CCC concerning offences that involve drinking and driving. Basic terms and concepts related to CCC definitions of "motor vehicle," "impaired driving," being "over 80," "operating" a vehicle, and "having care and control of a vehicle" are defined, as are the various standards of proof required to use the approved devices and methods to determine a person's blood alcohol level (BAC). These basic terms and concepts underlie the discussion that considers the circumstances where a lawful demand for breath or blood samples can be made or a warrant obtained for blood samples, and indicates how the evidence so obtained can be properly used to obtain a conviction. In this context, particular attention is paid to the timing issues and the investigative procedure to be followed. Finally, the different types of suspension and prohibition orders are explored with respect to the consequences for each type of order.

KEY TERMS

arrest

CVOR

forfeited to the Crown

legal presumption

prohibition order

suspension (HTA)

REVIEW QUESTIONS

■ TRUE OR FALSE

Place a "T" next to the statement if it is true, or an "F" if it is false.

F **1.** A farmer in Ontario who operates a farm tractor along the highway may be lawfully charged with the offence of driving while under suspension if his driver's licence is suspended in Ontario for a conviction for operating a motor vehicle while his or her ability is impaired.

F **2.** There is no difference between a charge and an arrest under the HTA.

T **3.** A person who is prohibited from driving a motor vehicle as a result of a conviction for operating a motor vehicle while his or her ability is impaired cannot lawfully operate a farm tractor on a highway in Ontario.

F **4.** Defacing or altering a permit, number plate, or evidence of validation (s. 12(1(a)) is not an arrestable offence under the HTA.

T **5.** A person whose Ontario driver's licence is suspended for unpaid fines and who is driving a car on a city street in Ontario is guilty of the offence of disqualified operation of a motor vehicle.

T **6.** If a police officer suspects that your number plate has been altered, he or she can seize it under the HTA, s. 14(1).

F **7.** A person whose Alberta's driver's licence has been suspended in Alberta for refusal to provide a breath sample may lawfully operate a farm tractor anywhere in Ontario.

T **8.** If a driver is stopped by the police while driving a friend's car and is asked to produce an insurance card, it is all right to produce his or her insurance card for a car that he or she owns.

T **9.** A person whose driver's licence is suspended for demerit points in Ontario is guilty of a provincial offence if he or she drives his or her car on a highway in Ontario.

T **10.** The driver of a pickup truck on a street in Ontario while under a 12-hour suspension is guilty of disqualified operation.

■ **SHORT ANSWER**

Briefly answer the following questions.

1. **a.** What is the difference between the definitions of "motor vehicle" in the HTA and the CCC?

   b. Why is the difference important?

2. How could you be "over 80" and not be "impaired"?

3. What is the difference between "reasonable suspicion" and "reasonable grounds to believe"?

4. Explain what the differences are between a "breathalyzer" and a "roadside screening device" in terms of function and purpose.

5. What are the grounds for a lawful demand for the following?

   a. A breath sample for a breathalyzer.

   b. A blood sample.

   c. A breath sample for a roadside screening device.

6. Explain the importance of the two-hour limit and the four-hour limit in determining the BAC.

7. May a police officer make a breathalyzer demand for someone he or she has grounds to believe is impaired by drugs? Explain your answer.

8. What is "double barrelling" and when can it be used in relation to an alcohol-related driving offence?

9. **a.** Site the statute and section number that authorizes the following:

    i. A demand for a breath sample for a roadside screening device.

    ii. A demand for a breath sample for a breathalyzer.

    iii. A demand for a blood sample.

    iv. An application for a warrant to obtain a blood sample.

    v. Suspension of a driver's licence for 12 hours.

    vi. Suspension of a driver's licence for 90 days.

    vii. Seizure of a radar warning device.

    viii. Seizure of number plates.

b. Explain what events must occur or what factors must be present before the police may validly take the steps described above.

■ DISCUSSION QUESTIONS

1. Rank the following four topics in the order in which they would occur sequentially and describe the basis for your ordering.

   a. blood warrant

   b. blood demand

   c. breathalyzer demand

   d. roadside screening device demand

2. "In drunk driving cases, timing is everything." Discuss this statement in terms of the nature of the offences, the requirements of the law, and any other relevant matter.

3. Discuss the following statements:

   a. Breathalyzer evidence is only corroborative evidence for a charge of operating a motor vehicle while ability is impaired by alcohol, but is essential evidence for a charge of operating a motor vehicle with over 80 mg of alcohol per 100 ml of blood.

   b. Failing a roadside screening test is not sufficient evidence by itself for a charge of operating a motor vehicle with over 80 mg of alcohol per 100 ml of blood.

   c. If a peace officer has the lawful grounds to make a breathalyzer demand, he or she also has the lawful grounds to make an arrest.

   d. If a person is arrested on the basis that there are reasonable grounds to believe that he or she is "over 80," an additional charge of "impaired" is not possible, but if the subject is arrested on reasonable grounds to believe that he or she is "impaired," an additional charge of "over 80" is possible.

NOTES

1   A 12-hour suspension may be given when a person blows "warn" on a roadside screening device, blows 50mg or more on a breathalyzer, or refuses a screening device demand, breathalyzer demand, or demand for a blood sample. A 12-hour suspension and related charges are discussed in more detail later in this chapter.

2   Counsel will also focus on whether the police were scrupulous in affording the right to counsel and whether the testing procedures were carried out properly. Because drunk driving is an offence that crosses the class and income spectrum, there are more offenders who have the money and resources to support an aggressive and imaginative defence than is the case for most criminal charges. For this reason, a disproportionately large number of reported criminal cases are "drunk driving" cases.

3   The CCC uses the more encompassing term "peace officer."

CHAPTER 6
Collision Investigation

CHAPTER OBJECTIVES

After completing this chapter, you should be able to:

Know the steps for investigating a collision.

Understand the process of mental role playing, and be able to use it to improve the pattern of response at a motor vehicle collision scene.

Know the information you need prior to responding to a collision, and be able to obtain it.

Develop a safe driving strategy for responding to emergency calls.

Understand how to evaluate a collision scene on arrival.

Prioritize steps to be taken at a collision scene.

Know and understand the significance of the signs and symbols for dangerous goods.

◆ Know what steps must be taken when dangerous goods are found at a collision scene.

Assess whether an injured person can be moved safely.

Know the circumstances where death can be assumed without determination by a physician.

Know your duty with respect to assisting injured persons.

Know when and how to close off and safeguard a collision scene.

◆ Know what to do if there are downed hydro lines at a scene.

Know what steps to take if there is a vehicle fire.

◆ Know what steps to take to safeguard the public if the road is icy.

Know how to handle fighting or argumentative drivers.

Know what questions to ask to determine who is hurt, who the drivers are, who the witnesses are, and, in general, how to obtain information voluntarily from persons involved at the scene.

◆ Understand and master appropriate witness and suspect interview techniques.

◆ Structure an interview to elicit relevant information from witnesses.

◆ Recognize the importance of developing good listening skills and become an active and effective listener.

◆ Recognize situations where a cautioned statement is required.

◆ Take a cautioned statement that will stand up to court scrutiny.

◆ Obtain information from a driver who has been cautioned and opted to remain silent.

◆ Deal with unruly spectators.

◆ Make a field sketch.

◆ Make a diagram of a collision scene.

◆ Make coordinate and triangulated measurements at a collision scene and accurately transfer the information to a diagram of the collision scene.

◆ Understand the importance of tire marks in a collision investigation.

◆ Recognize the significance of various types of tire marks, including skids and scuffs.

◆ Understand the effect of under- and overinflation of tires in a collision.

◆ Accurately measure and interpret skids and scuffs.

◆ Recognize wheel lock-up situations from an examination of skids and scuffs.

◆ Recognize and understand the significance of less-common skids.

◆ Recognize the significance of scratches and gouges at a collision scene.

◆ Obtain useful information from an examination of scratches and gouges at a collision scene.

◆ Understand the significance of debris in helping to determine what happened at a collision scene.

◆ Identify what can be determined from debris at a collision.

◆ Determine whether a vehicle has vaulted or been involved in a fall.

◆ Define and understand the terms used to describe a collision scene and be able to apply these terms in writing an accident report.

COLLISION, RECONSTRUCTION, AND INVESTIGATION

The police are required to investigate or receive a report of a collision from drivers involved in every motor vehicle collision in Ontario where a personal injury occurs or there is property damage valued at more than $1,000 (reg. 596, as amended by O. reg. 537/97, s. 11). Because even minor damage to motor vehicles is expensive to repair, the $1,000 reporting threshold is easily reached in most cases and as a result, the police investigate virtually every motor-vehicle collision in Ontario.

Some collisions will receive additional attention. Besides an investigation, a serious collision may also result in a collision reconstruction. If it appears that criminal or provincial charges may be laid, civil litigation is likely, or a coroner's inquest is called.

The reasons why police officers attend motor vehicle collisions are many. Police officers must record the identification of all persons involved, the type of injuries sustained, the registration of the vehicles involved, the insurance particulars of the vehicle owners, the type and amount of damage to vehicles and property, and the location and time of the collision. This information, recorded and saved by the police, is necessary to prevent incorrect or fraudulent claims, to provide a basis for statistical analysis by the Ministry of Transport, and to provide evidence for prosecutions and inquests.

Note that although police officers must investigate any violations of the law and collect evidence relevant to a prosecution, this is not necessarily the same as finding fault. A driver may be "at fault" for the purposes of a civil suit for negligence, but the conduct of the driver may fall far short of what is required for a prosecution under provincial legislation or under the CCC. "Fault" is a term of interest to insurance companies dealing with civil liability for negligence; it is not a term of interest to the police.

STEPS IN A COLLISION INVESTIGATION

The steps described here are general in nature and do not presume to apply to all situations. The steps that make up this approach to collision investigation should be considered a good starting framework that you can develop further as you become more experienced. The steps are set out and discussed below.

Mental Role Playing

Psychologists have determined that the mind cannot tell the difference between an imagined experience and a real one in some circumstances. Russian sports psychologists have exploited this idea by having their figure skaters and gymnasts visualize their routines repeatedly so that the pattern becomes imprinted in their minds; the athletes, thus, act more instinctively when performing their routines. This visualization technique also allows the athletes to practice much more in their minds than their bodies could manage physically.

A police officer can employ this mental role-playing technique to condition himself or herself to act more instinctively when confronting a collision scene. During quiet times on his or her shift, a police officer can imagine a collision scenario and then think of the correct response to the scene. The brain becomes used to the pattern of response and the officer will then act instinctively under the pressure of a collision situation.

The pattern of response can be improved over time if officers "debrief" themselves. After each collision, officers must ask themselves how they could improve their performances. Debriefing is an important way to reinforce and refine the skills used in carrying out a procedure.

Approaching the Scene

Obtain as Much Information as Possible

Prior to arrival, obtain as much information as possible to expedite an efficient and effective handling of the collision scene.

Find out the exact location of the collision, and determine the lane and lane direction, if it is a divided highway. Find out where the closest cross street is from your approach.

Ascertain whether there are any injuries and, if so, ask whether medical personnel have been dispatched. Ask whether any other emergency services are needed and, if so, ask whether they have been dispatched. These could include hydro (downed wires), the fire department, officers for traffic control, or environmental protection personnel.

Guarantee Arrival

At the Ontario Police College, new police recruits were given the task of driving a given route to a collision scene as fast as possible. Each recruit was timed with a stopwatch, and his or her time was recorded. The recruits invariably turned this exercise into a competition with other students. The recruits drove at excessive speeds and hit many of the pylons along the route. They were then asked to drive the same route again, using a car that cannot exceed a predetermined speed limit. Each recruit was again timed with a stopwatch and his or her time recorded. The recruits were surprised to discover that the second controlled run was always faster. The moral of this story is: *If you slow down and drive at a more controlled speed, you will actually get there faster and more safely.*

A section of the HTA that deals with rate of speed exempts police officers in the lawful performance of their duties from the speed limits imposed in the HTA or any speed bylaw. Responding to a motor vehicle collision is within the lawful performance of a police officer's duty, so police officers may exceed the speed limit when en route to a collision scene. However, considering the experiment at the Ontario Police College, driving *excessively* over the speed limit is inefficient and unnecessarily risky.

The HTA also authorizes the driver of an emergency vehicle, after stopping the vehicle at a red light, to proceed through the red light, if it is safe to do so. Emergency vehicles do not, however, have blanket authority to run through a red light. If the driver of an emergency vehicle is involved in a collision while proceeding through a red light, there is a presumption that it was not safe to run the light. The burden of proving it was safe is always on the driver of the emergency vehicle.

The HTA defines an emergency vehicle as a vehicle used by a police officer in the lawful performance of his or her duties on which a siren is continuously sounding, and from which intermittent flashes of red light are visible from all directions. This definition means that a police officer cannot lawfully proceed through a red light in an emergency situation unless the flashing red lights are on and the siren is continuously sounding. There could be insurance problems if the police vehicle does not match the definition of an emergency vehicle.

The HTA also permits a police department vehicle to drive off the roadway to overtake another vehicle. Passing on the shoulder is sometimes necessary when traffic stops on the roadway and no other lane is open. Obviously, care should be taken when driving onto the soft shoulder to prevent a rollover.

In the event that a motorist fails to pull over to permit an emergency vehicle to pass, there is not much that can be done at the time by the officer responding to a collision. However, all police officers can enforce the law when they see such an obstruction of other emergency vehicles. The HTA states that the driver of a vehicle, on the approach of an ambulance, fire, or police department vehicle on which a bell or siren is sounding or on which a lamp located on the roof of the vehicle is producing intermittent flashes of red light, shall immediately bring such a vehicle to a standstill, as near as practicable to the right-hand curb or edge of the roadway and parallel to it, and clear of any intersection. If the vehicle is on a roadway that has more than two lanes for traffic and is designated for the use of one-way traffic, the driver shall stop as near as practicable to the nearest curb or edge of the roadway, parallel to it, and clear of any intersection.

Arrival at the Scene

When officers arrive at a collision scene, they must stop to evaluate what they are confronting. They need time to determine which emergency, if left unattended, would cause the most serious consequences. From the safety of the police cruiser, an officer can buy time to determine his or her plan of action by picking up the car microphone and pretending to talk to the communications centre. This technique allows you to survey the scene without appearing to be inactive or uninvolved.

Prioritize Emergencies

When considering what action to take, the officer should be mindful of the priorities at all collision scenes: YOU, THEM, IT. Your first priority

ON ARRIVAL, BE SAFE

B   Before
E   Entering
S   Stop
A   and
F   First
E   Evaluate

should be your own safety. If you rush into a collision scene where there is a spill of dangerous goods or downed hydro lines, you may become another casualty. In order for you to be effective, you cannot become one of the injured. You may need to close the road to protect yourself as you walk into the scene and to prevent the situation from becoming worse. Second, if there are injured persons, attend to them. Last, concern yourself with property damage.

Situations that could cause the most serious consequences if left unattended are

◆   the presence of dangerous goods,

◆   injuries,

◆   scene protection and evidence preservation,

◆   downed hydro lines,

◆   vehicle fires,

◆   road conditions,

◆   theft protection, and

◆   fighting drivers.

Dangerous Goods

Transport Canada has developed a system of dangerous goods placards to be placed on all vehicles transporting dangerous goods, and a similar system of dangerous goods labels to be placed on containers of dangerous goods. The purpose of these placards and labels is to alert emergency response crews who can quickly identify the dangerous goods in question so that appropriate action can be taken to minimize damage and save lives when these goods are involved in a collision.

If emergency personnel are unsure of the dangers, there are emergency phone numbers at both the federal and provincial levels of government to obtain information about the appropriate response. Police officers should record these numbers for quick access.

The dangerous goods placards and labels use a three-part system to identify the goods:

◆   colour,

◆   symbols, and

◆   class numbers.

The first officer at a collision scene, when evaluating the situation from a distance, may recognize the category of dangerous goods by colour first. Colour is easily recognizable from afar. For example, colour recognition could warn of poison, explosives, or radioactive material. Symbols on the placards assist in interpreting the meaning of the colour of the placard. For example, a red placard is enhanced by a symbol of a flame to convey the message that the goods are flammable. Be aware that in failing light, colours are harder to recognize and to distinguish, one from another. A strong flashlight and a closer look may be necessary.

Binoculars may be necessary to identify the class number printed on the bottom of the placard. For example, a number two at the bottom of the placard tells the emergency personnel that the goods involve a compressed gas. This information, along with the condition of the vehicle or the containers, needs to be immediately relayed to the communications centre, which in turn should notify the appropriate authorities. If a tanker truck is ruptured and the compressed gas is poisonous, only emergency personnel with protective clothing and breathing apparatus may approach. They may be able to obtain the **bill of lading** from the cab of the vehicle to identify the specific cargo. Their job will also be to neutralize any danger, so that investigation and cleanup can be done safely and effectively. The responsibility of the police will be to secure the scene and evacuate the area downwind of the collision to minimize injury and damage.

Obviously, police officers need to know the meaning of the colour symbols and class numbers used on the dangerous goods placards and labels to prevent injury to themselves and others and to prevent further damage to property.

Dangerous goods placards can be initially identified from afar by colour, as the table below indicates.

bill of lading
a receipt for merchandise that accompanies the merchandise when it is being transported from one place to another; it should provide detailed information about the cargo carried by a commercial vehicle

Orange	explosives
Red	anything flammable
Green	non-flammable compressed gases
Blue	dangerous when wet
Yellow	**oxidizers**
White	poisonous and infectious substances
Yellow over white	radioactive materials
White over black	corrosives

oxidizer
a substance that combines with oxygen, which may be quite volatile, flammable, or otherwise chemically active and therefore dangerous

Dangerous goods placards and labels employ the use of 10 symbols that assist in the interpretation of the colour. See figure 6.1 for a breakdown. Below is a list of symbols and their meanings.

Explosive	Exploding bomb
Flammable	Flame
Compressed gas	Gas cylinders
Poison	Skull and crossbones
Oxidizers	Burning "O"
Harmful foodstuffs	Cross on wheat kernel
Infectious materials	Biomedical symbol
Radioactive materials	Trefoil
Corrosive	Acid attacking hand or metal
Miscellaneous	Exclamation mark

Dangerous goods are divided into nine classes. The class number is printed at the bottom of the placard or label. Transport Canada's chart of dangerous goods is reproduced in colour on the inside back cover of this book.

Class	Colour	Symbol
Class 1: Explosives	Orange	Exploding bomb
Class 2: Compressed gases	Red	Flame
	Green	Gas cylinder
	White	Skull
	White	Gas cylinder
Class 3: Flammable liquids	Red	Flame
Class 4: Flammable solids	Red and white stripes	Flame
	White over red	Flame
	Blue	Flame
Class 5: Oxidizers	Yellow	Burning "O"
Class 6: Poisonous/ infectious substances	White	Skull
	White	Food
Class 7: Radioactives	Yellow over white	Trefoil
Class 8: Corrosives	White over black	Acid on hand or metal
Class 9: Miscellaneous	White	Red "!"
	Red	Word "Danger"

■ **Figure 6.1   Dangerous Goods Symbols**

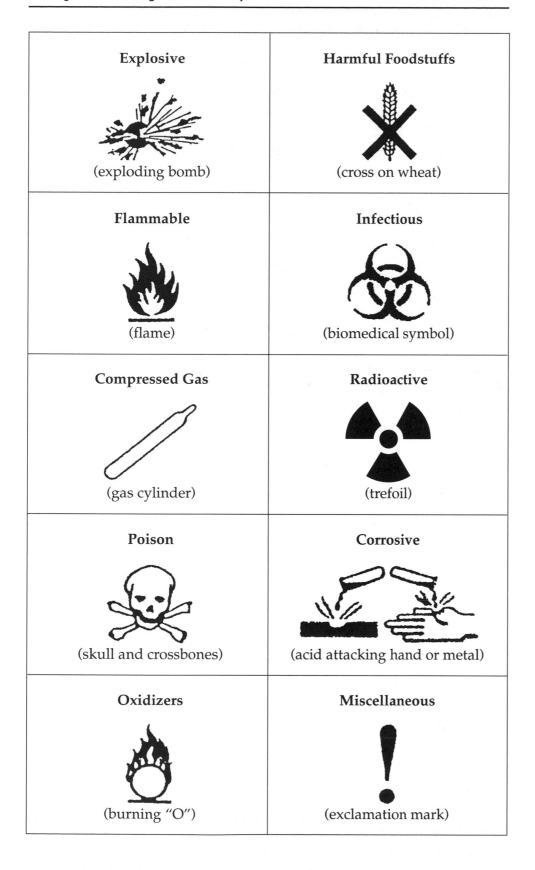

Explosive
(exploding bomb)

Harmful Foodstuffs
(cross on wheat)

Flammable
(flame)

Infectious
(biomedical symbol)

Compressed Gas
(gas cylinder)

Radioactive
(trefoil)

Poison
(skull and crossbones)

Corrosive
(acid attacking hand or metal)

Oxidizers
(burning "O")

Miscellaneous
(exclamation mark)

Hint for remembering class numbers on dangerous goods placards:

Class 2	Compressed gas (O_2)
Class 3	Liquids (more dense than gas)
Class 4	Solids (most dense)

A flammable compressed gas placard can look like a flammable liquid placard except for the class number.

Injuries

Injured persons should not be moved if there is a risk of aggravating the injury, but they may have to be moved if there is a danger of more serious consequences.

If a live victim needs to be removed from a vehicle, stabilization is required. Stabilization of the scene, stabilization of the vehicle, and stabilization of the victim must all be considered before a victim is moved. Ambulance and fire personnel are best equipped to treat and move injured persons so it is imperative to have these experts on scene as soon as possible.

Only medical practitioners (doctors) can pronounce someone dead. Police officers, however, can assume death in four circumstances:

1. decapitation,

2. trans-section of the body,

3. advanced decomposition, or

4. extreme circumstances.

According to the *Coroner's Act*, no person, including police officers, shall interfere with or move a dead body without a "warrant to take possession of the body of a deceased person" signed by the coroner. When a police officer can assume death, he or she should cover the body and its parts with a blanket until the coroner arrives.

Most motor-vehicle collisions will not have a victim that fits within the extreme circumstances category. Extreme circumstances are more than just severe blood loss. Police officers are qualified in first aid and CPR. With that qualification comes an obligation or duty. Police officers are obligated (if emergency medical personnel are not on the scene) to render first aid to every victim whom they cannot assume is dead. Failure to provide first aid can lead to a charge of neglect of duty under the *Police Services Act* and possibly a charge of criminal negligence causing death under the CCC. There is also the possibility of a civil action by the victim or his or her family.

Officers should make sure that each victim is identified before the victim is removed from a collision scene. Obviously, discretion is required to make sure that the attempt to identify the victim does not interfere with those persons rendering emergency medical services. Officers should also make sure that they know the name of the hospital where each victim is being taken and who is transporting the victim.

In a collision with multiple victims and there is a lack of emergency medical personnel, a police officer will have to prioritize who needs treatment. Officers will have to group victims into three categories; category one victims are top priority. These categories are as follows:

1. Victims whose injuries are life threatening and require immediate treatment.

2. Victims whose injuries are not life threatening and who can wait for treatment.

3. Victims whose injuries are so severe that death is imminent.

Hopefully, an officer will never have to make these kinds of decisions, but by clarifying the decision-making process, and using the mental role-playing technique, an officer can prepare himself or herself for such a situation.

If the collision involves only property damage, a police officer should make sure not to trivialize the collision. The collision may be routine for the police officer, but it is a dramatic life event for the victim. A little sympathy can go a long way to enhancing the image of the police service. Remember the officer's report is important, but it is not more important than public support.

Protecting the Scene

The HTA authorizes a police officer to close a highway or any part thereof to ensure the orderly movement of traffic, to prevent injury or damage to persons or property, or to permit proper action in an emergency. Every person shall obey the officer's directions (HTA, s. 134). Emergency and service vehicles are exempt from road-closure rules. For the purposes of closing a highway or any part of it, a police officer may post or cause to be posted signs to that effect, or may place or cause to be placed traffic control devices as prescribed by the regulations.

The regulations prescribe the use of a "Do Not Enter" sign and not fewer than three orange cones, or not fewer than two rectangular shapes with horizontal orange and black stripes mounted on posts, or not fewer than two barricades that are orange in colour with black bars. See Figure 6.2.

The HTA also authorizes police officers to direct traffic to ensure the orderly movement of traffic, to prevent injury or damage to persons or property, or to permit proper action in an emergency.

With these powers comes the responsibility to ensure that no further injury or damage occurs at a collision scene. This responsibility means that officers attending a collision scene must warn other traffic approaching the scene so that the traffic has time to slow down and stop, if necessary. Flares are usually used for this purpose and must be placed far enough ahead according to the circumstances. On a long straight road with no view obstructions, only the speed limit is a factor in determining

■ **Figure 6.2 Barricades**

Do Not Enter Sign
(60cm × 60cm)

Red reflective circle

White reflective background and bar

Black border

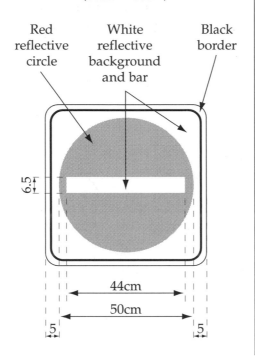

6.5

44cm

50cm

5

5

Orange Cone

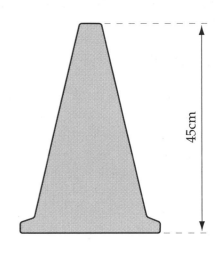

45cm

Post

20cm

9

6

60cm

100cm

Orange reflective background

Black bars

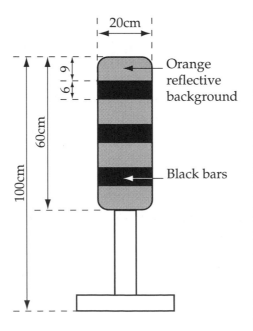

Barricade

100cm

90cm

15

Orange or orange with black bars

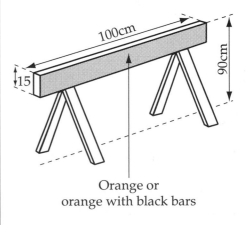

how far from the collision to place the flares. On a road with curves, hills, bridges, or other view obstructions of the collision scene, the flares may have to be placed much further ahead.

Until the proper road or lane closure devices are in place, or if none are available, officers will have to direct traffic manually. This may require several police officers. If other officers are not available, a police cruiser, with the red lights activated, may be used to close a lane. Especially at night, officers directing traffic should ensure that they are wearing the appropriate reflective vests to avoid personal injury.

Downed Hydro Lines

If hydro lines are down at a collision scene, hydro distribution companies recommend that the police officers stay in the police cruiser until the power can be shut off. If the road is wet, stepping onto the road could result in death by electrocution. The investigating officer should also take steps to keep other persons away from the collision scene and notify those involved in the collision to stay in their cars until the power has been shut off. Once the power has been shut off, the officer can continue to deal with other emergencies arising from the collision.

Vehicle Fires

If there are no dangerous goods involved, and a vehicle is on fire, the ignition should be turned off, if possible, and all people kept away until the fire department arrives. If the fire is small and can be extinguished, a dry-chemical extinguisher should be used. If no extinguisher is available, the fire should be smothered with dirt or a blanket. The officer should remember his or her priorities when trying to save a car that is on fire. Personal safety has priority over property. If occupants are still in the vehicle, rescue the occupants, if possible.

> In extinguishing a car fire, use a fire extinguisher.
> Do not attempt to extinguish a car fire with water.

Road Conditions

Often after an ice storm, the road conditions, if left unattended, may cause a serious emergency. Notify the communications centre to dispatch the road sanding and salting equipment to the scene to reduce the likelihood of further collisions. Failure to do this may result in a charge of neglect of duty and exposure to civil liability.

Theft Protection

Sometimes a valuable cargo is spilled on the road, and looting becomes a problem. In this case, the investigating officer should immediately call for assistance to help secure the scene. If the first officer on the scene runs after someone who has stolen some cargo, the scene is left unprotected. At least one officer must protect the cargo while the investigating officer attends to other aspects of the collision.

If the road must be closed to prevent other collisions and injuries, or if the present collision has resulted in injuries, the cargo is obviously secondary to attending to the injured. It would be extremely unprofessional for an officer to chase someone who has stolen a VCR or a case of beer from a spilled cargo if the driver is unconscious from injuries. Remember the motto YOU, THEM, IT; property is the last priority. An officer's first instinct may be to chase someone who is running from the scene with some cargo, but the officer must concern himself or herself first with the safety of others.

Fighting Drivers

The first officer on the scene must immediately call for backup if drivers are fighting. Obviously, the fight must be stopped and the drivers kept apart. It will be necessary to place each driver in the back of separate police cruisers until the officer finds out what happened. Criminal charges may need to be laid, and neither driver should be allowed to leave until the incident is fully understood by the officer on the scene. This temporary incarceration will allow each driver to cool down. The authority to arrest in this case is granted to prevent a continuing breach of the peace. There is no charge for breach of the peace and each driver may be released when he or she has calmed down, if there are no other charges pending.

Management of People at the Scene

All dealings with the public must be done in a manner that enhances the professionalism of the police service. Collision investigations are one of the most common situations when ordinary members of the public come into contact with the police. The police officer must not make a bad impression if the police service seeks to gain or maintain public support. The officer must be seen to be courteous, sympathetic, and fair.

Four Questions To Ask at a Collision Scene

1. Is anyone hurt?

When approaching people at a collision scene, the police officer should first ask if anyone is hurt. This initial question shows concern for people first, and demonstrates that the police are not just there to lay charges or assign blame. This question also has investigative merit because the investigating officer may be challenged by an insurance company at a later date about why the officer did not initiate medical treatment for an injured person. If a person later claimed that he or she had sustained neck or back problems, the investigating officer can truthfully state that no one reported any injuries when questioned at the time of the investigation.

The question also has the indirect value of helping to sort out the crowd that may have gathered. The crowd will usually direct the officer to the injured person(s) and react in other ways that give the officer clues about who is involved in the collision and who is just a spectator.

2. Who is the driver of this vehicle?

If there are no injuries, the police officer should walk over and touch one of the vehicles and ask, "Who is the driver of this vehicle?" The voluntary answer to this investigative question is admissible in court because there is no determination of a violation. The question is also of such a nature that there is no dispute that the response is voluntary. The admission is important because it may be the only evidence of who was driving the vehicle. Once the driver is identified, the officer should ask the driver for his or her driver's licence, registration, and evidence of insurance. The officer should develop the habit of placing these documents together in a predetermined place, such as a right-hand pocket. This will save the officer the embarrassment of not being able to find the documents when he or she is ready to return them to the driver.

The officer could then ask the driver if he or she was wearing a seatbelt. Again, the confession is admissible in court if there is no dispute that the response is voluntary. The officer should then direct the driver to stay with his or her vehicle or some other safer place until the officer returns.

If another vehicle is involved, the officer should walk over and touch that vehicle and ask, "Who is the driver of this vehicle?" Again, the voluntary admission is admissible in court because there is no talk of any charges at this stage. The officer should ask this driver for his or her licence, registration, and evidence of insurance, and place those documents in a predetermined place, perhaps in the left-hand pocket (so as not to mix them up with other drivers' documents). The officer should ask whether the driver was wearing his or her seatbelt and direct the driver to stay with his or her vehicle or another safer place, preferably away from the other driver, to avoid a confrontation. The officer now has all of the documents of both drivers; this reduces the likelihood that either driver will leave the scene, and provides the officer with basic information for accident reports and charges, if charges are necessary.

3. Did anyone witness the collision?

The identification of the drivers must not take very long because it is important to speak to any witnesses before they leave. The testimony of independent witnesses in court carries a lot of weight. The officer should approach the crowd and ask if anyone witnessed the collision. If witnesses come forth, the officer should thank them for their assistance. The officer should tell the witnesses that it should only take a few minutes to record their statements, and then the officer should speak to each witness separately. If one witness says that he or she must leave immediately because of a scheduled meeting or for some other urgent reason, record his or her name and a number where he or she can be reached by phone. Insisting that he or she stay will only produce a hostile witness, who is likely to give a poor quality statement and to be less helpful.

It is very important to listen to what each witness has to say before the officer records personal data. If the officer starts by asking questions about the witness's name, date of birth, address, phone number, place of employment, work phone number, and so on, the witness will likely fall into a question-and-answer mode, and may not offer information until he or she is asked for it. A better technique is for the officer to ask where the witness was in relation to the collision scene, and then ask the witness to recount, chronologically, what he or she saw. The officer should refrain from interrupting the witness with too many questions during the narrative, as it will disrupt the spontaneous flow of the witness's account and put the witness back into question-and-answer mode.

One technique to avoid interruptions, yet impose a chronological order to the witness statement is for the officer to hand the witness a card, and then ask the witness to please explain what he or she saw following the order of the items on the card:

◆ Description of the vehicle.

◆ Direction of travel.

◆ Name of street.

◆ Lane of travel.

◆ Approximate speed.

◆ What happened?

It is always best to listen to what a person says. People talk if they see that you are listening. This point is very important to remember when taking any statement. The officer's interest and facial expressions will encourage a more detailed answer than would otherwise be obtained.

> Hint: People will talk when you listen.

Listening involves continual eye contact and responding with facial expressions—*not* staring at your notebook and writing madly. If the investigating officer is looking only at his or her notebook, racing to record the witness's statement, and does not pay attention to the witness, the witness becomes focused on the officer's writing and actually speaks at the pace of the officer's hand-writing speed. Concentrating on the officer's problem will distract the witness and cause him or her to omit details in the statement. This is another reason for the officer to listen to the statement first, and then ask the witness to repeat the statement as the officer writes it down. Then the officer knows what to expect and can record the statement more effectively. Although this two-step procedure may appear to take more time, it really does not, because it reduces the time that it takes the officer to interrupt the witness to get the required detail. There are other advantages to this approach: the statement is in the witness's own words, and in telling the story twice, the witness has the opportunity to consider the accuracy of his or her statement more carefully.

These statements can be handled as formal statements or as **"will say" statements**, depending on the policy of the police service and the severity of the collision. The witness should be invited to read the statement, to make any changes that he or she wishes, and to sign the statement. Because the Crown and defence counsel are likely to see the document, and it may be questioned in court, some attention should be paid to grammar, spelling, and clarity of language.

"will say" statements
a brief description or summary from an officer's notebook of what the witness will say in court; its primary audience is the Crown Attorney and defence counsel, who will likely see the statement under evidentiary disclosure rules

4. Was anyone else involved in the collision?

It usually is not necessary to take statements from passengers in the vehicles involved in the collision. These statements do not carry much weight because they are considered to be biased. Identification, position in the vehicle, seatbelt use, and injury information is usually all that is necessary. If a person admits that he or she was not wearing a seatbelt, this voluntary answer to an investigative question is admissible in court because there was no determination of a charge before the question was asked. The question must be asked in a manner that ensures there is no dispute that the response is voluntary.

Cautioned Statements

If the physical evidence is overwhelming or independent witnesses supplied statements, the investigating officer may know beyond a reasonable degree of certainty that a violation of the HTA or CCC has occurred. The officer should interview the non-offending driver first. The procedure for taking a statement from this driver is the same as for other witnesses. Get the driver's story first, and record the information from the driver's licence, registration, and insurance card last.

When the officer approaches the suspect driver, the officer should follow the **Judge's Rules** and read the caution first, because this driver is suspected of a violation. The suggested language for the caution is as follows:

Judge's Rules
rules that were developed by the English courts in the early 20th century, which govern the questioning of suspects; they have generally been applied in Canada and some of the rules have been incorporated into the **Charter of Rights,** *particularly s. 10, which requires that a suspect be cautioned and advised of a right to counsel*

You are to be charged with _____. Do you wish to say anything in answer to the charge? You are not obliged to say anything in answer to the charge unless you wish to do so, but whatever you do say may be given in evidence.

If the suspect driver does make a "cautioned" statement, it may be tendered as evidence at the trial. Prior to giving the contents of the statement as evidence, there will usually be a **voir dire** to ensure that the statement was voluntary and made without any inducements. The caution will go a long way to demonstrate that any subsequent statement

voir dire
a "trial within a trial" conducted by a trial judge to determine whether evidence to be tendered is admissible in the main proceeding; an officer may have to give evidence whether the accused was given a warning and whether his or her statement was voluntary and not compelled or coerced

was given voluntarily. Having the suspect driver read the statement over and make corrections before signing it also supports the case that the statement was given voluntarily.

If the driver refuses to make a statement after being cautioned, the officer may still charge the driver on the strength of physical evidence, on the evidence of the other driver, and on the evidence of independent witnesses. If there are no independent witnesses, the statement of the driver may be more important. Extra care should be made in taking this cautioned statement because its admission in court may be vital to the case.

Statements Required by Statute

If the suspect driver does not wish to make a cautioned statement at that time, he or she should be told of the statutory requirement in the HTA (ss. 199-200) to supply evidence necessary for the completion of the accident report. Failure to supply this information could result in a charge of failing to report a collision. However, care should be taken to explain to the suspect driver that the statutory requirement invalidates the statement for use in court as evidence against the driver because it is a forced statement, not a voluntary one. Anything the suspect driver says in providing information to complete the accident report cannot be used in court against the driver, but is required by the Ministry of Transportation for the planning of public safety. However, although the statement itself is not admissible in evidence against the driver, the information may provide useful insights that will assist the officer in gathering evidence that is admissible.

If a collision occurred at an intersection controlled by traffic lights and there is not enough physical evidence or statements from any independent witnesses, statements by statutory requirement will at least help determine the truth. In these cases, no charges are feasible. Remember that the investigating officer should be more concerned with determining what happened than with laying charges.

Unruly Spectators

If spectators become unruly, it is necessary to dispatch other police officers to the scene to assist. If spectators obstruct the officer in the lawful execution of his or her duty, a criminal charge of obstructing the police (CCC, s. 129) is possible, although this detracts from the primary purpose of the investigation and is best handled by other officers.

Moving spectators back on the sidewalk can be accomplished with an authoritative command. If people do not instantly obey the officer, an explanation of the consequences, given in a professional manner, is required. People who do not comply with this order are not necessarily "obstructing a peace officer"; there must be more evidence of interference with the collection of evidence or with other duties related to the collision investigation. Officers must not be overzealous in their wish to have everyone jump to their commands and immediately arrest those who do not. Arrests for this purpose diminish the professionalism of the police service and give the public the impression that the police are capricious and "power hungry."

SKETCHING, MEASURING, AND DIAGRAMMING A COLLISION SCENE

Field Sketch

A field sketch consists of drawings and notes made at a collision scene that show the road configuration, the position of vehicles and relevant objects, and the measurement lines illustrating the system of measurement used and the corresponding measurements.

A field sketch must be factual. The sketch must only show what was visible to the investigating officer and not include opinions, such as the point of impact. However, evidence that might suggest the point of impact, such as gouges in the roadway and offset skid marks, should be shown.

Because the field sketch is **contemporaneous with the event** and factual, it can be used in court and introduced as evidence. Therefore, a field sketch should not be redrawn or altered after the officer leaves the scene.

A field sketch should be drawn before the officer starts measuring. Figuring out the system of measurement to be employed on the field sketch minimizes the time spent measuring and improves the accuracy of the finished product.

There are some further points to note with regard to sketches:

◆   A field sketch is a freehand drawing, and is not drawn to scale or with the aid of a ruler.

◆   If the objects in the sketch are relatively proportional, it is easier to interpret the sketch visually.

◆   To distinguish between the roadway edges and measurement lines, roadway edges could be drawn using solid lines, and dotted lines could be used for the measurement lines.

◆   The field sketch should also include north direction for reference, the name of the investigating officer who made the sketch, the names of any assistants, the case or identifying number, and the date and time of the collision.

contemporaneous with the event
usually used to describe notes or other records of an event made at the time the event occurred; it may be used to refresh a witness's memory, and the record itself may be introduced in evidence

Forensic Measuring

The measurement systems described here are applicable to any scene and not just to collision scenes. The number of measurements depends on the detail required. The amount of detail depends on the severity of the scene and the type of court proceedings. Many measurements may be necessary for the accurate location of all the evidence required to produce a detailed scale diagram of a fatal collision. Such a diagram may be required for criminal prosecutions or civil litigation. The diagram may be important to the outcome of the case, and a poorly constructed diagram reflects badly on the police service. Few measurements may suffice if an officer is just testifying in Provincial Offences Court. In fact, the diagram may not be needed, but, if challenged, the officer can respond with accuracy and confidence if some measurements were taken.

If an officer is testifying in court, he or she should begin his or her description of a scene by generally describing the overall scene and then adding the detail. A description of the road configuration should precede the location of the vehicles and other relevant information, such as the location of objects, debris, and tire marks. The coordinate and triangulation measurement methods described in the next section of this chapter provide the basis for the creation and use of diagrams of the collision scene for **demonstrative evidence**, and as an aid in giving clear and comprehensible oral evidence, provided it is done in an orderly fashion.

demonstrative evidence
visual, physical evidence that often supplements oral evidence; includes photographs, diagrams, maps, models, and charts

In taking measurements, temporary evidence must be measured first. Temporary evidence is evidence that will disappear or move in a short time. Temporary evidence could be the location of the vehicles, bodies of victims, collision debris, or pools of liquid.

Permanent evidence can be measured last, even at a later date, if necessary. Permanent evidence can consist of the road configuration, the location of relevant trees, signs, buildings, and other reference points.

Use reference points from which to measure. Reference points are one or more points from which the location of evidence can be measured. Reference points may be tangible or intangible.

Tangible reference points are real locations on permanent or fixed objects that will not move over a reasonable period of time. Examples of tangible reference points are the corner of a building, a hydro pole, or a bridge abutment.

Intangible reference points are not readily observable points, but are calculated points. These points are usually temporary marks that are founded on something permanent, and can be referenced again, if the same formula for their creation is used. Some examples of intangible reference points include the point of intersection of lines extending from the cement curbs at a corner, or the point 10 m due south of the west wall of, for example, a hockey arena. See figure 6.3.

coordinate measurement
also called right-angle measurement; involves the use of a baseline reference, with measurements taken along the baseline and along a line at right angles to the baseline so that an object can be located in relation to known reference points located on the baseline

triangulation measurement
a form of measurement used to locate an object on a map or diagram by connecting the object to two known reference points on a baseline with two lines, forming a triangle

There are two types of measurements that a police officer should be able to make at a collision scene, using a tape measure: **coordinate measurements** and **triangulation measurements**. The introduction of electronic measuring devices is simplifying the taking of the actual measurements, but this process will still require the use of tangible and intangible reference points. An officer may use one or both, depending on the nature of the collision scene. In making a diagram and measuring, remember to do the following:

◆   Determine which direction is north; conventionally this is shown with an arrow point toward the top of the page with a small "n" next to it.

Figure 6.3   Example of Intangible Reference Point

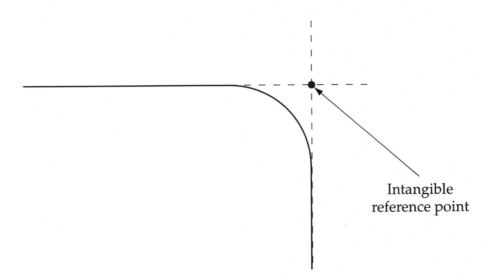

Intangible
reference point

◇ Sketch the road configuration.

◆ Position the vehicles, debris, and so on.

◇ Determine the system of measurement to be used.

◇ Establish reference points, lines, and measurement lines.

◇ Make actual measurements after the procedure has been determined on paper.

◇ How many measurements are taken depends on what needs to be measured. For example, a vehicle should be located in reference to its final position on the roadway, but you may also wish to establish the position of debris in reference to the edge of the roadway and in reference to the position of the vehicle.

Coordinate or Right-Angle Measuring

Coordinate measurement involves nothing more than the imposition of a grid system on a diagram of the collision scene. See figure 6.4.

To take coordinate measurements, you must do the following:

◇ Establish a baseline (try to make it a tangible base line).

◇ Establish a zero point on that baseline.

◆ From the zero point, measure along the baseline to a point from which a right angle would extend out to the point you wish to locate.

◆ Measure the length of the right-angle arm from the baseline out to the point you wish to locate.

■ **Figure 6.4 Example of Coordinate Measurement**

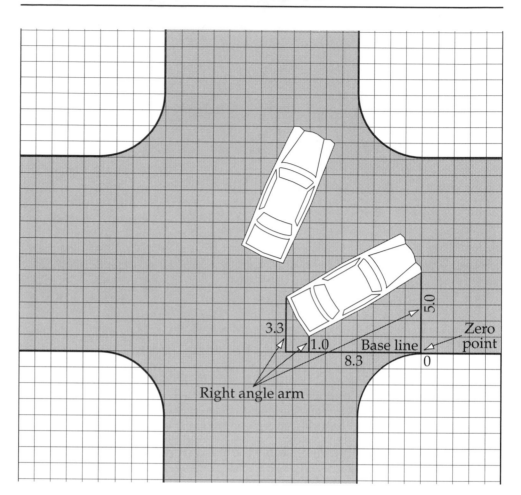

Triangulation

In order to measure by triangulation, do the following:

◆ Establish a baseline between two reference points, preferably tangible ones.

◆ Measure the length of the baseline.

◆ Create a triangle by drawing and measuring a straight line from each reference point at each end of the base line out to the object that you wish to locate. See figure 6.5.

Remember that it is wise to use tangible reference points. If you use tangible reference points, like stop signs, to measure the location of a vehicle in an intersection, you must measure the location of the stop signs in reference to the intersection. Also keep in mind that you are trying to locate vehicles in reference to the roadway. If you locate a vehicle using reference points that are off the road, you must measure where these points are in relation to the road. It usually takes two measurements to locate any point using the coordinate measurement system. See figure 6.6.

Figure 6.5   Examples of Triangulation Measurements

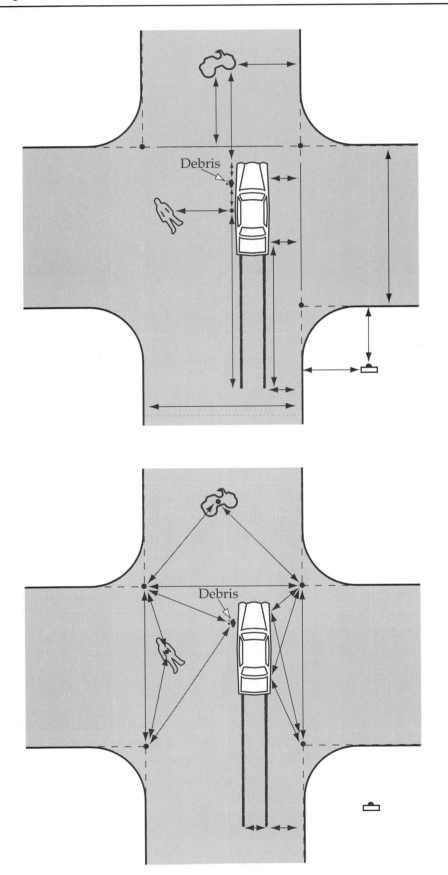

■ **Figure 6.6   Example of Triangulation Measurement Using "Off Road" References**

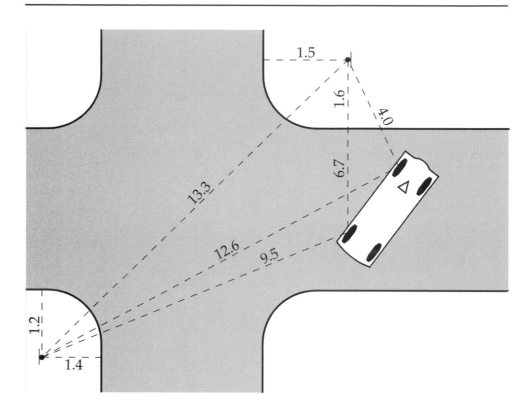

Measuring Road Configurations

Because measurements of vehicles and objects in the road are made in reference to the road, it is necessary to measure the roadway. Measuring most road configurations is relatively simple. Measuring lane and road-way widths may be sufficient. If the collision occurs at an intersection, most intersections are at right angles, in which case, measuring could still be as simple as recording the road and land widths. See figure 6.7.

If a collision scene involves an intersection where one or more roads are not in alignment, additional measurements are required to show how much the roads are out of alignment. See figure 6.8.

Measuring Irregular Road Configurations

Because most officers only have a tape measure for taking linear mea-surements, a system of straight lines must be used for measuring curves and angles. Where roads do not meet at right angles or are curved, a sys-tem of straight-line measurement can provide enough data to accurately reproduce the road configuration on a diagram.

Measuring an irregular road configuration is usually achieved by es-tablishing a baseline and then measuring at right angles from the baseline to the road at predetermined intervals. The right-angle measure-ments are called offset measurements. The intervals are determined

■ **Figure 6.7   Example of Measurement of Simple Road Configuration**

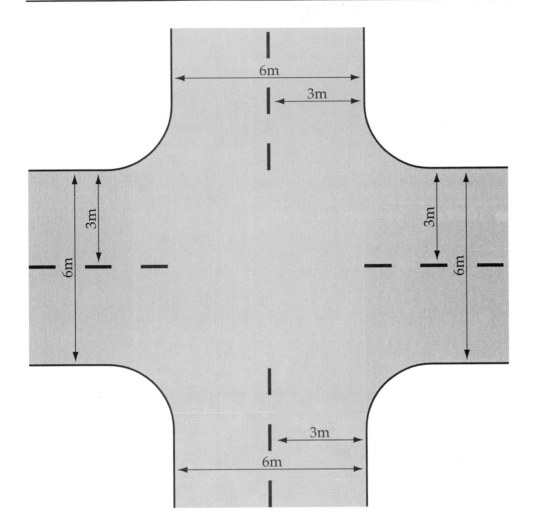

according to the complexity or irregularity of the road. For example, a road shape that is not too irregular may only require offset measurements every 20 m. A more irregular road may require offset measurements be taken every 5 m. The intervals start at a zero reference point on the baseline, as shown in figure 6.9.

COLLECTION OF PHYSICAL EVIDENCE

Tire Marks

Tire marks are made in three different ways (see figure 6.10):

1. *Skid Marks* are made when the wheels are not rotating and the tires are sliding on the road surface.

2. *Scuff Marks* are made when the wheels are rotating while the tires are sliding.

■ **Figure 6.8 Example of Measurement of Road Configuration Where Roads Not Aligned**

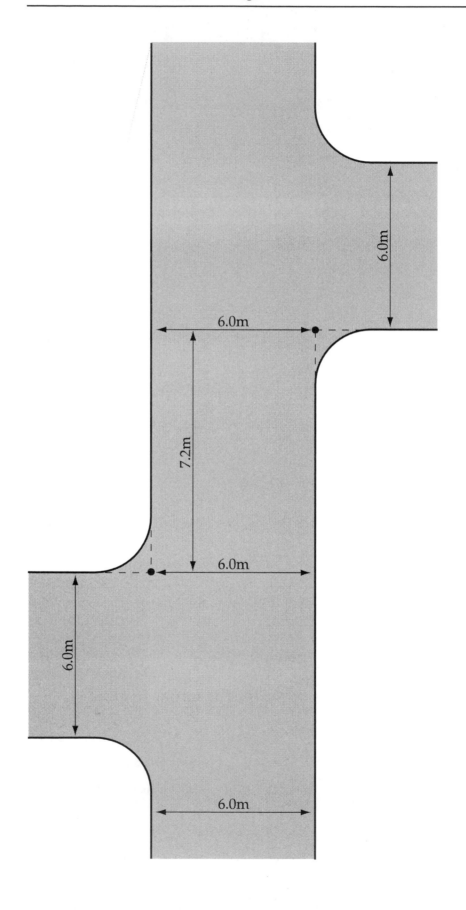

Figure 6.9   Example of Measurement of Irregular Road Configuration

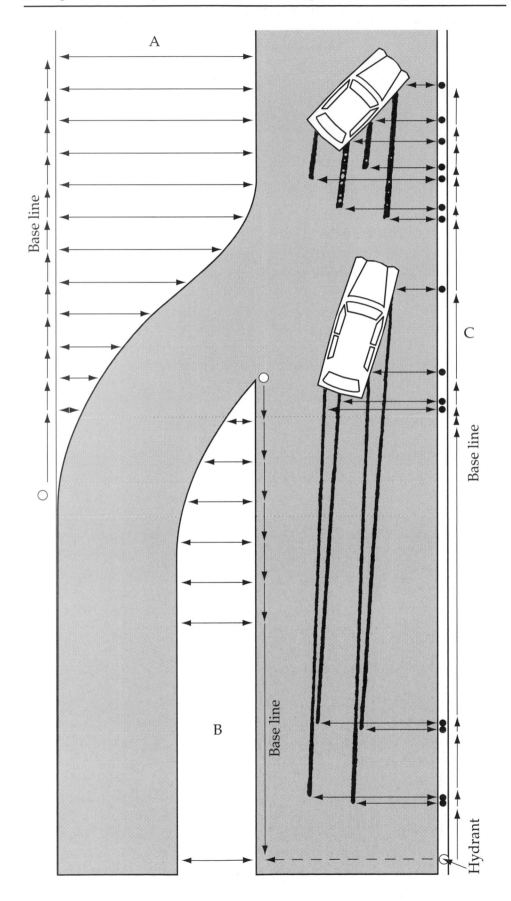

3. *Tire Prints* are made when the wheels are rotating and the tires are not sliding.

Tire Mark	Wheels Rotating	Wheels Sliding
skid marks	no	yes
scuff marks	yes	yes
prints	yes	no

Effect of Overdeflection and Underdeflection on Tire Marks

Tires are designed with thicker treads on the outside edges so that more tread pattern is in contact with the road surface under normal inflation and vehicle weight distribution. See figure 6.11. As vehicle weight distribution shifts, as it can when the brakes are applied hard, tires can become overinflated (underdeflection) or underinflated (overdeflected) for the moment. There is a consequent change in the tire shape and the amount of tread that is in contact with the road surface when a tire becomes over- or underinflated. In a skid, these changes cause different types of skids that can tell an investigator about the driver's actions and the vehicle's movements at the time of the collision.

Underinflated (Overdeflected) Tires

When the brakes are applied, the inertia of the vehicle causes the vehicle's weight to shift forward, adding extra weight to the front tires. You probably have experienced how a vehicle takes a nose dive when the brakes are applied abruptly. The front tires now have more weight on them than usual. The extra weight on the front tires causes them to be underinflated for the moment. The extra weight presses down on the outside edges of the tire, and the centre of the tread actually lifts. Consequently, front-tire skid marks have dark outer edges and nothing in the centre. As the vehicle slows down and the weight distribution returns closer to normal, the middle part of the front-tire mark starts to fill in. See figure 6.12.

Overinflated (Underdeflected) Tires

As weight shifts to the front tires when the brakes are applied, it is taken off the rear tires, causing them to become overinflated for the moment. When tires are overinflated, the outer edges leave the road surface and only the centre area of tread contacts the road. Consequently, rear-tire skid marks are dark in the middle with little or no marks left by the outer edges. As the vehicle slows down, the weight distribution begins to return to normal, and the outer edges will come into contact with the road and create full-width skid marks. However, an overloaded vehicle, or tires with too little air pressure in them, can also leave skid marks that resemble the skid marks left by front tires. Where full-width skid marks

■ **Figure 6.10   Tire Marks**

Skid marks

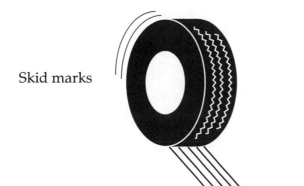

Scuff marks

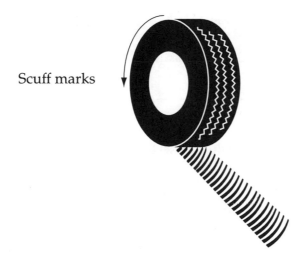

Prints

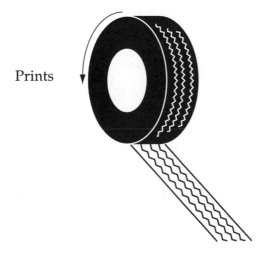

■ **Figure 6.11   Normally Inflated Tire**

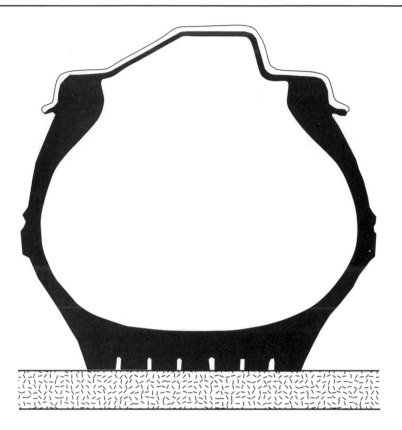

■ **Figure 6.12   Underinflated (Overdeflected) Tire**

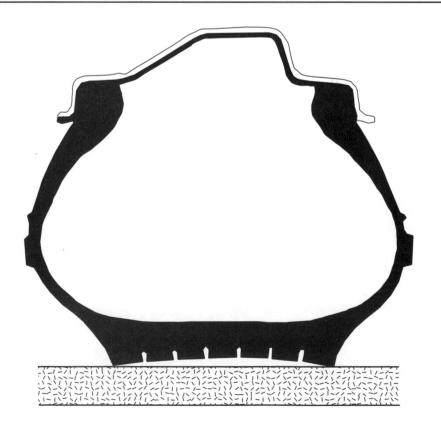

■ **Figure 6.13   Overinflated (Underdeflected) Tire**

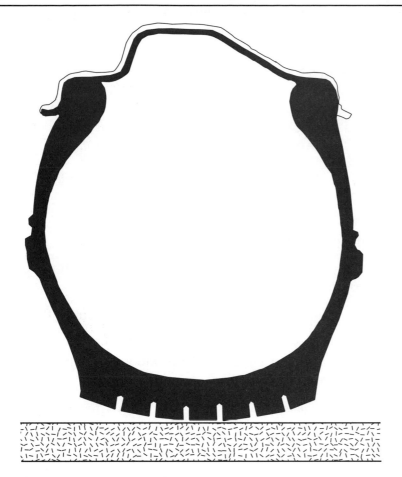

on both front and rear tires occur, overloading or low air pressure may be the cause. See figure 6.13.

Impending Skid

Impending skid (also called "shadow" or "incipient" skid) occurs at the beginning of a skid mark. When the brakes are applied and the tires start to slow down, but have not yet stopped rotating, the tires will lightly clean the road surface before creating darker skid marks. Braking is most effective at the time the tires are still rotating, so this impending skid mark must be located and measured. The distance that it takes a vehicle to stop after the brakes are applied is critical to the determination of the vehicle's speed.

Skid Marks: Light to Dark

Skid marks go from light to dark in colour. The front tires, which become underinflated, leave outer edge marks. Because there is more weight on the front tires, front-tire skid marks are darker than rear-tire marks. As the vehicle slows down and the weight distribution on the tires returns closer to normal, the tires return closer to normal inflation, and more of the front and rear tire treads come into contact with the road. As this happens, the skid marks become darker in colour. See figure 6.14.

Types of Skid Marks

Skid marks are more than just black marks on the road surface. The different types of mark can provide information about what occurred during a collision. There are eight classifications of skid marks:

1. *Pavement Grinding*: Hard material embedded in the tire treads scratches in the road.

2. *Tire Grinding*: Small bits of rubber are ground off the sliding tire and deposited on the road.

3. *Erasing*: The sliding tire cleans dirt or other solid material from the road surface.

4. *Squeegee Marks*: The sliding tire rubs off moisture from the road surface.

5. *Smear of Soft Material*: The sliding tire smoothes or spreads snow, mud, or debris on the road surface.

6. *Smear of Bituminous Material (Tar)*: The sliding tire spreads warm tar on the road surface.

7. *Tire Smear*: Rubber is melted from the sliding tire rather than the road surface being melted.

8. *Ploughing*: The sliding tire ploughs a depression in a soft material with the material piled up on each side and at the end of the skid.

It is important to measure all of the skid marks, and not just the black marks, because the total distance that the brakes were applied is required to calculate speed.

Skid Patterns

Just as there are differences in skid marks, there are also differences is skid patterns. An examination of skid patterns can help determine the vehicle's behaviour and the cause of that behaviour. The different skid patterns are the results of differential wheel lockup or different coefficients of friction on different road surfaces. The six patterns discussed here do not apply to vehicles equipped with **ABS brakes**. ABS brakes are computerized, and release a wheel the moment that it starts to lock.

ABS brakes
anti-lock braking system; a computer controls the application of braking pressure, releasing the wheel when it is about to lock up, with the goal of reducing or preventing skidding

Front-Wheel Lockup

If both front wheels lock up, the front wheels will slide straight and the vehicle cannot be steered. Even if the driver, as illustrated in figure 6.15,

Figure 6.14   Change in Skid Marks

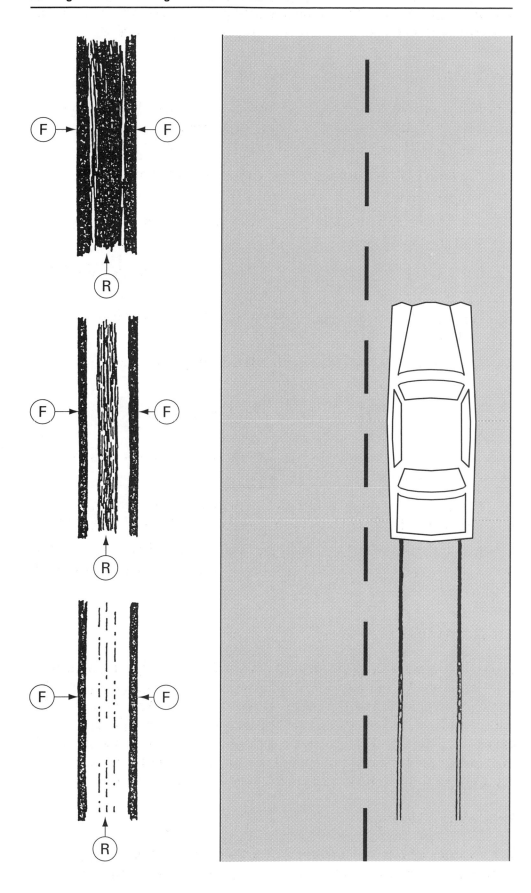

■ **Figure 6.15   Front-Wheel Lockup**

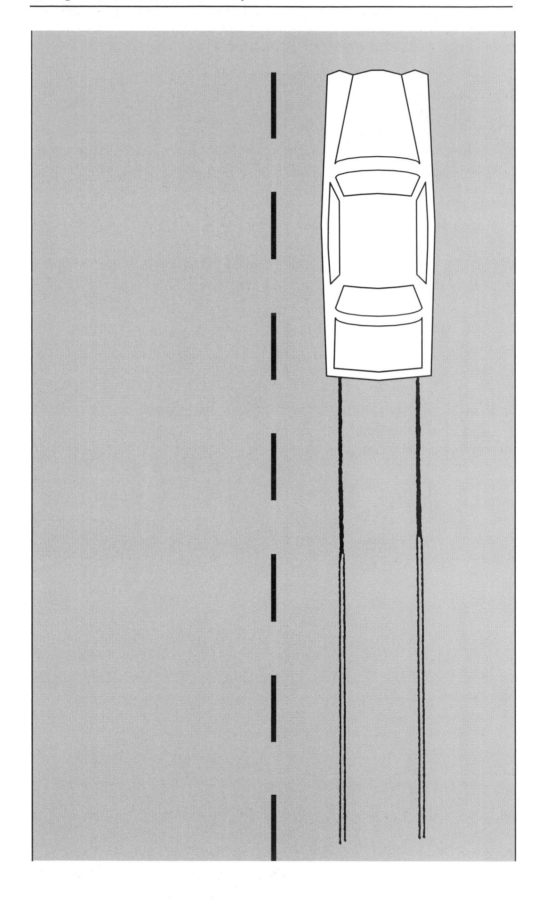

turns the front wheels, the vehicle will continue to slide straight ahead in the direction of its momentum because the sliding front wheels cannot steer the vehicle. The rear wheels are still rolling and still have some grip on the road, so the rear of the vehicle is kept in line.

Rear-Wheel Lockup

If both rear wheels lock up, the rear wheels slide. The front wheels are still rolling and maintaining a grip on the road. If the road surface is not completely horizontal or the driver turns the steering wheel, the rear of the vehicle will swing 180°. The skid marks from this manoeuvre are distinctive. The skid marks from both front tires cross each other approximately half way through the skid, as do the rear tires. See figure 6.16.

Road Crown (Camber)

Most roads are crowned (**cambered**) for water drainage; the middle of the road is higher than the edges. When a vehicle is skidding, gravity will pull the vehicle and cause it to drift to the low side. The gradual curve in the skid mark is often not from steering, because if the front wheels are locked, as is often the case when a vehicle brakes hard and the front wheels lock up, steering is impossible. See figure 6.17.

camber
the convex curve of the road's surface, with the highest part at the centre of the road and the lowest at the road edge

Side-Wheel Lockup

When two wheels lock up on one side, the vehicle will turn toward the locked side. The side with the locked wheels is attempting to stop the vehicle while the other side is still rolling forward. The situation is comparable to grabbing the arm of a person who is walking by you. When you grab the person's arm, the person will spin toward you. See figure 6.18.

One Wheel Not Locked

If one front wheel is not locked, the vehicle tends to turn as though only the rear wheels are locked (180° turn), but will rotate toward the side of the locked front wheel because of the friction from the locked-up wheel. Some steering is still possible from the rolling tire, which should also create some yaw scuff marks.

If one rear wheel is not locked, there is little difference in the vehicle's behaviour. The vehicle will turn slightly toward the side with both locked wheels. See figure 6.19.

Wheels on Different Surfaces

If the wheels on one side of the vehicle are on a different surface than the wheels on the other side and the brakes are applied, the vehicle will turn

■ **Figure 6.16   Rear-Wheel Lockup Skid**

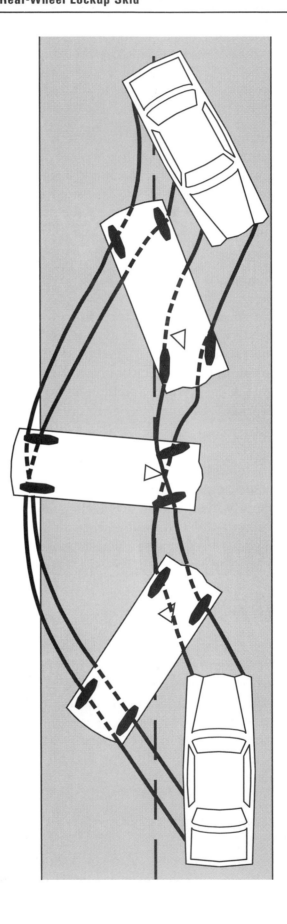

■ **Figure 6.17   Effect of Camber on a Skid**

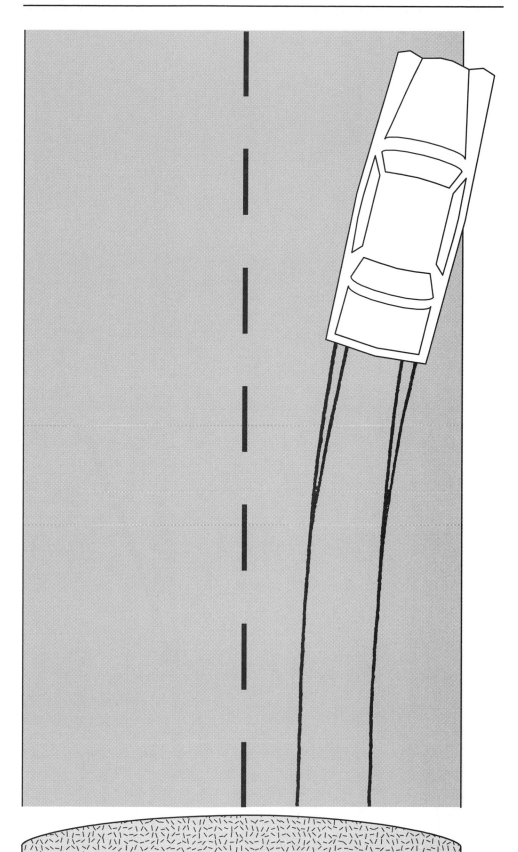

■ Figure 6.18   Effect of Side-Wheel Lockup

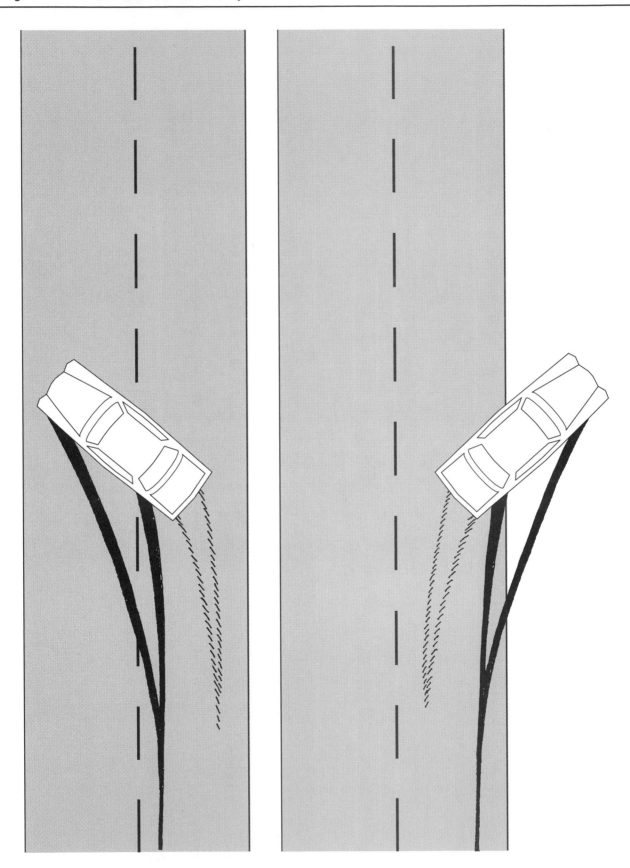

■ **Figure 6.19   One Wheel Not Locked**

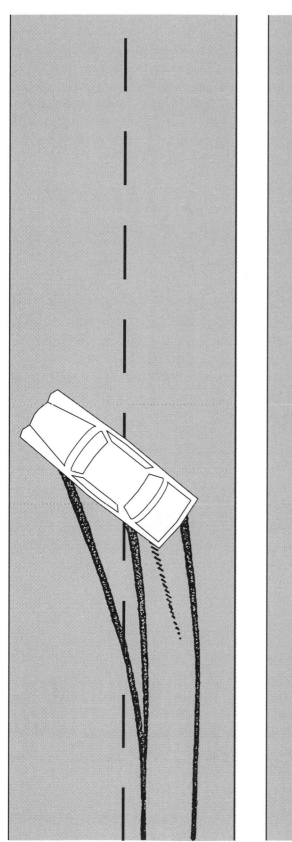

One front wheel not locked.

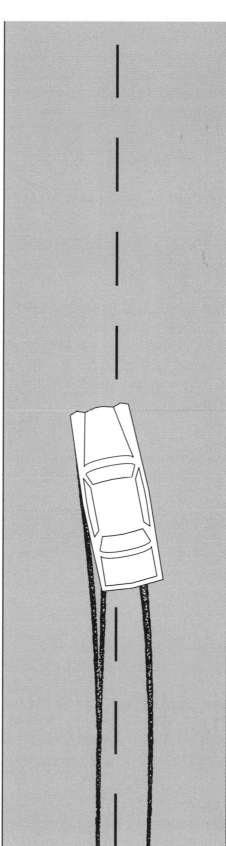

One rear wheel not locked.

toward the surface with the most friction. The analogy of causing a passerby to turn toward you by grabbing his or her arm also applies to this situation. On a highway, if the right front and rear wheels are on the gravel shoulder, and the left front and rear wheels are on the paved roadway, and the brakes are applied hard, the right-hand side will slide on the gravel and the left-hand side, where there is more friction, will grip the road. The vehicle will turn toward the surface with more friction, as illustrated in figure 6.20.

Scuff Marks

Scuff marks are made when the tires are still rotating, but also sliding. There are two kinds of scuff marks: yaw marks and acceleration scuff marks.

Yaw Marks

Yaw marks are often called critical speed marks because they are created when a vehicle is travelling too fast to negotiate a curve and the vehicle starts to slide sideways. This will happen when the brakes are not applied, the wheels are still rotating, and the tire starts sliding sideways.

Yaw marks are always curved and contain oblique or slanting striations. The radius of the curve changes through the length of the yaw mark. The width of yaw marks is less than the width of the tire treads. The tires on the outside of the curve will leave darker marks because of the weight shifted by centrifugal force.

Yaw marks illustrate the path of the vehicle during side slip. They provide key evidence in proving that a vehicle was going too fast to make a curve. The length of the yaw mark is not critical but the distance and height of the yaw mark are important. These two measurements are used in a mathematical formula to determine the speed of the vehicle. See figures 6.21 and 6.22.

Acceleration Scuff Marks

Acceleration scuff marks are the tire marks created when a vehicle quickly accelerates from a stopped position. These are the marks created when a driver "squeals" his or her tires. In this situation, the wheels rotate and slip at the same time. If these marks are curved, rather than straight, the vehicle has "fishtailed." Acceleration scuff marks look like skid marks, except that they start dark and fade to a lighter colour.

Flat-Tire Marks

When a tire is deflated, the tire collapses and the loose rubber flops from side to side as the wheel is rotating. The flopping back and forth creates a wavy mark on the roadway. See figure 6.23.

■ **Figure 6.20   Wheels on Different Surfaces**

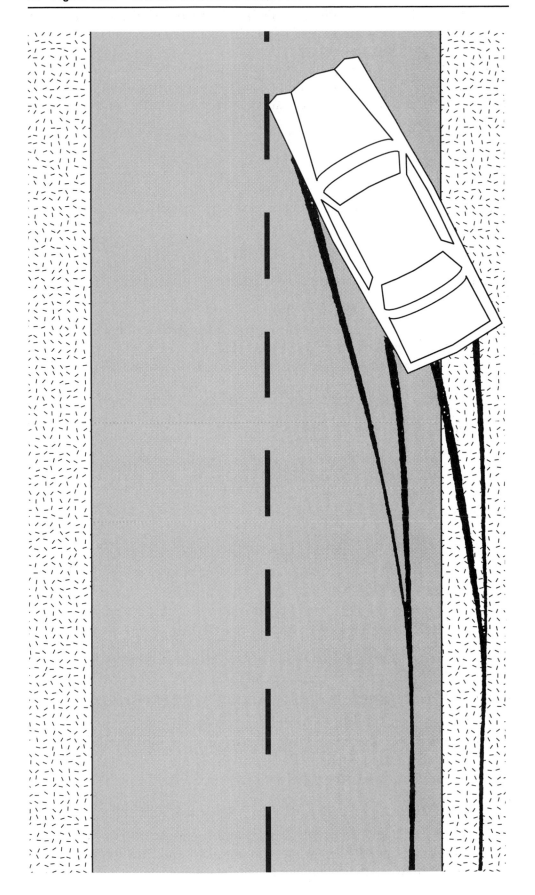

■ **Figure 6.21   Measuring a Yaw Mark**

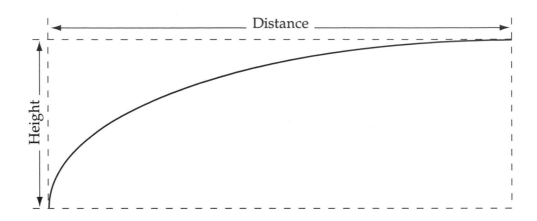

Tire Prints

Tires that are rotating without sliding leave no friction marks in the form of scuffs or skids. These tires may leave a tread impression in soft material or, if the tires are wet, may print the tread pattern on dry pavement. These prints are useful for proving that the wheels did not lock and for proving the direction of travel.

Unusual Skid Patterns

So far, we have examined skid and scuff marks that are likely to occur at a collision scene. We now turn to three skid patterns that occur less frequently.

Offset Skids

Offset skids occur when some outside force causes the vehicle to change direction abruptly. These skid marks are useful in determining the direction of application of the outside force. They are also useful in determining the location of the tires of the vehicle that was struck and, indirectly, can help to establish the point of impact. See figure 6.24.

Skip Skids

Skip skids occur when a locked wheel bounces because it has struck a hole, debris, or another vehicle or object. The spaces between the skids are usually shorter than one metre. The whole length of the skip skid—skids and spaces—is measured because the brakes were applied throughout the whole distance, and other tires are carrying the load.

Gap Skids

Gap skids occur when locked wheels are released and then relocked. This often happens when a driver pumps the brakes. The gaps are not measured

■ **Figure 6.22   Yaw Marks—Critical Speed Marks**

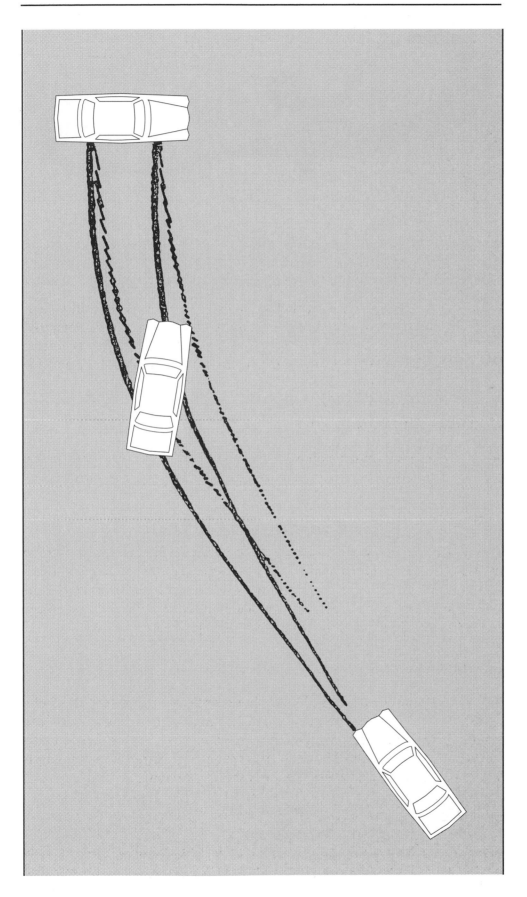

■ **Figure 6.23 Flat Tire Mark**

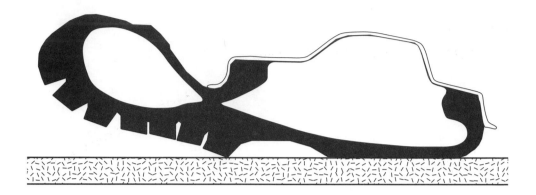

because the brakes are not applied when the gaps are made. The gaps are usually between four and six metres in length. The visible skid marks plus the total length of the stopping distance (the skids plus the gaps) are measured.

Skid and Tire Marks—Length and Position on the Road

Do not forget to measure both the length of the skid and the position of the beginning and the end of the skid on the road. In measuring the position of the skid on the road, the officer will need measurements to locate each end point, if the coordinate measurement system is used, and three measurements, if the triangulation measurement is used. If the skid

---

TIRE MARKS CAN TELL

Skid marks indicate
◆ that brakes were applied;
◆ the speed of vehicle, determined from the total skid length;
◆ the vehicle's position in the lane on the road; and
◆ the point of impact, if skid marks take an abrupt change in direction.

Scuff marks indicate
◆ excessive speed from start, if acceleration scuff marks.

Yaw marks indicate
◆ excessive speed through turn;
◆ speed, determined from the measurement of yaw marks; and
◆ that brakes were not applied.

Prints indicate
◆ that brakes were not applied;
◆ the position of the vehicle on the road; and
◆ which vehicle made the prints, if there is sufficient print detail.

■ **Figure 6.24   Unusual Skid Patterns**

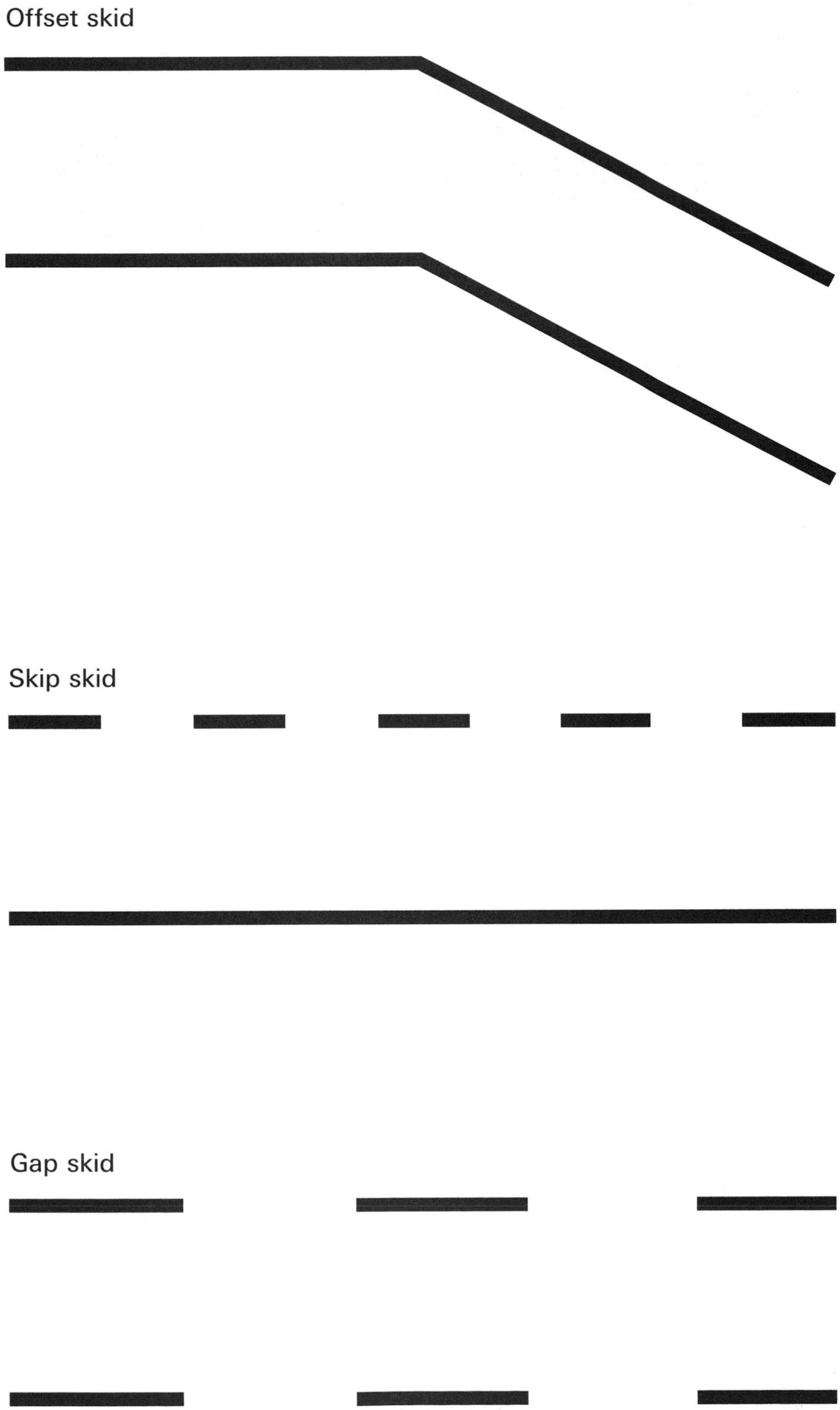

Offset skid

Skip skid

Gap skid

marks are not straight, offset measurements must be taken to measure the irregular shape of the skid mark. The length of the skid mark and the end points still have to be located with measurements, using either coordinate or triangulation measurement. See figure 6.25.

Metal Scars

There are two types of metal scars, scratches, and gouges. Information obtained from them can be useful in identifying hit-and-run vehicles and in tracing the path of a vehicle after impact.

Scratches

Scratches are marks made on the surface of the roadway by sliding parts of vehicles (other than tires). Scratches can be matched to the part of the vehicle that made the scratches, and are, therefore, useful in determining the path of the vehicle after collision and in identifying a vehicle involved in a hit-and-run collision.

Gouges

Locard Principle

when one person comes into contact with another person or object, a cross-transfer of evidence occurs; that is, a person will leave some trace evidence from him or her at a scene and will take some trace evidence from the scene

Gouges are different from scratches; they are not surface scratches, but holes or grooves dug into the road material. Gouges are obviously caused by strong impacts with the road by hard parts of the vehicle. There is always part of the road material stuck to the car and, conversely, when you apply the "**Locard Principle**," you should find part of the vehicle in the gouge; usually this would consist of paint or particles of the vehicle body.

Debris

Debris is the most common evidence at a collision scene. Debris is not just vehicle parts, but underbody pieces, vehicle fluids, and solid cargo as well. Fluids spatter, dribble, puddle, and run off to lower ground. Each fluid activity can help interpret what happened to the vehicle. Debris is not useful in determining the point of impact because debris is knocked off an object or vehicle, and flies some distance as a result of the impact before coming to rest. Debris is useful in identifying hit-and-run vehicles as the debris can often be matched to a specific vehicle. Debris can also be useful in determining the vehicle's direction of travel or the direction of the force that was applied to the vehicle. Debris usually fans out in the direction that the debris was travelling. This direction can be used to interpret the direction in which the vehicle was travelling and the direction of the force that was applied. See figure 6.26.

Signs that a Vehicle Has Left the Road: Flips and Falls

If a vehicle leaves the road and is airborne for a short time, the takeoff and landing points and the distance between them provide important

■ **Figure 6.25   Measuring and Locating Skid Marks on Roadway**

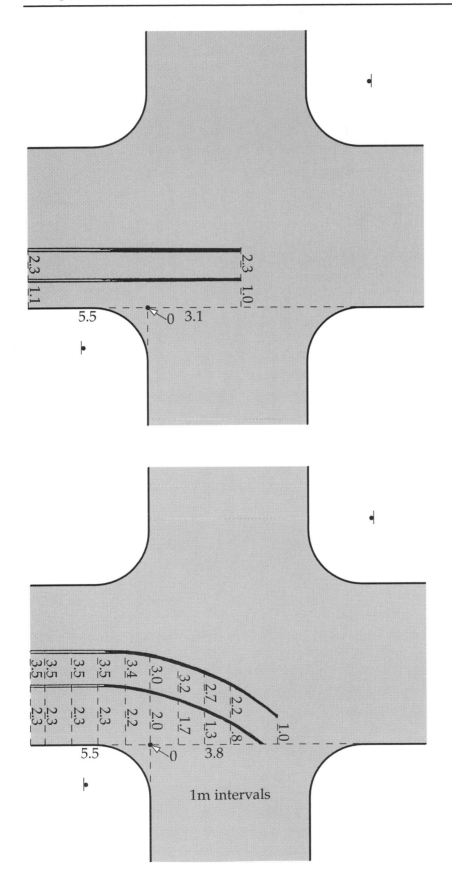

1m intervals

■ **Figure 6.26 Metal Scars and Debris**

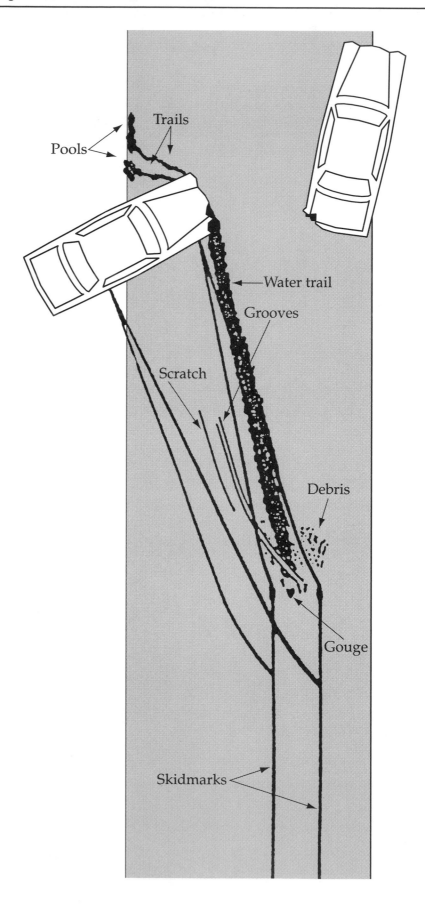

information for determining the speed and the sequence of events in the collision. This information is important for collision reconstruction.

Flips or Vaults

This occurs when the moving vehicle is "tripped" by an object, such as a curb, so that it flips onto its side, roof, or completely over onto its wheels again. As well as the takeoff mark and the landing mark, the point on the vehicle that made the mark should be determined. See figure 6.27.

Falls

A fall occurs when a vehicle runs off a bridge or embankment and falls through the air. The fall distance is critical for determining speed.

SERIES OF EVENTS IN COLLISION RECONSTRUCTION

There are a series of points, intervals of time, distances, and actions that are described here in sequence and that are considered in the reconstruction of a collision. Knowledge of this series of events can provide guidance for the collection of evidence and taking statements.

Point of Possible Perception

The point of possible perception is the earliest time when the hazard could have been perceived.

Perception Delay

The perception delay is the time from the point of possible perception to the point of actual perception.

Perception Distance

The perception distance is the distance travelled during the perception delay.

Point of Perception

The point of perception is the place where the hazard was actually perceived. It is not always discernible in a series of events in a collision.

Reaction

The reaction is the voluntary or involuntary response to the perceived hazard—for example, a driver "freezes" with fear.

■ **Figure 6.27 Flips or Vaults**

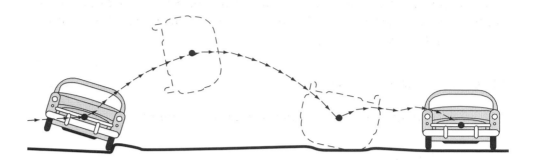

OVERVIEW OF STEPS AND TECHNIQUES IN COLLISION INVESTIGATION

MENTAL ROLE PLAYING

Approach
◆ Obtain as much information as possible.
◆ Guarantee arrival.

Arrival
◆ Follow BE SAFE motto.
◆ Prioritize emergencies.
◆ Deal with the presence of dangerous goods, if any.
◆ Assess injuries.
◆ Protect the scene and preserve evidence.
◆ Determine whether there are downed hydro lines, and take the necessary precautions.
◆ Extinguish vehicle fires, if feasible, or call for assistance.
◆ Assess road conditions.
◆ Protect cargo from theft.
◆ Deal with fighting drivers.

Management of People at the Scene
◆ Determine whether anyone is hurt.
◆ Determine who the drivers are.
◆ Determine who the witnesses are.
◆ Determine who else was involved in the collision.
◆ Obtain cautioned statements.
◆ Obtain statements required by statute (accident report).
◆ Control unruly spectators.

Sketching, Measuring, and Diagramming a Collision Scene
◆ Prepare a field sketch.
◆ Take forensic measurements.

Collection of Physical Evidence
◆ Measure tire marks.
◆ Determine metal scars.
◆ Assess debris.

Reaction Time

The reaction time is the length of time between the point of actual perception and the action point. For example, reaction time is the number of seconds that the driver "froze."

Reaction Distance

The reaction distance is the distance travelled during the reaction time.

Action Point

The action point follows the reaction, and is the point where the driver starts evasive action. For example, when the driver snaps out of the "frozen" state and applies the brakes.

Evasive Action

Evasive action describes the combination of actions made with the intention of avoiding the collision, such as steering and braking.

Evasive Action Distance

Evasive action distance is the distance travelled after the action point to the point of impact or avoidance of the collision.

True (Safe) Area

The true or safe area is the area leading to the point of no escape during which evasive action *could have been* initiated to avoid collision. The area begins from the point of possible perception and ends at the point of no escape.

Encroachment

Encroachment is the area where a vehicle has entered into the rightful path of another vehicle.

Point of Impact

The point of impact is the place where one vehicle strikes another vehicle or other object.

Primary Contact

Primary contact is the first contact between two vehicles or between a vehicle and another object.

■ **Figure 6.28 Overview of Events in a Collision Reconstruction**

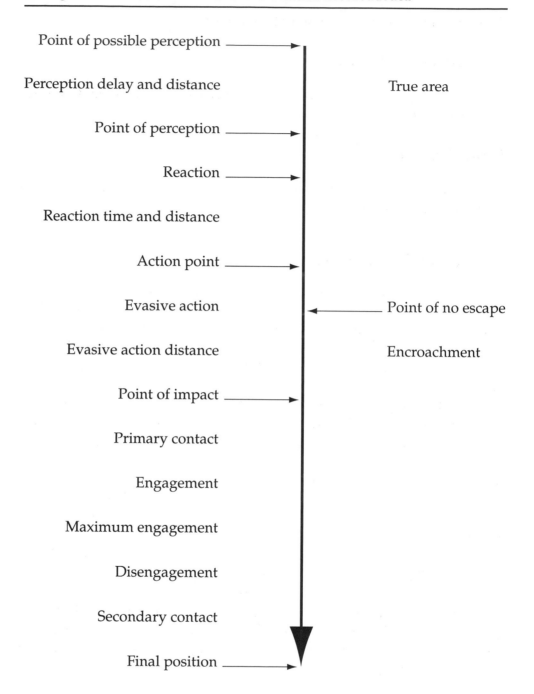

Point of possible perception

Perception delay and distance

    True area

Point of perception

Reaction

Reaction time and distance

Action point

Evasive action

    Point of no escape

Evasive action distance

    Encroachment

Point of impact

Primary contact

Engagement

Maximum engagement

Disengagement

Secondary contact

Final position

Engagement

Engagement is the penetration of one object into another during a collision.

Maximum Engagement

Maximum engagement is the maximum penetration by one object into another.

Disengagement

Disengagement is the separation of the units involved.

Secondary Contact

Secondary contact is the second contact between a vehicle and another vehicle or object.

Final Position

The final position is the position where the vehicles or bodies come to rest after the collision. See figure 6.28.

CHAPTER SUMMARY

This chapter considers the role played by police officers at a motor-vehicle collision scene, and provides information on how an officer manages and investigates a collision scene. Once an officer is dispatched to a collision, he or she must obtain as much advance information as possible, and then take steps to arrive quickly but safely at the scene. On arrival at the scene, the officer prioritizes emergencies and may have to deal with the presence of dangerous goods, injuries, downed hydro lines, fighting drivers, and vehicle fires. The officer also needs to take steps to ensure the protection of the collision scene, preserve evidence, and safeguard goods.

One of the officer's most important tasks is "people management." The officer must determine whether anyone is hurt, who the drivers are, who the witnesses are, and if necessary, obtain cautioned statements and witness statements, using various interview techniques designed to elicit accurate information efficiently and effectively.

The officer may need to prepare a field sketch and, using coordinate and triangulation measurements, take appropriate measurements for a more detailed diagram that may be used in court, if required. The officer must collect physical evidence (such as debris) and observe and measures tire marks (such as skids and scuffs) and gouges and scratches in the roadway, and use this information in investigating the collision and writing an accident report.

KEY TERMS

bill of lading	demonstrative evidence
oxidizer	coordinate measurement
"will say" statements	triangulation
Judge's Rules	ABS brakes
voir dire	camber
contemporaneous with the event	Locard Principle

REVIEW QUESTIONS

■ SHORT ANSWER

1. What would you do if you arrived at a collision scene and discovered

    a. that hydro lines were down?

    b. that a damaged tanker truck has a placard coloured red, with a flame and a number "3"?

    c. that two drivers are punching each other in the middle of the road?

    d. that an injured person is badly cut, has bled profusely, and has no pulse, and a second person is sitting dazed on the side of the road, and appears to be in shock.

2. Explain what the following colours represent on dangerous goods placards:

    a. yellow

b. white

c. yellow over white

d. green

e. blue

f. white over black

3. Briefly describe the six classes of dangerous goods.

4. In what circumstances may an officer presume a person at a collision scene is dead?

5. If the officer cannot presume an injured person is dead, what must he or she do?

6. Suppose the collision scene is on a two-lane road, with one lane in each direction. Both lanes are blocked by the collision. Describe what you would do to close the road, and indicate the tools or devices you would use to do it.

7. What are the four questions you should ask at most collision scenes?

   a.

   b.

   c.

   d.

8. If a driver declines to answer your questions after being cautioned, is there any way to get information from that driver? Can that information be used in court?

9. Briefly describe what is missing or wrong with the sketch in figure 6.29.

■ Figure 6.29   What Is Missing in This Sketch?

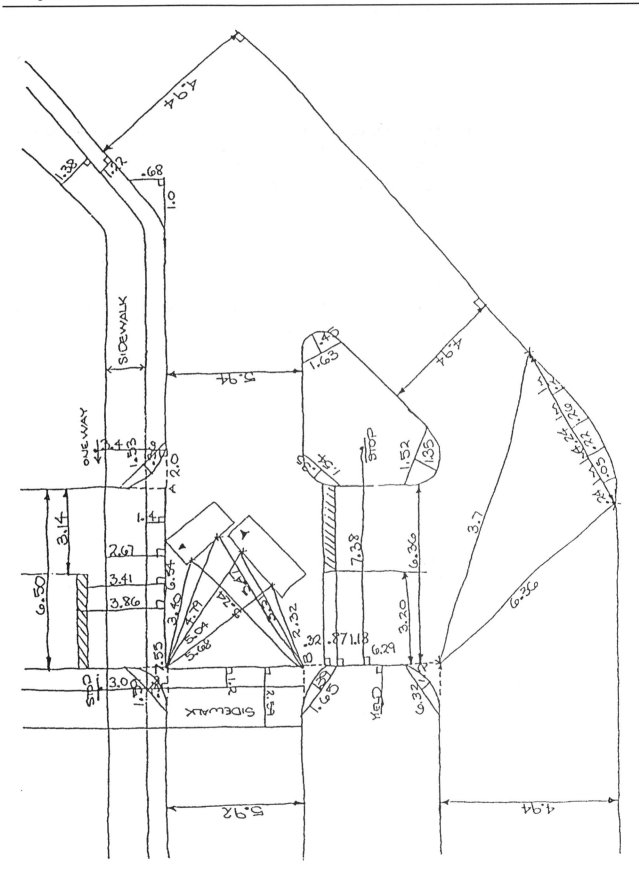

10. Using coordinate measurements, establish the location of the motor vehicles in the collision scenes in the diagram labelled figure 6.30.

11. To determine total stopping distance, what would you measure if you observed the following series of marks:

   a. A tire print, ploughing, and smearing on a snow-covered road.

   b. Pavement grinding, erasing, tire smear, and smearing of bituminous material on a dry pavement.

   c. Squeegee marks, pavement grinding, and tire smear on wet pavement.

   d. Skid marks, gap skid, and yaw marks on curved pavement.

■ **Figure 6.30   Two Collision Scene Diagrams**

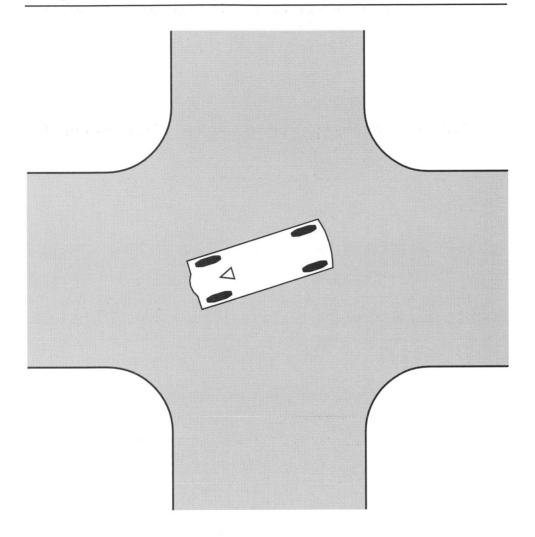

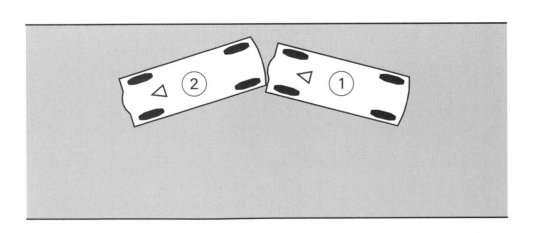

12. Briefly describe six items of information that an investigator might obtain from an examination of tire marks.

   a.

   b.

   c.

   d.

   e.

   f.

■ DISCUSSION QUESTIONS

1. Using graph paper, sketch a diagram with measurements of the following collision described in evidence given in court:

The collision occurred in a "T" shaped intersection. King Street is the through street and runs east and west. Princess Street is the stop street and runs south from King Street, so northbound traffic on Princess Street has to stop at King Street. King Street is a two-way two lane street and is 9 metres wide. Princess Street is a two way two lane street and is also 9 metres wide.

There are two passenger cars involved in the collision, a red Ford and a blue Chevrolet. Both vehicles are located on King Street. Both vehicles are located according to the south-east corner of the intersection. The red Ford will be located first. The right rear wheel of the red Ford is located 1 metre east and 1 metre north of the south-east corner. The right front wheel is located 5 metres east and 2.5 metres north of the south-east corner. Therefore, the Ford is pointing north-east across the east bound lane. The right rear wheel of the blue Chev is located 1.5 metres east and 6 metres north of the south-east corner. Therefore the Chev is eastbound and angled slightly to the south in the westbound lane of King Street.

2. Given the following facts, explain what steps you would take as the first officer on the scene, in order.

You arrive at the scene of a collision at the intersection of two provincial highways in cottage country on a Friday night at 10 p.m. in summer. It is dark and beginning to rain. The intersection is controlled by traffic signals and is lit by two overhead street lights. There appear to be three vehicles involved. On the shoulder is a 48-passenger public commercial bus, with the front end demolished. The engine is still running, and a number of passengers appear to be injured. Some passengers are still on the bus, unable to get out through the doors on the smashed front end. About 15 people are gathered around the bus, some bleeding and dishevelled, and others appearing to be unhurt. The driver, it appears, is still in his seat, but he appears to be unconscious, and his clothing is covered with blood.

The second vehicle is a truck. It is in the intersection, lying on its side. It has completely blocked the roadway of both highways. Some of its cargo of red canisters has spilled. On the side of the truck you can see a red placard with the number 2 on it.

Lastly, there is a van behind the truck. Its front end is badly damaged. A man, woman, and two small children are standing next to the van. None of them appear to be injured.

The summer weekend traffic is snarled because vehicles cannot get through the intersection. Some vehicles are pulling onto the shoulder to try to inch past, others are trying to turn around and find an alternate route, and others are pulling onto the grass to stop, either to help or merely to watch. Your communications centre only told you that there was a collision for which they had no details. You and an ambulance are the only emergency vehicles dispatched to answer this call.

CHAPTER 7

Motor Vehicle Offences Arising from Collision Investigation

CHAPTER OBJECTIVES

After reading this chapter, you should be able to:

◆ Distinguish between civil negligence and criminal charges involving negligence, carelessness, and dangerous driving.

◆ With respect to hit-and-run law, understand the elements of, and the circumstances to which the following charges may be applied:

- ■ s. 252, CCC—failure to stop at the scene of an accident

- ■ s. 199(1), HTA—failure to report an accident

- ■ s. 200(1), HTA—failure to remain at the scene of an accident

- ■ s. 201, HTA—failure to report damage to property.

◆ Know which hit-and-run offences are arrestable, are "anywhere" offences, are owner-liability offences, must be reported to the police, and require an officer to stop and render assistance.

◆ Recognize report forms for non-reportable and reportable accidents.

◆ Understand the elements of, and the circumstances to which the following charges may be applied:

- ■ s. 130, HTA—careless driving

- ■ s. 249, CCC—dangerous operation of a motor vehicle

- ■ ss. 219-221, CCC—criminal negligence causing death or injury.

INTRODUCTION

This chapter examines charges that commonly follow a collision. We examined the two classes of charges: those involving hit-and-run situations, and those involving careless driving. The term "careless" is used here in a general way to describe charges involving mental components, ranging from negligence and carelessness through to recklessness and deliberate willfulness.

HIT-AND-RUN LAW

In the investigation of hit-and-run collisions, officers can take advantage of provisions in both the CCC and the HTA. There is one offence in the CCC and three offences in the HTA that are applicable to hit-and-run investigations.

Failure To Stop at the Scene of an Accident, CCC, Section 252(1)

Failure to stop at the scene of an accident is a s. 536 dual or hybrid offence, and can be prosecuted, at the Crown's discretion, either by indictment or summarily. If the Crown elects to proceed by indictment, the accused has the right to elect the mode of trial and, therefore, it is possible that this charge could come before a Superior Court Judge and jury. In most cases, the Crown proceeds summarily, with a trial before an Ontario Court judge.

If the Crown proceeds by indictment, the maximum penalty is five years' imprisonment. If the charge is tried as a summary conviction offence, the maximum penalty is six months' imprisonment, a $2,000 fine, or both.

The subsection states that every person who has the care, charge, or control of a vehicle, vessel, or aircraft will be charged with failure to stop when he or she is involved in a collision with another person, vehicle, vessel, or aircraft and

fails to stop the vehicle, vessel or where possible, the aircraft, give his or her name and address and, where any person has been injured or appears to require assistance, offer assistance.

No location has been specified for this offence, so its occurrence is not restricted to highways, and it may occur anywhere. No quantification of the damage is required to trigger the offence, so even if no property damage occurs, the offence may be successfully prosecuted.

The offence uses the term "vehicle" and not "motor vehicle" and, therefore, muscular-powered vehicles and vehicles running on rails are also included.

Because this is a hybrid offence, it is treated as an indictable offence for arrest purposes, no matter how the Crown later elects to proceed with the charge. This means that an officer may make an arrest if he or she has reasonable grounds to believe that the offence was committed.

Failure To Report an Accident, HTA, Section 199(1)

Section 199(1) states that every person in charge of a motor vehicle or streetcar who is directly or indirectly involved in an accident shall, if the accident results in personal injury or damage to property apparently exceeding the amount prescribed by regulation (currently $1,000), report the accident forthwith to the nearest provincial or municipal police officer and furnish him or her with information concerning the accident for the Ministry of Transportation Accident Report.

The application of this subsection is not limited to highway property, and applies to vehicles and other property damaged in the collision. The section also applies to a person who may not have been directly involved in the collision, but who may have caused the collision by his or her driving.

This is an owner liability offence that is listed in s. 207(2) and, therefore, the owner could be charged if the driver cannot be identified. This offence is not included in the list of arrestable offences, possibly because the registered owner can be found and charged without a need to use arrest powers.

The offence is limited in its application to drivers and owners and passengers of a vehicle as defined in the HTA and passengers of a streetcar. If the driver is unable to make the report, s. 199(2) requires a passenger to make the report. The report must be submitted by the police to the Ministry of Transportation within 10 days of the collision.

Failure To Remain at the Scene of an Accident, HTA, Section 200(1)

Where a collision occurs on a highway, every person in charge of a vehicle or streetcar that is directly or indirectly involved in a collision shall

a) remain at or immediately return to the scene of the accident;

b) render all possible assistance; and

c) upon request, give in writing to anyone sustaining loss or injury or to any police officer or to any witness his or her name, address, driver's licence number and … name and address of the registered owner of the vehicle and the vehicle permit number.

Section 200(2) determines the penalty to be not less than $200 or more than $1,000, imprisonment for not more than six months, or both. The person's driver's licence or permit can also be suspended for a period of not more than two years.

Section 200(1)(a), "failure to remain at the scene," is included in the list of arrestable offences in s. 217(2). Therefore, if an officer has reasonable grounds to believe that a person has failed to remain at the scene of a collision, the officer may arrest the person.

This offence is not restricted to motor vehicles, and includes the broader category of "vehicle." The offence is restricted to collisions located on highways. There is no damage limit in this offence; it applies to every collision on the highway, whether or not there is property damage or injury.

Persons indirectly involved in a collision must also remain at the scene. For example, a driver who cuts off another vehicle and causes a collision is obliged to remain at the collision scene. Only a driver may be charged with this offence; an owner is not liable, possibly because there is an authority to arrest a driver to identify that person so that he or she can be charged.

Report of Damage, HTA, Section 201

Every person who, as a result of a collision or otherwise, operates or drives a vehicle, or leads, rides, or drives an animal on a highway and thereby damages any shrub, tree, pole, light, sign, sod, other property on the highway, or a fence bordering the highway, shall forthwith report the damage to a police officer.

The purpose of this section is to make it possible for the government to recover the costs of repairing damage caused by a vehicle (or animal) to the highway. A driver who crashes into a roadside barrier is obliged to report the damage to the police in addition to stopping and remaining at the scene. However, a driver who drives off the shoulder onto the grass and damages the sod is also required to report the damage, even though there was no collision. Arrests are not permitted for failing to report damage, and neither can an owner be held liable if he or she is not the driver.

Some Tips for Learning Hit-and-Run Law

If a subject is confusing, organize it. This can be done in several ways. Generalizations can be made about complex material, and complex material can be broken down to more manageable components. The subject matter can be organized in chart form and memory aids can be developed to recall the content of each subsection. See figure 7.1.

Some Generalizations About Hit-and-Run Law

◆   There are two highway offences and two "anywhere" offences:

   ■   anywhere—*fail to stop* and *fail to report*.

   ■   highway—*fail to remain* and *fail to report damage*.

◆   There are two arrestable offences—*fail to stop* and *fail to remain*.

◆   Only one offence specifies that the damage must be over $1,000—*fail to report*. All other offences include situations where there is damage.

◆   Only one offence is an owner liability offence—*fail to report*. All other offences require that the driver be identified.

◆   Only one offence uses the HTA definition of "motor vehicle"—*fail to report*.

◆   Only two provisions require only that a report be made to the police—*fail to report* and *damage to property*.

■ Figure 7.1   Hit-and-Run Table

Section	Location	Type of vehicle	Type of damage	Duties	Person liable	Time limit	Arrestable (yes or no)
CCC, 252(1) Fail to stop	Anywhere	Vehicle, vessel, or aircraft	Any	Stop; give name and address; offer assistance where persons are injured	Driver	IND: forever S/C: 6 months	Yes; CCC authorities
HTA, 199(1) Fail to report	Anywhere	Motor vehicle or streetcar	Personal injury or damage exceeding $700	Report forthwith to the nearest police officer	Driver or owner	6 months	No
HTA, 200(1) Fail to remain	Highway	Vehicle or streetcar	Any	Remain at or immediately return; render all possible assistance; on request, give in writing • driver name and address, • owner name and address, and • permit number	Driver	6 months	Yes, for not remaining
HTA, 201 Damage to property	Highway	Vehicle or animal	Any	Report any damage to shrub, tree, pole, light sign, sod, or other property	Driver	6 months	No

IND Indictment.   S/C Summary conviction.

Two other provisions require stopping, rendering assistance, and providing identification—*fail to stop* and *fail to remain*. As people are more important than paper, it is not surprising that "stopping offences" are arrestable and carry higher penalties.

◆ One stopping offence is limited to collisions on a highway—*fail to remain*—and one is an "anywhere" offence—*fail to stop*.

Police Responsibility for Reporting "Non-Reportable" and "Reportable" Accidents

Because a driver does not have to report a collision, it does not mean that an officer is exempted from submitting a report. Officers are required to complete and file reports for virtually every collision. Most police services have a non-reportable accident report form that must be completed by officers who are called to investigate a collision where there are no personal injuries or where the property damage does not exceed $1,000. The non-reportable accident form is much less detailed than the ministry report, and has been designed to simply record location, drivers, vehicles, and insurance particulars. See figures 7.2 and 7.3.

Collisions where there are personal injuries or property damage apparently in excess of $1,000 must be reported to the Ministry of Transportation, as required by s. 199 of the HTA. The Motor Vehicle Accident Report supplied by the ministry is used for this purpose. Some police services also use the Motor Vehicle Accident Report supplied by the Ministry for any collisions that involve a charge because it is structured for a more detailed investigation, which is necessary when charges are laid and evidence must be given in court. The Motor Vehicle Accident Report is not admissible in court, however, because it is not a document that is made contemporaneously with the event. Instead, it is usually assembled from an officer's notes some time after the collision.

The Motor Vehicle Accident Report must be completed as described in the accident report manual so that data from it can be correctly analyzed and interpreted by ministry analysts who use the data for public safety purposes. Failure to complete the report can result in a conviction based on s. 199(1) of the HTA for failing to report a collision.

CARELESS DRIVING OFFENCES

Many traffic offences involve specific acts, such as speeding, failing to stop at a stop sign (under the HTA), or being "over 80" (under the CCC). If there is evidence that a person has performed an act that is specifically prohibited, police should pursue a conviction for that specific offence where the act is done voluntarily.

In some cases, a person may engage in a course of conduct where more than one specific offence is committed. As a result, in addition to the specific offences, the person's course of conduct may indicate a lack

■ Figure 7.2   Non-Reportable Motor Vehicle Accident Report

Non-Reportable Motor Vehicle Accident Report

	Report Completed ☐	Accident Number
Name of Investigating Officer / No. / Detachment		Date of Accident

LOCATION

Road 1	Street, Road, Highway, etc.	Time Officer Arrived or Agency Reported to
	House Number or Distance ☐ Metres ☐ Kilometres ☐ N ☐ S ☐ E ☐ W	**Road Jurisdiction**
Road 2	**Intersection, Key point, Patrol Area or Other Reference**	☐ Municipal (Excl. Twp. Rd.) ☐ Regional Municipality
		☐ Provincial Highway ☐ Private Property
	Municipality / **County**	☐ Township ☐ County/Dist. ☐ Other

Driver#1 (Surname First) / Telephone No. / Vehicle Make / Year / Colour / Model / Permit No. / Prov./State / Valid ☐ Yes ☐ No

Address / Owner (Surname First) / ☐ As Driver / Telephone No.

Postal Code / Address / Postal Code

Proper Lic. to Drive ☐ Yes ☐ No	Driver Lic. Number	Insured ☐ Yes ☐ No	Insurance Company and Policy Number
Prov./State	Date of Birth	Sex / Class / Cond.	Description of Damage to Vehicle

Driver#2 (Surname First) / Telephone No. / Vehicle Make / Year / Colour / Model / Permit No. / Prov./State / Valid ☐ Yes ☐ No

Address / Owner (Surname First) / ☐ As Driver / Telephone No.

Postal Code / Address / Postal Code

Proper Lic. to Drive ☐ Yes ☐ No	Driver Lic. Number	Insured ☐ Yes ☐ No	Insurance Company and Policy Number
Prov./State	Date of Birth	Sex / Class / Cond	Description of Damage to Vehicle

Property Owner (Surname First) / Telephone / Address / Postal Code

Description of Damage / Owner Notified ☐ Yes ☐ No

Charges Laid ☐ Yes ☐ No / Person Charged, Act and Section No. / P.O.T. No.

Weather Conditions (Diagram or description - if required by district or detachment policy)

	Signature of Investigating Officer
Signature of Supervisor	Date and Time

■ Figure 7.3 Ministry Motor Vehicle Accident Report (Top Half)

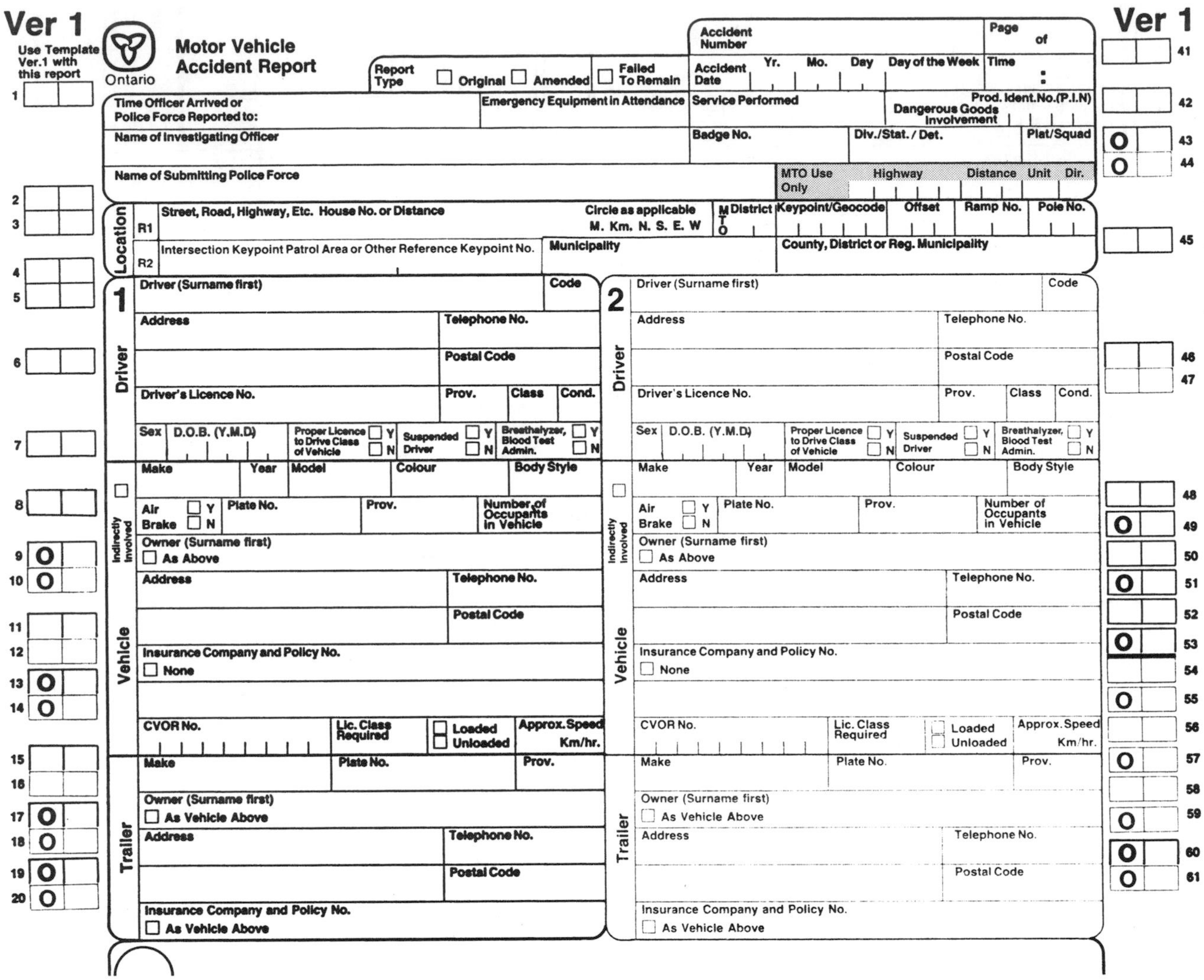

Ver 1
Use Template Ver.1 with this report

Ontario

Motor Vehicle Accident Report

Report Type ☐ Original ☐ Amended ☐ Failed To Remain

Accident Number | Page of

Accident Date Yr. Mo. Day | Day of the Week | Time :

Ver 1

Time Officer Arrived or Police Force Reported to: | Emergency Equipment in Attendance | Service Performed | Dangerous Goods Involvement | Prod. Ident.No.(P.I.N)

Name of Investigating Officer | Badge No. | Div./Stat./Det. | Plat/Squad

Name of Submitting Police Force | MTO Use Only | Highway | Distance | Unit | Dir.

Location

R1 Street, Road, Highway, Etc. House No. or Distance | Circle as applicable M. Km. N. S. E. W | MTO | District | Keypoint/Geocode | Offset | Ramp No. | Pole No.

R2 Intersection Keypoint Patrol Area or Other Reference Keypoint No. | Municipality | County, District or Reg. Municipality

1 | **Driver**

Driver (Surname first) | Code

Address | Telephone No.

Postal Code

Driver's Licence No. | Prov. | Class | Cond.

Sex | D.O.B. (Y.M.D) | Proper Licence to Drive Class of Vehicle ☐ Y ☐ N | Suspended Driver ☐ Y ☐ N | Breathalyzer, Blood Test Admin. ☐ Y ☐ N

Vehicle ☐ Indirectly Involved

Make | Year | Model | Colour | Body Style

Air Brake ☐ Y ☐ N | Plate No. | Prov. | Number of Occupants in Vehicle

Owner (Surname first) ☐ As Above

Address | Telephone No.

Postal Code

Insurance Company and Policy No. ☐ None

CVOR No. | Lic. Class Required | ☐ Loaded ☐ Unloaded | Approx. Speed Km/hr.

Trailer

Make | Plate No. | Prov.

Owner (Surname first) ☐ As Vehicle Above

Address | Telephone No.

Postal Code

Insurance Company and Policy No. ☐ As Vehicle Above

2 | **Driver**

Driver (Surname first) | Code

Address | Telephone No.

Postal Code

Driver's Licence No. | Prov. | Class | Cond.

Sex | D.O.B. (Y.M.D) | Proper Licence to Drive Class of Vehicle ☐ Y ☐ N | Suspended Driver ☐ Y ☐ N | Breathalyzer, Blood Test Admin. ☐ Y ☐ N

Vehicle ☐ Indirectly Involved

Make | Year | Model | Colour | Body Style

Air Brake ☐ Y ☐ N | Plate No. | Prov. | Number of Occupants in Vehicle

Owner (Surname first) ☐ As Above

Address | Telephone No.

Postal Code

Insurance Company and Policy No. ☐ None

CVOR No. | Lic. Class Required | ☐ Loaded ☐ Unloaded | Approx. Speed Km/hr.

Trailer

Make | Plate No. | Prov.

Owner (Surname first) ☐ As Vehicle Above

Address | Telephone No.

Postal Code

Insurance Company and Policy No. ☐ As Vehicle Above

1 2 3 4 5 6 7 8 9 10 11 12 13 14 15 16 17 18 19 20

41 42 43 44 45 46 47 48 49 50 51 52 53 54 55 56 57 58 59 60 61

◼ **Figure 7.3   Ministry Motor Vehicle Accident Report (Bottom Half)**

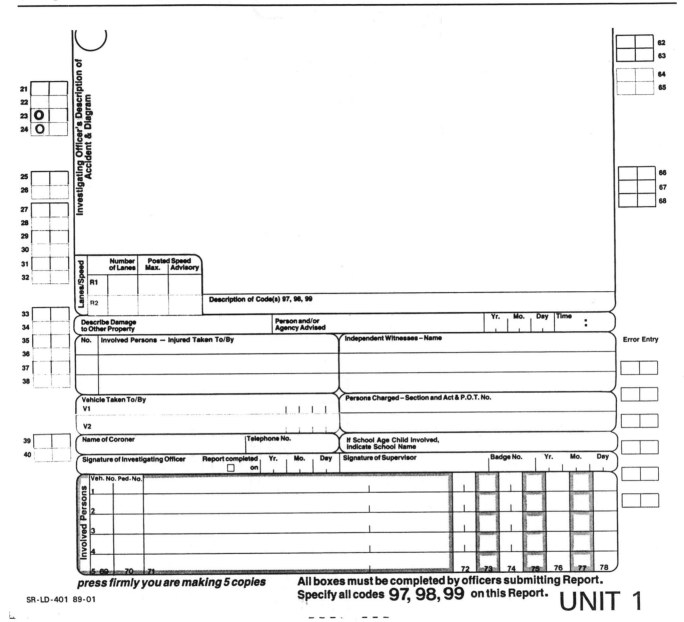

■ Figure 7.3 Ministry Motor Vehicle Accident Report Template* (Top Half)

Ver 1

Accident Location

On Highway

		Off Highway
01-Non intersection	05-At railway crossing	08-Trail
02-Intersection related	06-Underpass or tunnel	09-Frozen lake or river
03-At intersection	07-Overpass or bridge	10-Parking lot
04-At/near private drive	98-Other	99-Other

1

Impact Location

01-Within intersection	07-Passing lane	11-Not on roadway – right side
02-Thru lane	08-Left shoulder	
03-Left turn lane	09-Right shoulder	12-Off highway
04-Right turn lane	10-Not on roadway- left side	99-Other
05-Right turn channel		
06-Two-way left turn lane		

2

3 If 02 used above, enter Thru Lane No.

Environment Condition Multiple Choices Allowed

01-Clear	04-Freezing rain	07-Fog, mist, smoke, dust
02-Rain	05-Drifting snow	
03-Snow	06-Strong wind	99-Other

4
5

Light

01-Daylight	04-Dawn, artificial	07-Dark
02-Daylight, artificial	05-Dusk	08-Dark, artificial
03-Dawn	06-Dusk, artificial	99-Other

6

Traffic Control

01-Traffic signal	05-Police control	09-Traffic controller
02-Stop sign	06-School guard	10-No control
03-Yield sign	07-School bus	99-Other
04-Ped. crossover	08-Traffic gate	

7

Traffic Control Condition

01-Functioning	03-Obscured
02-Not functioning	04-Missing/Damaged

8

Road Character

01-Undivided – one-way	04-Divided - no barrier	07-Express lane
02-Undivided – two-way	05-Ramp	08-Transfer lane
03-Divided with restraining barrier	06-Collector lane	

9 R1
10 R2

Road Surface

01-Asphalt	04-Concrete	07-Steel
02-Oil treated gravel	05-Earth	08-Brick/interlocking stone
03-Gravel or crushed stone	06-Wood	99-Other

11 R1
12 R2

Road Condition

01-Good	02-Poor	03-Under repair or construction

13 R1
14 R2

Road Surface Condition

01-Dry	05-Packed snow	09-Spilled liquid
02-Wet	06-Ice	99-Other
03-Loose snow	07-Mud	
04-Slush	08-Loose sand or gravel	

15 R1
16 R2

Road Alignment

01-Straight on level	03-Curve on level
02-Straight on hill	04-Curve on hill

17 R1
18 R2

Road Pavement Markings

01-Exist	03-Obscured
02-Non - existent	04-Faded

19 R1
20 R2

Road Jurisdiction

01-Municipal (excl. Twp. Rd.)	04-County or district	07-Federal
02-Provincial highway	05-Regional municipality	99-Other
03-Township	06-Private property	

41

Classification of Accident

01-Fatal injury	03-P.D. only	99-Other
02-Non-fatal injury	04-Non-reportable	

42

Initial Direction of Travel

01-North	03-East
02-South	04-West

V1 43
V2 44

Initial Impact Type

01-Approaching	05-Turning movement
02-Angle	06-SMV unattended vehicle
03-Rear end	07-SMV other
04-Sideswipe	99-Other

45

Vehicle Manoeuver

01-Going ahead	09-Reversing
02-Slowing or stopping	10-Stopped
03-Overtaking	11-Parked
04-Turning left	12-Disabled
05-Turning right	13-Pulling away from shoulder or curb
06-Making "U" turn	14-Pulling onto shoulder or toward curb
07-Changing lanes	00-Unknown
08-Merging	99-Other

V1 46
V2 47

Sequence of Events Multiple Choices Allowed

Moveable Objects

01-Other motor vehicle	06-Street car
02-Unattended vehicle	07-Farm tractor
03-Pedestrian	08-Animal — domestic
04-Cyclist	09-Animal — wild
05-Railway train	97-Other

Other Events

20-Ran off road	25-Submersion
21-Skidding/sliding	26-Rollover
22-Jackknifing	27-Debris on road
23-Load spill	28-Debris falling off vehicle
24-Fire/explosion	98-Other

Fixed Objects

50-Cable guide rail	60-Ditch
51-Concrete guide rail	61-Curb
52-Steel guide rail	62-Crash cush/end treat.
53-Pole (utility, tower)	63-Building or wall
54-Pole (sign, parking meter)	64-Water course
55-Fence/noise barrier	65-Construction marker
56-Culvert	66-Tree, shrub, stump
57-Bridge support	99-Other
58-Rock face	
59-Snowbank/drift	

V1 1st **48** Offset **49** 2nd **50** Offset **51** 3rd **52** Offset **53**

V2 1st **54** Offset **55** 2nd **56** Offset **57** 3rd **58** Offset **59**

Fixed Object Offset

Left of Roadway	Right of Roadway
01- Less than 3.1m	05- Less than 3.1m
02- 3.1m to 6.0m	06- 3.1m to 6.0m
03- 6.1m to 9.0m	07- 6.1m to 9.0m
04- Greater than 9.0m	08- Greater than 9.0m

Vehicle Damage

01-None	03-Moderate	05-Demolished
02-Light	04-Severe	

V1 60
V2 61

* This is a cardboard template that fits over the Motor Vehicle Accident Report reproduced on pp. 212–213.

■ **Figure 7.3   Ministry Motor Vehicle Accident Report Template (Bottom Half)**

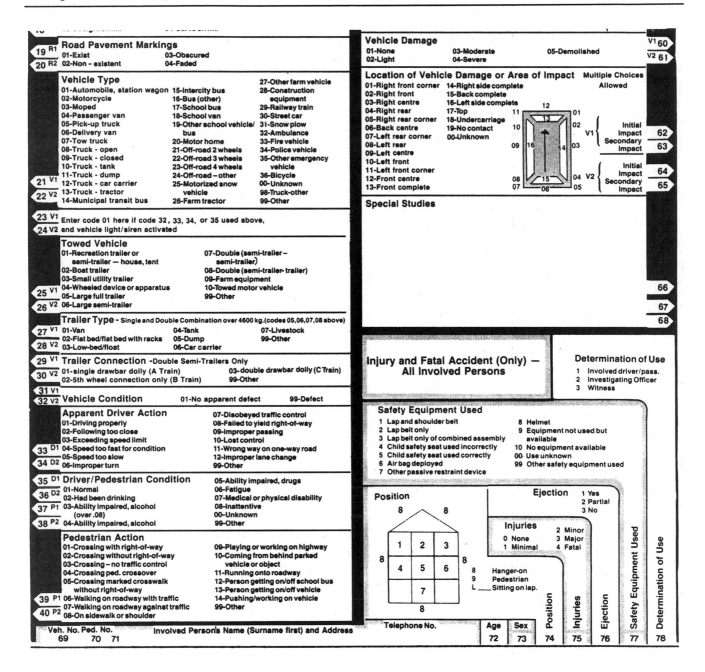

of attention to the duty of care owed to others on the highway. The failure to take care may arise from carelessness, negligence, recklessness, indifference, or be intentional. We now turn to an examination of the mental elements that determine civil liability and liability for certain criminal offences.

Civil Negligence

Civil negligence occurs when a driver fails to meet the duty that he or she owes to others on the highway. That duty is to drive with the skill and care shown by a reasonable driver in that situation. The "reasonable driver" is a legal fiction. No such person actually exists. The standard of care expected of the fictional reasonable driver is not the standard of the perfect driver who always does everything right and never makes a mistake. Rather, it is the standard of a reasonably careful and reasonably skilled driver who, on objective analysis, meets the licensing requirements and exercises a reasonable degree of care and skill. The fact that a driver is young and inexperienced does not entitle him or her to be compared to other young and inexperienced drivers. The standard remains objectively and more generally defined as the reasonable driver. This standard is commonly invoked in situations where a person must possess skills that meet the minimum requirements of a licensing system.[1]

Negligence is the basis for most civil lawsuits against "at fault" drivers. A plaintiff who can persuade a court that it is more probable than not that the defendant was negligent may win his or her lawsuit. The civil standard of proof—the balance of probability—means that on a scale of 0 to 100, where 0 is a complete absence of proof and 100 is absolute proof, the plaintiff must convince the court that his or her proof measures 51, just beyond the half-way point, and that it is more probable than not that the plaintiff's evidence can be proven. Compare this measurement to the standard of proof in criminal and provincial offences cases, where proof beyond reasonable doubt is required. Here, the Crown must convince the court that its proof measures well beyond the 50 mark, to about 90, on every element of the offence. The Crown need not reach 100 and prove its case absolutely, but the standard is much higher than it is in civil cases.

Under the HTA, a plaintiff has two years from the time of the collision to commence proceedings by issuing a claim (HTA, s. 206). A plaintiff may not sue for physical injury unless the injury is very serious. A plaintiff may sue for property damage, although this is usually covered by insurance. The insurance company pays its insured client for property damage where the other driver is at fault, and then may commence a lawsuit in the name of its insured client to recover what the insurance company has paid out to its clients. This does not happen often, as insurance adjusters usually negotiate the percentage of fault of one or both drivers, and settle on that basis. In the course of negotiating a settlement of a civil matter, charges laid by the police are of more than passing interest to the insurance company and its insured clients. Although it is not automatic, conviction for a charge arising from the collision is often presumed to be proof of fault in the civil proceeding.

CIVIL AND CRIMINAL STANDARDS OF PROOF

0	51	90	100
absolutely not proved	proved on the balance of probability	proof beyond reasonable doubt	absolutely proved
	Civil Trials	Criminal Trials	

Careless Driving, HTA, Section 130

Anyone who drives a vehicle or streetcar on a highway without due care and attention or without reasonable consideration for other persons using the highway may be convicted of careless driving.

Note that the broad HTA definition of "vehicle" is used so that drivers of vehicles other than motor vehicles may be liable for this offence. The offence can only be committed on a highway. On conviction, a driver may be fined between $200 and $1,000, imprisoned for up to six months, or be both fined and imprisoned. In addition, the court may suspend the driver's licence for up to two years.

In *R v. Glogoki*, the judge stated that the prosecution must show "a sufficient departure from the standard of a prudent and reasonable driver to make the driving 'deserving of punishment.'" The prosecution must be able to prove more than just a minor act of negligence.

Where there is evidence of a single specific offence, the officer should proceed to charge that offence. Evidence of a single offence is not usually enough to sustain a conviction for careless driving as well. However, a pattern of two or more HTA offences arising out of a single driving episode, collision, or event may provide the basis for a charge of careless driving. For example, a driver who is speeding and changing lanes abruptly without signalling could be departing significantly from the standard of the reasonable and prudent driver, whether or not he or she causes a collision. This pattern of conduct might justify a careless driving charge.

The fact that a collision results in serious damage does not justify laying a careless driving charge; the amount of damage speaks to the result of a collision, not its cause. A mere non-negligent error in judgment can result in a collision with serious property damage. It is the conduct that caused the collision that the officer must consider, not the results, when considering what charge should be laid.

Inattentiveness can give rise to a careless driving charge. However, a rear-end collision may result from a driver looking away from the road for a split second, but that, in itself, is not a sufficient enough departure from paying attention to warrant the charge of careless driving. There must be evidence of prolonged inattentiveness to support a "careless" charge.

Because this charge is general rather than specific in nature, officers tend to misuse it where, for example, a collision has serious results, the officer cannot find the appropriate specific charge, or a collision results from a momentary distraction.

Dangerous Operation of a Motor Vehicle, CCC, Section 249(1)(a)

Everyone who operates a motor vehicle in a manner that is dangerous to the public, having regard to all the circumstances, including the nature, condition, and use of the location where the vehicle is being driven, and the usual traffic volume at that location, may be charged with an indictable offence or be charged summarily, at the Crown's prerogative. If the Crown proceeds by indictment, the accused is liable to imprisonment for up to 5 years; if the accused, as a result of dangerous operation of a motor vehicle, causes another person's death or bodily harm, the charge under s. 249(1)(a) must proceed by indictment, and carries a maximum sentence of 10 years.

This is an "anywhere" offence, and is not restricted to driving on highways only. To determine whether someone's driving is "dangerous," the officer must consider the "nature and use of the place" where the vehicle is operated and "the amount of traffic at the time, or the traffic that might be expected in that place." There must also be a danger to "the public who are present, or could be expected to be present." Endangering the public and traffic volume need not be proved if it can be shown that the reasonable person would expect the public to be present or expect significant traffic volume in that location.

The mental element of this offence rests on an objective standard of what a reasonable person would do in the accused's position. The normal inference is that a person who commits an obviously dangerous act (as defined in s. 249) failed to consider the risk and the need to take care to avoid the harm. In other words, the driver engaging in this behaviour should have known better. This inference can be negated if the driver lacked the capacity to appreciate the situation, but strictly personal factors, such as youth or inexperience, are not considered to be defences and, therefore, the standard remains objective. (See *R v. Creighton*, [1993] 3 SCR 3; 83 CCC (3d) 346, per McLachlin J.)

Examples of dangerous driving include fleeing the police in a high-speed chase, driving at high speed across an area restricted to pedestrians, and driving down a one-way street the wrong way at 4 a.m., wearing a blindfold.

Criminal Negligence Causing Death or Injury, CCC, Sections 219-221

Section 219 states that everyone is criminally negligent who, in doing anything, or omitting to do anything that it is his or her duty to do, shows wanton or reckless disregard for the lives or safety of other persons.

DRIVING OFFENCES

Criminal Negligence Causing Injury or Death, ss. 219-221 CCC:

◆ the operator of the motor vehicle knows the consequences of his or her acts, and *doesn't care* or *is willfully blind to the consequences*

Dangerous Operation of a Motor Vehicle, s. 249 CCC

◆ the operator of the motor vehicle *should have known the consequences of his or her actions, and should have known better*

Careless Driving, s. 130 HTA

◆ *prolonged inattentiveness*

In other words, the person knows the consequences of his or her actions and simply does not care or is willfully blind to the risk. This charge carries a higher standard and implies a higher level of intention than that for dangerous driving or careless driving. For a dangerous driving charge, the driver is liable because he or she *should have known* that the act was dangerous. For a careless driving charge, *inattention or carelessness* is the basis for liability.

Although the level of intent does not require proof of deliberateness or willfulness in deciding to act or failing to act where there is a duty to act, the case law is not clear whether the standard is objective or subjective. One view is that factors such as age, inexperience, mental development, and education should be considered. A stricter view is that an objective examination of the conduct provides a sufficient measure to infer a reckless or wanton disregard that is sufficient to provide the basis for a conviction.[2]

Where death results from an act of criminal negligence, s. 220 requires the charge to proceed by indictment. On conviction, the accused is liable to life imprisonment. Where bodily harm, rather than death, results, s. 221 requires the offence to proceed by indictment with a sentence of imprisonment for up to 10 years. These are "anywhere" offences and can be committed with any type of vehicle.

CHAPTER SUMMARY

This chapter is concerned with the identification of the charges that are appropriate in hit-and-run cases and "at fault" drivers, following a collision investigation.

If a driver fails in his or her obligation to stop, render assistance, and meet reporting requirements, it is necessary to distinguish between the CCC charge of failing to stop at the scene of a collision and the HTA charges of failing to report a collision, failing to remain at the scene, and failing to report damage. The officer must be familiar with the elements of these offences and the differences between them in order to decide which charge is appropriate.

Where there is a single specific offence, it is appropriate to charge for that offence. However, where the investigation uncovers a pattern in driver conduct that ranges from negligence and carelessness to recklessness and deliberate willfulness, an officer must be able to determine which charge is appropriate to the driver's level of intention. The chapter examines the components of the offences of careless driving, dangerous driving, and criminal negligence, identifies the circumstances in which one or another of these charges might be laid, and distinguishes these charges from civil negligence.

REVIEW QUESTIONS

■ MULTIPLE CHOICE

You are a police officer investigating the following collision scenarios. Circle the most correct answer to each question.

1. Ms Smith is driving her moped on a plaza parking lot. Farmer Akinido is coming to town to do his weekly shopping; he sideswipes Ms Smith with his implement of husbandry that he is towing behind his farm tractor. He stops, looks at Ms Smith, and leaves the scene. You arrive at the scene, and Ms Smith states that the farm tractor has an unusual paint job. She can positively identify the tractor, but not the driver. You question the owner of the tractor, but he denies driving it.

    What charge(s) could you lay?

    a. CCC, s. 252(1)

    b. HTA, s. 199(1)

    c. HTA, s. 200(1)

    d. HTA, s. 201

2. Mr. Armani is walking to town along the side of the highway. Ms Kahn comes racing along on her motorized snow vehicle and hits Mr. Armani. She stops and splints his broken arm. Mr. Armani asks her name, but Ms Kahn refuses to identify herself and leaves. Mr. Armani can identify the driver because she took off her helmet to assist him.

    What charge(s) could you lay?

    a. CCC, s. 252(1)

    b. HTA, s. 199(1)

    c. HTA, s. 200(1)

    d. HTA, s. 201

3. Ms Delgado has a job painting guard rails along the highway. A self-propelled implement of husbandry, operated by Mr. Nkrumah, drives past and damages about 30 m of guard rail. Ms Delgado saw Mr. Nkrumah's vehicle coming and jumped out of the way. She tells you that the driver did not stop and she cannot identify Mr. Nkrumah. You do get a good description of the implement of husbandry, and trace it to Mr. Nkrumah.

    What charge(s) could you lay?

    a. CCC, s. 252(1)

    b. HTA, s. 199(1)

    c. HTA, s. 200(1)

    d. HTA, s. 201

4. Ms Offenbach is crossing Main Street when she is clipped by Mr. Chen. Mr. Chen stops immediately, gets out of his vehicle, and renders assistance to Ms Offenbach. Mr. Chen then leaves the scene before anyone asks for the driver's name. You locate the vehicle, but because Ms Offenbach broke her glasses, she cannot identify Mr. Chen.

   What charge(s) could you lay?

   a. CCC, s. 252(1)

   b. HTA, s. 199(1)

   c. HTA, s. 200(1)

   d. HTA, s. 201

5. Mr. Grieg is hitchhiking on the shoulder of the road. Ms Ducharme is driving a flatbed truck, and as it passes Mr. Grieg, a bail of hay falls off and hits him. Ms Ducharme fails to stop. Mr. Holst, a passenger in the truck, looks back and sees that Mr. Grieg is injured. You locate the vehicle, but Mr. Grieg cannot identify the driver, just the passenger that he saw looking back at him.

   What charge(s) could you lay?

   a. CCC, s. 252(1)

   b. HTA, s. 199(1)

   c. HTA, s. 200(1)

   d. HTA, s. 201

6. Ms Schwartz is riding her dog sled along the shoulder of the highway. Mr. Karagianis comes along on his motorized snow vehicle and hits her sled. The sled is damaged, but Ms Schwartz is not injured. Mr. Karagianis leaves the scene. You locate the motorized snow vehicle, but you are unable to identify the driver, Mr. Karagianis. Total damage is $400.

   What charge(s) could you lay?

   a. CCC, s. 252(1)

   b. HTA, s. 199(1)

   c. HTA, s. 200(1)

   d. HTA, s. 201

7. Mr. Djugashvili's 14-year-old son is riding a soapbox racer down a hill. He collides with a street sign, doing about $100 worth of damage to the sign. Ms Fujiwara witnesses the collision while sitting on her porch, and can identify the driver of the soapbox racer.

   What charge(s) could you lay?

   a. CCC, s. 252(1)

   b. HTA, s. 199(1)

   c. HTA, s. 200(1)

   d. HTA, s. 201

8. Mr. Pilsudski is driving his car on a residential street. He hits an icy patch and loses control of his car. He strikes Ms Hassan's car. Mr. Pilsudki gets out, looks at the damage, which totals about $2,000, sees no witnesses, and leaves. Through an observant officer on your shift, you locate a possible suspect vehicle. You make a physical match with a piece of broken direction signal lens that was left at the scene.
   What charge(s) could you lay?

   a. CCC, s. 252(1)

   b. HTA, s. 199(1)

   c. HTA, s. 200(1)

   d. HTA, s. 201

9. Morris is driving east on a four-lane divided highway. He suddenly realizes that he forgot his wallet. Because he is late for an appointment, he pulls off on the left shoulder, drives over the grass centre strip, and drives immediately onto the left-hand shoulder of the west-bound side of the highway. He then drives directly into the left-hand lane, hitting a vehicle already driving in that lane. No one is injured, but there is considerable property damage.
   What charge(s) could you lay?

   a. HTA, s. 130

   b. CCC, s. 249

   c. CCC, s. 220

   d. CCC, s. 221

10. Demetrius is driving, and Diana is sitting next to him. Demetrius says his right foot is tired and asks Diana to use her left foot to operate the accelerator while he handles the other controls. It is about 4 a.m., and the highway has very little traffic. As they come to a traffic light, Diana mistakenly presses the accelerator harder. The car shoots through a red light and hits a man on a bicycle, causing him serious injury.
   What charge(s) could you lay?

   a. HTA, s. 130

   b. CCC, s. 249

   c. CCC, s. 220

   d. CCC, s. 221

11. Mr. Bordelaise is driving his catering van along the highway. He discovers that a bee has flown in. While continuing to drive, he attempts to swat the bee, weaving all over the road and into the opposing lane. While he is flailing about after the bee, he fails to notice that he has just run a stop sign, and smashes into the side of another vehicle legally travelling through the intersection on the cross street.

    What charge(s) could you lay?

    a. HTA, s. 130

    b. CCC, s. 249

    c. CCC, s. 220

    d. CCC, s. 221

12. Dougal Doofus decides he is going to get home before 6 p.m., come hell or high water. To do this, the rush hour notwithstanding, he speeds up, braking hard and blasting on his horn when other cars are in the way and changes lanes abruptly without signalling. After a kilometre or two of this behaviour, one of his horn blasts frightens another driver, who panics and turns abruptly to the right, into a third vehicle.

    What charge(s) could you lay?

    a. HTA, s. 130

    b. CCC, s. 249

    c. CCC, s. 220

    d. CCC, s. 221

■ DISCUSSION QUESTIONS

1. A 16-year-old male is driving home with his girlfriend. It was raining heavily. There were road signs with symbols indicating that the road is slippery when wet. The normal speed limit is 80 km/h, but under the slippery-when-wet sign, there is a posted speed limit of 70 km/h. The driver is in a hurry and is driving 110 km/h. When the road is dry, this is a safe speed, although it is above the speed limit. The driver loses control of the vehicle, it goes off the road, and crashes, causing the death of his passenger. He is charged with criminal negligence causing death.

   a. Should the standard to judge this case be that of a sane and sober 16-year-old driver, or should another standard be used?

   b. Does the conduct amount to a marked and substantial departure from the standard you identified in (a), above?

   For a discussion of these issues, see *R v. Barron* (1985), 23 CCC (3d) 544; 48 CR (2d) 344 (Ont. CA).

2. Mr. Kolovoski is trying to flee the police car chasing his vehicle. He turns into a shopping plaza, travelling the wrong way on a one-way exit ramp. His motor vehicle strikes the side of Ms Ngomo's vehicle, damaging her vehicle and slightly injuring her. Mr. Kolovoski continues driving, exits the plaza, and re-enters the highway, where he sideswipes and damages a light post. He speeds on, runs a red light, and hits a pedestrian in the intersection, killing him.

   Discuss the charges that could be laid against Mr. Kolovoski in this situation.

NOTES

1   It could be argued that a driver with a G1 or G2 licence should only have to meet the standards of the reasonable driver holding a graduated licence, and not be subjected to the standard expected of a G licence holder. On the other hand, it can also be argued that the standard to be met by a G1 or G2 driver is the same as a G driver's standard, and that the graduated system merely eliminates situations that would expose the holder of a G1 or G2 to risks that an inexperienced driver cannot yet manage at the G level (for example, driving at night or driving on a 400-series highway).

2   *R v. Waite*, [1989] 1 SCR 1436; *R v. Tutton*, [1989] 1 SCR 1392. There was no clear majority and no consensus as to the components of the mental element for criminal negligence.

APPENDIX A

Short-Form Wordings and Set Fines from the Provincial Offences Act

The short-form wordings of charges as set out in the *Provincial Offences Act* are an aid in locating topics in the *Highway Traffic Act*. Users of this device must be aware that only charges are listed here. If police officers use the list of short-form wordings as a device for determining an appropriate charge, they must recognize that the short-form wordings do not adequately reflect all the facts in issue for an offence. The actual section, subsection, and clause should be referenced to determine whether a specific charge is appropriate. As long as users understand the limitations of this device, the short-form wordings are invaluable as an overview of all charges in the Act.

Selected short-form wordings for offences relating to licences and to speeding and rules of the road are set out below.

PROCEEDINGS COMMENCED BY CERTIFICATE OF OFFENCE, RRO 1990, REG. 950

SCHEDULE 43
HIGHWAY TRAFFIC ACT

Item	Column 1	Column 2 Section	Set Fine (Includes Costs)
...			
84.	Drive motor vehicle—no licence	32(1)	$265.00
84.1	Drive commercial motor vehicle—no license	32(1)	$315.00
85.	Drive motor vehicle—improper licence	32(1)	$265.00
85.1	Drive commercial motor vehicle—improper licence	32(1)	$315.00
86.	Drive streetcar—no licence	32(2)	$265.00
87.	Drive vehicle with air brakes—no endorsement	32(3)	$205.00

87.1	Drive commercial motor vehicle with air brake—no endorsement	32(3)	$315.00
88.	Drive motor vehicle in contravention of conditions	32(9)	$90.00
88.1	Drive commercial motor vehicle in contravention of conditions	32(9)	$315.00
89.	Permit unlicensed person to drive motor vehicle	32(10)	$205.00
89.1	Permit unlicensed person to drive commercial motor vehicle	32(10)	$315.00
90.	Permit person with improper licence to drive motor vehicle	32(10)	$205.00
90.1	Permit person with improper licence to drive commercial motor vehicle	32(10)	$315.00
91.	Permit unlicensed person to drive	32(10)	$205.00
91.1	Permit operation of vehicles with air brakes—no endorsement on licence	32(11)	$205.00
91.2	Permit novice driver to drive in contravention of condition or restriction	32(11.1)	$205.00
92.	Driver fail to surrender licence	33(1)	$90.00
92.1	Accompanying driver fail to surrender licence	33(2)	$90.00
93.	Driver fail to give identification	33(3)	$90.00
93.1	Accompanying driver fail to give identification	33(3)	$90.00
94.	Possess illegal licence	35(1)(a)	N.S.F.
95.	Use illegal licence	35(1)(a)	N.S.F.
96.	Possess non-Photo Card portion of cancelled, revoked or suspended licence	35(1)(b)	N.S.F.
97.	Use non-Photo Card portion of cancelled, revoked or suspended licence	35(1)	N.S.F.
98.	Permit another person to use all or part of licence	35(1)(c)	N.S.F.
98.1	Use other person's licence	35(1)(d)	N.S.F.
98.2	Apply for more than one licence	35(1)(e)	N.S.F.
98.3	Secure more than one licence	35(1)(e)	N.S.F.
98.4	Possess more than one licence	35(1)(e)	N.S.F.
98.5	Fail to surrender suspended, revoked or cancelled license	35(1)(f)	N.S.F.

99.	Driving under licence of other jurisdiction while suspended in Ontario	36	N.S.F.
100.	Employ person under 16 to drive	37(2)	N.S.F.
101.	Permit person under 16 to drive	37(2)	N.S.F.
102.	Let unlicensed driver hire vehicle	39(1)	N.S.F.
103.	Fail to produce licence when hiring vehicle	39(3)	$90.00
104.	Apply for permit while prohibited	47(5)	N.S.F.
105.	Procure permit while prohibited	47(5)	N.S.F.
106.	Possess permit while prohibited	47(5)	N.S.F.
107.	Apply for licence while prohibited	47(6)	N.S.F.
108.	Procure licence while prohibited	47(6)	N.S.F.
109.	Possess licence while prohibited	47(6)	N.S.F.
110.	Procure CVOR certificate while suspended	47(7)	$265.00
111.	Apply for CVOR certificate while suspended	47(7)	$265.00
112.	Operate commercial motor vehicle—fleet limitation certificate not carried	47(8)(a)	N.S.F.
113.	Operate commercial motor vehicle— CVOR certificate	47(8)(b)	N.S.F.
113.1	Novice driver fail to provide breath sample	48.1(3)	$90.00
113.2	Novice driver refuse to provide breath sample	48.1(4)	$90.00
113.3	Novice driver fail to provide breath sample	48.1(4)	$90.00
113.4	Novice driver refuse to provide breath sample	48.1(4)	$90.00
113.5	Novice driver fail to surrender licence	48.1(5)	$90.00
113.6	Accompanying driver fail to provide breath sample	48.2(2)	$90.00
113.7	Accompanying driver refuse to provide breath sample	48.2(2)	$90.00
114.	Operate vehicle for which permit suspended	51	N.S.F.
115.	Operate vehicle for which permit cancelled	51	N.S.F.
116.	Driving while under suspension	53	N.S.F.
...			
340.	Speeding	128	Schedule B
340.1	Speeding—liability of owner where evidence obtained through photo-radar	128	Schedule C

340.2	Speeding—community safety zone	128	Schedule D
340.3	Owner—speeding pursuant to section 207—community safety zone	128	Schedule D
341.	Careless driving	130	$265.00
341.1	Careless driving—community safety zone	130	N.S.F.
342.	Unnecessary slow driving	132	$90.00
342.1	Unnecessary slow driving—community safety zone	132	$125.00
343.	Disobey officer directing traffic	134(1)	$90.00
343.1	Disobey officer directing traffic—community safety zone	134(1)	$125.00
344.	Drive on closed highway	134(3)	$90.00
344.1	Drive on closed highway—community safety zone	134(3)	$125.00
345.	Fail to yield—uncontrolled intersection	135(2)	$90.00
345.1	Fail to yield—uncontrolled intersection—community safety zone	135(2)	$155.00
346.	Fail to yield to vehicle on right	135(3)	$90.00
346.1	Fail to yield to vehicle on right—community safety zone	135(3)	$155.00
347.	Disobey stop sign—stop wrong place	136(1)(a)	$90.00
347.1	Disobey stop sign—stop wrong place—community safety zone	136(1)(a)	$125.00
348.	Disobey stop sign—fail to stop	136(l)(a)	$90.00
348.1	Disobey stop sign—fail to stop—community safety zone	136(1)(a)	$155.00
349.	Fail to yield to traffic on through highway	136(1)(b)	$90.00
349.1	Fail to yield to traffic on through highway—community safety zone	136(1)(b)	$155.00
350.	Traffic on through highway—fail to yield	136(2)	$90.00
350.1	Traffic on through highway—fail to yield—community safety zone	136(2)	$155.00
351.	Fail to yield—yield sign	138(1)	$90.00
351.1	Fail to yield—yield sign—community safety zone	138(1)	$155.00

352.	Fail to yield from private road	139(1)	$90.00
352.1	Fail to yield from private road—community safety zone	139(1)	$155.00
353.	Fail to yield from driveway	139(1)	$90.00
353.1	Fail to yield from driveway—community safety zone	139(1)	$155.00
354.	Fail to yield to pedestrian	140(1)(a)	$90.00
354.1	Fail to yield to pedestrian—community safety zone	140(1)(a)	$155.00
355.	Fail to yield to pedestrian approaching	140(1)(b)	$90.00
355.1	Fail to yield to pedestrian approaching—community safety zone	140(1)(b)	$155.00
356.	Fail to yield to person in wheelchair	140(1)(a)	$90.00
356.1	Fail to yield to person in wheelchair—community safety zone	140(1)(a)	$155.00
357.	Fail to yield to person in wheelchair approaching	140(1)(b)	$90.00
357.1	Fail to yield to person in wheelchair approaching—community safety zone	140(1)(b)	$155.00
358.	Pass stopped vehicle at crossover	140(2)	$90.00
358.1	Pass stopped vehicle at crossover—community safety zone	140(2)	$155.00
359.	Pass stopped street car at crossover	140(2)	$90.00
359.1	Pass stopped street car at crossover—community safety zone	140(2)	$155.00
360.	Stopped vehicle at crossover—fail to yield to pedestrian	140(2)(a)	$90.00
360.1	Stopped vehicle at crossover—fail to yield to pedestrian—community safety zone	140(2)(a)	$155.00
361.	Stopped street car at crossover—fail to yield to pedestrian	140(2)(a)	$90.00
361.1	Stopped street car at crossover—fail to yield to pedestrian—community safety zone	140(2)(a)	$155.00
362.	Stopped vehicle at crossover—fail to yield to person in wheelchair	140(2)(a)	$90.00
362.1	Stopped vehicle at crossover—fail to yield to person in wheelchair—community safety zone	140(2)(a)	$155.00

363.	Stopped street car at crossover—fail to yield to person in wheelchair	140(2)	$90.00
363.1	Stopped street car at crossover—fail to yield to person in wheelchair—community safety zone	140(2)(a)	$155.00
364.	Stopped vehicle at crossover—fail to yield to pedestrian approaching	140(2)(b)	$90.00
364.1	Stopped vehicle at crossover—fail to yield to pedestrian approaching—community safety zone	140(2)(b)	$155.00
365.	Stopped street car at crossover—fail to yield to pedestrian approaching	140(2)(b)	$90.00
365.1	Stopped street car at crossover—fail to yield to pedestrian approaching—community safety zone	140(2)(b)	$155.00
366.	Stopped vehicle at crossover—fail to yield to person in wheelchair approaching	140(2)(b)	$90.00
366.1	Stopped vehicle at crossover—fail to yield to person in wheelchair approaching—community safety zone	140(2)(b)	$155.00
367.	Stopped street car at crossover—fail to yield to person in wheelchair approaching	140(2)(b)	$90.00
367.1	Stopped street car at crossover—fail to yield to person in wheelchair approaching—community safety zone	140(2)(b)	$155.00
368.	Pass front of vehicle within 30 m of crossover	140(3)	$90.00
368.1	Pass front of vehicle within 30 m of crossover—community safety zone	140(3)	$155.00
369.	Pass front of street car within 30 m of crossover	140(3)	$90.00
369.1	Pass front of street car within 30 m of crossover—community safety zone	140(3)	$155.00
370.	Pedestrian fail to yield at crossover	140(4)	$40.00
371.	Person in wheelchair—fail to yield at crossover	140(4)	$40.00
371.1	Cyclist—ride in crossover	140(6)	$90.00

372.	Improper right turn	141(2)	$90.00
372.1	Improper right turn—community safety zone	141(2)	$125.00
373.	Improper right turn—multi-lane highway	141(3)	$90.00
373.1	Improper right turn—multi-lane highway—community safety zone	141(3)	$125.00
374.	Left turn—fail to afford reasonable opportunity to avoid collision	141(5)	$90.00
374.1	Left turn—fail to afford reasonable opportunity to avoid collision—community safety zone	141(5)	$155.00
375.	Improper left turn	141(6)	$90.00
375.1	Improper left turn—community safety zone	141(6)	$125.00
376.	Improper left turn—multi-lane highway	141(7)	$90.00
376.1	Improper left turn—multi-lane highway—community safety zone	141(7)	$125.00
377.	Turn—not in safety	142(1)	$90.00
377.1	Turn—not in safety—community safety zone	142(1)	$155.00
378.	Change lane—not in safety	142(1)	$90.00
378.1	Change lane—not in safety—community safety zone	142(1)	$155.00
379.	Fail to signal for turn	142(1)	$90.00
379.1	Fail to signal for turn—community safety zone	142(1)	$125.00
380.	Fail to signal—lane change	142(1)	$90.00
380.1	Fail to signal—lane change—community safety zone	142(1)	$125.00
381.	Start from parked position—not in safety	142(2)	$90.00
381.1	Start from parked position—not in safety—community safety zone	142(2)	$155.00
382.	Start from stopped position—not in safety	142(2)	$90.00
382.1	Start from stopped position—not in safety—community safety zone	142(2)	$155.00
383.	Start from parked position—fail to signal	142(2)	$90.00
383.1	Start from parked position—fail to signal—community safety zone	142(2)	$125.00

384.	Start from stopped position—fail to signal	142(2)	$90.00
384.1	Start from stopped position—fail to signal—community safety zone	142(2)	$125.00
385.	Improper arm signal	142(4)	$90.00
385.1	Improper arm signal—community safety zone	142(4)	$125.00
386.	Improper signal device	142(6)	$90.00
386.1	Improper signal device—community safety zone	142(6)	$125.00
387.	Use turn signals improperly	142(7)	$90.00
387.1	Use turn signals improperly—community safety zone	142(7)	$125.00
388.	Fail to signal stop	142(8)	$90.00
388.1	Fail to signal stop—community safety zone	142(8)	$125.00
389.	Fail to signal decrease in speed	142(8)	$90.00
389.1	Fail to signal decrease in speed—community safety zone	142(8)	$125.00
390.	Improper signal to stop	142(8)	$90.00
390.1	Improper signal to stop—community safety zone	142(8)	$125.00
391.	Improper signal to decrease in speed	142(8)	$90.00
391.1	Improper signal to decrease in speed—community safety zone	142(8)	$125.00
392.	Brake lights—improper colour	142(8)(b)	$90.00
392.1	Brake lights—improper colour—community safety zone	142(8)(b)	$125.00
393.	U-turn on a curve—no clear view	143(a)	$90.00
393.1	U-turn on a curve—no clear view—community safety zone	143(a)	$155.00
394.	U-turn—railway crossing	143(b)	$90.00
394.1	U-turn—railway crossing—community safety zone	143(b)	$155.00
395.	U-turn near crest or grade—no clear view	143(c)	$90.00

395.1	U-turn near crest or grade— no clear view—community safety zone	143(c)	$155.00
396.	U-turn—bridge—no clear view	143(d)	$90.00
396.1	U-turn—bridge—no clear view— community safety zone	143(d)	$155.00
397.	U-turn—viaduct—no clear view	143(d)	$90.00
397.1	U-turn—viaduct—no clear view— community safety zone	143(d)	$155.00
398.	U-turn—tunnel—no clear view	143(d)	$90.00
398.1	U-turn—tunnel—no clear view— community safety zone	143(d)	$155.00
399.	Improper stop—traffic signal at intersection	144(5)	$90.00
399.1	Improper stop—traffic signal at intersection—community safety zone	144(5)	$125.00
400.	Improper stop—traffic signal not at intersection	144(6)	$90.00
400.1	Improper stop—traffic signal not at intersection—community safety zone	144(6)	$125.00
401.	Fail to yield to pedestrian	144(7)	$90.00
401.1	Fail to yield to pedestrian— community safety zone	144(7)	$155.00
402.	Fail to yield to traffic	144(8)	$90.00
402.1	Fail to yield to traffic— community safety zone	144(8)	$155.00
403.	Proceed contrary to sign at intersection	144(9)	$90.00
403.1	Proceed contrary to sign at intersection—community safety zone	144(9)	$125.00
404.	Disobey lane light	144(10)	$90.00
404.1	Disobey lane light—community safety zone	144(10)	$125.00
405.	Green light—fail to proceed as directed	144(12)	$90.00
405.1	Green light—fail to proceed as directed— community safety zone	144(12)	$125.00
406.	Flashing green light—fail to proceed as directed	144(13)	$90.00

406.1	Flashing green light—fail to proceed as directed—community safety zone	144(13)	$125.00
407.	Green arrow—fail to proceed as directed	144(14)	$90.00
407.1	Green arrow—fail to proceed as directed—community safety zone	144(14)	$125.00
408.	Amber light—fail to stop	144(15)	$155.00
408.1	Amber light—fail to stop—community safety zone	144(15)	$305.00
409.	Amber arrow—fail to stop	144(16)	$90.00
409.1	Amber arrow—fail to stop—community safety zone	144(16)	$125.00
410.	Amber arrow—fail to proceed as directed	144(16)	$90.00
410.1	Amber arrow—fail to proceed as directed—community safety zone	144(16)	$125.00
411.	Flashing amber light—fail to proceed with caution	144(17)	$90.00
411.1	Flashing amber light—fail to proceed with caution—community safety zone	144(17)	$125.00
412.	Red light—fail to stop	144(18)	$155.00
412.1	Red light—fail to stop—community safety zone	144(18)	$305.00
413.	Red light—proceed before green	144(18)	$155.00
413.1	Red light—proceed before green—community safety zone	144(18)	$305.00
414.	Turn on red light—fail to yield	144(19)	$90.00
414.1	Turn on red light—fail to yield—community safety zone	144(19)	$155.00
415.	Emergency vehicle—proceed when unsafe	144(20)	$90.00
416.	Flashing red light—fail to stop	144(21)	$90.00
416.1	Flashing red light—fail to stop—community safety zone	144(21)	$155.00
417.	Flashing red light—fail to yield	144(21)	$90.00
417.1	Flashing red light—fail to yield—community safety zone	144(21)	$155.00
418.	Pedestrian fail to use cross-walk	144(22)	$40.00

419.	Pedestrian disobey flashing green light	144(24)	$40.00
420.	Pedestrian disobey red light	144(25)	$40.00
421.	Pedestrian disobey amber light	144(25)	$40.00
422.	Pedestrian disobey "don't walk" signal	144(27)	$40.00
422.1	Cyclist—ride in or along crosswalk	144(29)	$90.00
423.	Disobey portable amber light fail to stop	146(3)	$155.00
423.1	Disobey portable amber light—fail to stop—community safety zone	146(3)	$305.00
424.	Disobey portable red light—fail to stop	146(4)	$155.00
424.1	Disobey portable red light—fail to stop—community safety zone	146(4)	$305.00
425.	Disobey portable red light—proceed before green	146(4)	$155.00
425.1	Disobey portable red light—proceed before green—community safety zone	146(4)	$305.00
426.	Disobey portable red light—stop wrong place	146(5)	$90.00
426.1	Disobey portable red light—stop wrong place—community safety zone	146(5)	$125.00
427.	Disobey portable amber light—stop wrong place	146(5)	$90.00
427.1	Disobey portable amber light—stop wrong place—community safety zone	146(5)	$125.00
428.	Remove portable lane control signal system	146(6)	$90.00
428.1	Remove portable lane control signal system—community safety zone	146(6)	$155.00
429.	Deface portable lane control signal system	146(6)	$90.00
429.1	Deface portable lane control signal system—community safety zone	146(6)	$125.00
430.	Interfere with portable lane control signal system	146(6)	$90.00
430.1	Interfere with portable lane control signal system—community safety zone	146(6)	$125.00
431.	Fail to keep right when driving at less than normal speed	147(1)	$90.00
431.1	Fail to keep right when driving at less than normal speed—community safety zone	147(1)	$125.00

432.	Fail to share half roadway—meeting vehicle	148(1)	$90.00
432.1	Fail to share half roadway—meeting vehicle—community safety zone	148(1)	$125.00
433.	Fail to turn out to right when overtaken	148(2)	$90.00
433.1	Fail to turn out to right when overtaken—community safety zone	148(2)	$125.00
434.	Fail to share roadway—meeting bicycle	148(4)	$90.00
434.1	Fail to share roadway—meeting bicycle—community safety zone	148(4)	$125.00
435.	Fail to turn out to left to avoid collision	148(5)	$90.00
435.1	Fail to turn out to left to avoid collision—community safety zone	148(5)	$125.00
436.	Bicycle—fail to turn out to right when overtaken	148(6)	$90.00
436.1	Bicycle—fail to turn out to right when overtaken—community safety zone	148(6)	$125.00
437.	Fail to turn out to left to avoid collision with bicycle	148(6)	$90.00
437.1	Fail to turn out to left to avoid collision with bicycle—community safety zone	148(6)	$125.00
438.	Motor assisted bicycle—fail to turn out to right when overtaken	148(6)	$90.00
438.1	Motor assisted bicycle—fail to turn out to right when overtaken—community safety zone	148(6)	$125.00
439.	Fail to turn out to left to avoid collision with motor assisted bicycle	148(6)	$90.00
439.1	Fail to turn out to left to avoid collision with motor assisted bicycle—community safety zone	148(6)	$125.00
440.	Fail to stop to facilitate passing	148(7)	$90.00
440.1	Fail to stop to facilitate passing—community safety zone	148(7)	$125.00
441.	Fail to assist in passing	148(7)	$90.00
441.1	Fail to assist in passing—community safety zone	148(7)	$125.00

442.	Pass—roadway not clear—approaching traffic	148(8)(a)	$90.00
442.1	Pass—roadway not clear—approaching traffic—community safety zone	148(8)(a)	$155.00
443.	Attempt to pass—roadway not clear—approaching traffic	148(8)(b)	$90.00
443.1	Attempt to pass—roadway not clear—approaching traffic—community safety zone	148(8)(a)	$155.00
444.	Pass—roadway not clear—overtaking traffic	148(8)(b)	$90.00
444.1	Pass—roadway not clear—overtaking traffic—community safety zone	148(8)(b)	$155.00
445.	Attempt to pass—roadway not clear—overtaking traffic	148(8)(b)	$90.00
445.1	Attempt to pass—roadway not clear—overtaking traffic—community safety zone	148(8)(b)	$155.00
446.	Drive left of centre—approaching crest of grade	149(1)(a)	$90.00
446.1	Drive left of centre—approaching crest of grade—community safety zone	149(1)(a)	$155.00
447.	Drive left of centre—on a curve	149(1)(a)	$90.00
447.1	Drive left of centre—on a curve—community safety zone	149(1)(a)	$155.00
448.	Drive left of centre within 30 m of bridge—no clear view	149(1)(a)	$90.00
448.1	Drive left of centre within 30 m of bridge—no clear view—community safety zone	149(1)(a)	$155.00
449.	Drive left of centre within 30 m of viaduct—no clear view	149(1)(a)	$90.00
449.1	Drive left of centre within 30 m of viaduct—no clear view—community safety zone	149(1)(a)	$155.00
450.	Drive left of centre within 30 m of tunnel—no clear view	149(1)(a)	$90.00
450.1	Drive left of centre within 30 m of tunnel—no clear view—community safety zone	149(1)(a)	$155.00

451.	Drive left of centre within 30 m of level railway crossing	149(1)(b)	$90.00
452.	Drive left of centre within 30 m of level railway crossing—community safety zone	149(1)(b)	$155.00
453.	Pass on right—not in safety	150(1)	$90.00
453.1	Pass on right—not in safety—community safety zone	150(1)	$155.00
454.	Pass—off roadway	150(2)	$90.00
454.1	Pass—off roadway—community safety zone	150(2)	$155.00
455.	Disobey official sign	151(1)	$90.00
455.1	Disobey official sign—community safety zone	151(1)	$125.00
456.	Drive wrong way—one way traffic	153	$90.00
456.1	Drive wrong way—one way traffic—community safety zone	153	$155.00
457.	Fail to drive in marked lane	154(1)(a)	$90.00
457.1	Fail to drive in marked lane—community safety zone	154(1)(a)	$125.00
458.	Unsafe lane change	154(1)(a)	$90.00
458.1	Unsafe lane change—community safety zone	154(1)(a)	$155.00
459.	Use centre lane improperly	154(1)(b)	$90.00
459.1	Use centre lane improperly—community safety zone	154(1)(b)	$125.00
460.	Fail to obey lane sign	154(1)(c)	$90.00
460.1	Fail to obey lane sign—community safety zone	154(1)(c)	$125.00
461.	Drive wrong way—divided highway	156(1)(a)	$90.00
461.1	Drive wrong way—divided highway—community safety zone	156(1)(a)	$155.00
462.	Cross divided highway—no proper crossing provided	156(1)(b)	$90.00
462.0.1	Cross divided highway—no proper crossing provided—community safety zone	156(1)(b)	$125.00
462.1	Backing on roadway—divided highway	157(1)	$90.00
462.1.1	Backing on roadway—divided highway—community safety zone	157(1)	$125.00
462.2	Backing on shoulder—divided highway	157(1)	$90.00

462.3	Backing on shoulder—divided highway—community safety zone	157(1)	$125.00
463.	Follow too closely	158(1)	$90.00
463.1	Follow too closely—community safety zone	158(1)	$125.00
464.	Commercial vehicle—follow too closely	158(2)	$90.00
464.1	Commercial vehicle—follow too closely—community safety zone	158(2)	$125.00
465.	Fail to stop on right for emergency vehicle	159(1)(a)	$90.00
465.1	Fail to stop on right for emergency vehicle—community safety zone	159(1)(a)	$125.00
466.	Fail to stop—nearest curb—for emergency vehicle	159(1)(b)	$90.00
466.1	Fail to stop—nearest curb—for emergency vehicle—community safety zone	159(1)(b)	$125.00
467.	Fail to stop—nearest edge of roadway—for emergency vehicle	159(1)(b)	$90.00
467.1	Fail to stop—nearest edge of roadway—for emergency vehicle—community safety zone	159(1)(b)	$125.00
468.	Follow fire department vehicle too closely	159(2)	$90.00
468.1	Follow fire department vehicle too closely—community safety zone	159(2)	$125.00
469.	Permit attachment to vehicle	160	$90.00
469.1	Permit attachment to vehicle—community safety zone	160	$125.00
470.	Permit attachment to street car	160	$90.00
470.1	Permit attachment to street car—community safety zone	160	$125.00
471.	Draw more than one vehicle	161	$90.00
471.1	Draw more than one vehicle—community safety zone	161	$125.00
472.	Drive while crowded	162	$90.00
472.1	Drive while crowded—community safety zone	162	$125.00
473.	Disobey railway crossing signal—stop wrong place	163	$90.00
473.1	Disobey railway crossing signal—stop wrong place—community safety zone	163	$125.00

474.	Disobey railway crossing signal— fail to stop	163	$90.00
474.1	Disobey railway crossing signal— fail to stop—community safety zone	163	$155.00
475.	Disobey railway crossing signal— proceed unsafely	163	$90.00
475.1	Disobey railway crossing signal— proceed unsafely—community safety zone	163	$155.00
476.	Disobey crossing gate	164	$90.00
476.1	Disobey crossing gate— community safety zone	164	$155.00
477.	Open vehicle door improperly	165(a)	$90.00
478.	Leave vehicle door open	165(b)	$90.00
479.	Pass street car improperly	166(1)	$90.00
479.1	Pass street car improperly— community safety zone	166(1)	$155.00
480.	Approach open street car door too closely	166(1)	$90.00
480.1	Approach open street car door too closely— community safety zone	166(1)	$155.00
481.	Pass street car on the left side	166(2)	$90.00
481.1	Pass street car on the left side— community safety zone	166(2)	$125.00
482.	Frighten animal	167	$90.00
482.1	Frighten animal—community safety zone	167	$125.00
483.	Fail to ensure safety of person in charge of animal	167	$90.00
483.1	Fail to ensure safety of person in charge of animal—community safety zone	167	$125.00
484.	Fail to use lower beam—oncoming	168(a)	$90.00
484.1	Fail to use lower beam—oncoming— community safety zone	168(a)	$125.00
485.	Fail to use lower beam—following	168(b)	$90.00
485.0.1	Fail to use lower beam—following— community safety zone	168(b)	$125.00
485.1	Prohibited use of alternating highbeam headlights	169(2)	$90.00

485.2	Prohibited use of alternating highbeam headlights—community safety zone	169(2)	$125.00
486.	Fail to take precaution against vehicle being set in motion	170(9)	$55.00
487.	Fail to have warning lights	170(10)(a)	$55.00
488.	Fail to use warning lights	170(11)	$55.00
489.	Interfere with traffic	170(12)	$55.00
490.	Interfere with snow removal	170(12)	$55.00
490.1	Offer tow truck services on King's Highway within 200 m of accident or apparent accident	171(1)(a)	$90.00
490.2	Offer tow truck services on King's Highway within 200 m of vehicle involved in accident	171(1)(b)	$90.00
490.3	Park tow truck on King's Highway within 200 m of accident or apparent accident—sufficient tow trucks available	171(2)(a)	$90.00
490.4	Stop tow truck on King's Highway within 200 m of accident or apparent accident—sufficient tow trucks available	171(2)(a)	$90.00
490.5	Park tow truck on King's Highway within 200 m of vehicle involved in accident—sufficient tow trucks available	171(2)(b)	$90.00
490.6	Stop tow trucks on King's Highway within 200 m of vehicle involved in accident—sufficient tow trucks available	171(2)(b)	$90.00
491.	Race a motor vehicle	172(1)	N.S.F.
491.1	Race a motor vehicle—community safety zone	172(1)	N.S.F.
492.	Race an animal	173	$90.00
493.	Fail to stop at railway crossing— public vehicle	174(1)	$90.00
494.	Stop wrong place at railway crossing— public vehicle	174(1)(a)	$90.00
495.	Fail to look both ways at railway crossing— public vehicle	174(1)(b)	$90.00
496.	Fail to open door at railway crossing— public vehicle	174(1)(c)	$90.00

497.	Cross tracks using gear requiring change—public vehicle	174(1)(d)	$90.00
497.1	Change gears while crossing railway track—public vehicle	174(1)(e)	$90.00
497.2	Fail to stop at railway crossing—school bus	174(2)	$90.00
497.3	Stop wrong place at railway crossing—school bus	174(2)(a)	$90.00
497.4	Fail to look both ways at railway crossing—school bus	174(2)(b)	$90.00
497.5	Fail to open door at railway crossing—school bus	174(2)(c)	$90.00
497.6	Cross tracks using gear requiring change—school bus	174(2)(d)	$90.00
497.7	Change gears while crossing railway track—school bus	174(2)(e)	$90.00
498.	Bus not used to transport adults with developmental handicaps or children, painted chrome yellow	175(3)	$90.00
499.	Prohibited markings	175(4)	$90.00
499.1	Prohibited equipment—school bus stop arm	175(4)	$90.00
500.	Drive chrome yellow vehicle, not used to transport adults with developmental handicaps or children	175(5)	$90.00
501.	Drive vehicle with prohibited school bus markings	175(5)	$90.00
502.	Drive vehicle with prohibited school bus stop arm	175(5)	$90.00
503.	Fail to actuate school bus signals	175(6)	$90.00
504.	Improperly actuate school bus signals	175(8)	$90.00
505.	Improperly actuate school bus signals at intersection controlled by operating traffic control system	175(9)(a)	$90.00
506.	Improperly actuate school bus signals at location, other than an intersection, controlled by operating traffic control system—at sign or roadway marking indicating stop to be made	175(9)(b)(i)	$90.00

507.	Improperly actuate school bus signals at location, other than an intersection, controlled by operating traffic control system—in area immediately before entering cross-walk	175(9)(b)(ii)	$90.00
507.1	Improperly actuate school bus signals at location, other than an intersection, controlled by operating traffic control system—within 5 m of traffic control system	175(9)(b)(iii)	$90.00
507.2	Improperly actuate school bus signals within 60 m of location controlled by operating traffic control system	175(9)(c)	$90.00
507.3	Stop school bus opposite loading zone	175(10)(a)	$90.00
507.5	Fail to stop for school bus—meeting	175(11)	$405.00
507.6	Fail to stop for school bus—overtaking	175(12)	$405.00
508.	Guard fail to properly display school crossing stop arm	176(2)	$90.00
509.	Fail to obey school crossing stop sign	176(3)	$90.00
509.1	Fail to obey school crossing stop sign—community safety zone	176(3)	$155.00
510.	Improper use of school crossing stop sign	176(4)	$90.00
511.	Unauthorized person display school crossing stop sign	176(5)	$90.00
512.	Solicit a ride	177(1)	$55.00
513.	Solicit business	177(2)	$55.00
514.	Attach to vehicle	178(1)	$90.00
515.	Attach to streetcar	178(1)	$90.00
516.	Ride 2 on a bicycle	178(2)	$90.00
517.	Ride another person on a motor assisted bicycle	178(3)	$90.00
518.	Person—attach to vehicle	178(4)	$40.00
519.	Person—attach to streetcar	178(4)	$40.00
520.	Pedestrian fail to walk on left side of highway	179	$40.00
521.	Pedestrian on roadway fail to keep to left edge	179	$40.00
522.	Litter highway	180	$90.00
523.	Deposit snow or ice on roadway	181	$90.00
524.	Disobey sign	182(2)	$90.00
524.1	Disobey sign—community safety zone	182(2)	$125.00

525.	Disobey sign at tunnel	183(2)	$90.00
526.	Deface notice	184	N.S.F.
527.	Remove notice	184	N.S.F.
528.	Interfere with notice	184	N.S.F.
529.	Deface obstruction	184	N.S.F.
530.	Remove obstruction	184	N.S.F.
531.	Interfere with obstruction	184	N.S.F.
532.	Fail to remove aircraft	187(1)	N.S.F.
533.	Move aircraft improperly	187(2)	N.S.F.
534.	Aircraft unlawfully take off	187(3)	N.S.F.
535.	Draw occupied trailer	188	$90.00
536.	Operate air cushioned vehicle	189	$90.00
537.	Fail to maintain daily log	190(3)	$315.00
538.	Fail to carry daily log	190(3)	$315.00
539.	Fail to surrender daily log	190(4)	$315.00
540.	Driver in possession of more than one daily log	190(5)	$315.00
540.1	Permit person to drive commercial motor vehicle not in accordance with the regulations	190(6)	$315.00
540.2	Fail to produce proof of exemption	191(7)	$90.00
540.3	Drive motor vehicle—toll device improperly affixed	191.2(1)	$90.00
540.4	Drive motor vehicle—no toll device	191.2(1)	$90.00
540.5	Drive motor vehicle—invalid toll device	191.2(1)	$90.00
540.6	Engage in activity to evade toll system	191.3(1)	$90.00
540.7	Engage in activity to obstruct toll system	191.3(1)	$90.00
540.8	Engage in activity to interfere with toll system	191.3(1)	$90.00
540.9	Use device to evade toll system	191.3(1)	$90.00
540.10	Use device to obstruct toll system	191.3(1)	$90.00
540.11	Use device to interfere with toll system	191.3(1)	$90.00
540.12	Sell device designed to interfere with toll system	191.3(4)	$90.00

540.13	Offer to sell device designed to interfere with toll system	191.3(4)	$90.00
540.14	Advertise for sale device designed to interfere with toll system	191.3(4)	$90.00
540.15	Sell device intended to interfere with toll system	191.3(4)	$90.00
540.16	Offer to sell device intended to interfere with toll system	191.3(4)	$90.00
540.17	Advertise for sale device intended to interfere with toll system	191.3(4)	$90.00

08/98

SCHEDULE B
HIGHWAY TRAFFIC ACT
SPEEDING

Kilometres		**Set Fines**
a)	1-19 kilometres per hour over the maximum speed limit	$2.50 per kilometre plus costs of $5.00
b)	20-34 kilometres per hour over the maximum speed limit	$3.75 per kilometre plus costs of $5.00
c)	35-49 kilometres per hour over the maximum speed limit	$6.00 per kilometre plus costs of $5.00
d)	50 kilometres per hour or more over the maximum speed limit	No out of court settlement

09/98

SCHEDULE C
HIGHWAY TRAFFIC ACT
SPEEDING—PHOTO RADAR

Kilometres		**Set Fines**
a)	1-19 kilometres per hour over the maximum speed limit	$2.50 per kilometre plus costs of $5.00
b)	20-34 kilometres per hour over the maximum speed limit	$3.75 per kilometre plus costs of $5.00
c)	35-49 kilometres per hour over the maximum speed limit	$6.00 per kilometre plus costs of $5.00
d)	50-60 kilometres per hour over the maximum speed limit	$8.00 per kilometre plus costs of $5.00
e)	61+ kilometres per hour over the maximum speed limit	no set fine

09/98

SCHEDULE D
HIGHWAY TRAFFIC ACT
SPEEDING—COMMUNITY SAFETY ZONE

Kilometres	**Set Fines**
a)	1-19 kilometres per hour over the maximum speed limit	$5.00 per kilometre plus costs of $5.00
b)	20-34 kilometres per hour over the maximum speed limit	$7.50 per kilometre plus costs of $5.00
c)	35-49 kilometres per hour over the maximum speed limit	No out of court settlement

09/98

APPENDIX B

Provincial Offence Ticket and Summons

A blank Provincial Offence Ticket and a blank Provincial Offence Summons are reproduced on the following pages. Identifying numbers have been removed. Make photocopies of the ticket and the summons to practise filling them out properly.

■ Provincial Offence Ticket   Top Page

ICON LOCATION CODE CODE DE LOCALISATION RIII	OFFENCE NUMBER N° D'INFRACTION

FORM 1 PROVINCIAL OFFENCES ACT ONTARIO COURT OF JUSTICE
FORMULE 1 LOI SUR LES INFRACTIONS PROVINCIALES COUR DE JUSTICE DE L'ONTARIO

CERTIFICATE OF OFFENCE / *PROCÈS-VERBAL D'INFRACTION*

I/JE SOUSSIGNÉ(E) _____

BELIEVE AND CERTIFY
THAT ON THE DAY OF
CROIS ET ATTESTE
QUE LE JOUR DE

(PRINT NAME / NOM EN LETTRES MOULÉES)
Y/A   M/M   D/J   TIME/À (HEURE)   M

NAME
NOM _____
FAMILY/NOM DE FAMILLE

GIVEN/PRÉNOM   INITIALS/INITIALES

ADDRESS
ADRESSE _____
NUMBER AND STREET/N° ET RUE

MUNICIPALITY/MUNICIPALITÉ   P.O./C.P.   PROVINCE   POSTAL CODE/CODE POSTAL

DRIVER'S LICENCE NO./NUMÉRO DE PERMIS DE CONDUIRE   PROV ON

BIRTHDATE/DATE DE NAISSANCE   SEX   MOTOR VEHICLE INVOLVED
Y/A   M/M   D/J   SEXE   VÉHICULE IMPLIQUÉ

1 9   ☐ YES/OUI ☐ NO/NON

AT/À _____

MUNICIPALITY/MUNICIPALITÉ

DID COMMIT THE OFFENCE OF:
A COMMIS L'INFRACTION SUIVANTE : _____

CONTRARY TO:
CONTRAIREMENT À : _____

SECT./ART. _____

PLATE NUMBER N° DE PLAQUE D'IMMATRICULATION	YEAR/ ANNÉE	PROV	MAKE/ MARQUE	COLLISION INVOLVED COLLISION IMPLIQUÉE	WITNESSES TÉMOINS	CODE
		ON		☐Y/O ☐N	☐Y/O ☐N	

COMMERCIAL   CVOR / CECVU   C.V.O.R. NUMBER /N° DU CECVU
☐ YES/OUI   ☐ YES/OUI

AND I FURTHER CERTIFY THAT I SERVED AN OFFENCE NOTICE
PERSONALLY UPON THE PERSON CHARGED
JE CERTIFIE EN OUTRE QUE J'AI SIGNIFIÉ UN AVIS D'INFRACTION
EN MAINS PROPRES À L'ACCUSÉ(E)   ☐ ON THE OFFENCE DATE
LE JOUR DE L'INFRACTION.
☐ OTHER
AUTRE

SIGNATURE OF ISSUING PROVINCIAL OFFENCES OFFICER SIGNATURE DE L'AGENT DES INFRACTIONS PROVINCIALES	OFFICER NO. N° DE L'AGENT	PLATOON PELOTON	UNIT UNITÉ

SET FINE OF
L'AMENDE FIXÉE DE
$ $ **TOTAL PAYABLE**
$ $
MONTANT TOTAL EXIGIBLE

TOTAL PAYABLE INCLUDES COSTS AND APPLICABLE
VICTIM FINE SURCHARGE.
LE MONTANT TOTAL EXIGIBLE COMPREND LES
FRAIS ET LA SURAMENDE COMPENSATOIRE
QUI S'APPLIQUE

SUMMONS ISSUED. YOU ARE
REQUIRED TO APPEAR IN
COURT ON
Y/A   M/M   D/J   TIME/À (HEURE)   M

ASSIGNATION DÉLIVRÉE. VOUS
DEVEZ COMPARAÎTRE LE
CT.ROOM / SALLE D'AUDIENCE   ONTARIO COURT OF JUSTICE P.O.A. OFFICE AT/
COUR DE JUSTICE DE L'ONTARIO BUREAU - L.I.P. À
279 WELLINGTON STREET, KINGSTON, ONTARIO /
279, RUE WELLINGTON, KINGSTON (ONTARIO)

CONVICTION ENTERED. SET FINE (INCLUDING COSTS) IMPOSED.
CONDAMNATION INSCRITE. AMENDE FIXÉE (Y COMPRIS LES FRAIS) IMPOSÉE.

Y/A   M/M   D/J

JUSTICE/JUGE DE PAIX

■ **Provincial Offence Ticket   Top Page (Reverse)**

AFFIDAVIT OF SERVICE UPON DEFENDANT

I, _____, MAKE OATH AND

SAY THAT ON THE _____ DAY OF _____ YR. _____ , I PERSONALLY

SERVED THE OFFENCE NOTICE/SUMMONS* ISSUED WITH THE ATTACHED
CERTIFICATE OF OFFENCE UPON THE DEFENDANT NAMED IN THE ATTACHED
CERTIFICATE OF OFFENCE.

* (STRIKE OUT INAPPLICABLE TERM)

THE CORPORATE DEFENDANT NAMED IN THE ATTACHED CERTIFICATE OF
OFFENCE BY LEAVING IT WITH _____
                                          PERSON SERVED
_____ AT _____
          POSITION   ADDRESS

_____
SIGNATURE OF PROVINCIAL OFFENCES OFFICER

_____   _____
     BADGE NUMBER   UNIT

SWORN BEFORE ME AT _____

THIS _____ DAY OF _____ YR. _____

A JUSTICE OF THE PEACE IN AND FOR THE PROVINCE OF ONTARIO / COMMISSIONER FOR TAKING AFFIDAVITS

COURT RECORD

DATE	ADJOURNED TO	REQUESTED BY	ON CONSENT

DATE	PLEADS	☐ GUILTY	☐ NOT GUILTY
	☐ FAIL TO APPEAR - DEEMED NOT TO DISPUTE		☐ SECTION 9.1 CONVICTION
	☐ OTHER _____		

DATE	**FINDING OF COURT**	
	☐ GUILTY/CONVICTED	REASONS: _____
	☐ DISMISSED	_____
	☐ WITHDRAWN	FINE IMPOSED _____
	☐ SUSPENDED SENTENCE	COSTS _____
	☐ QUASHED	TIME TO PAY

THE APPLICABLE VICTIM FINE SURCHARGE PURSUANT TO 60.1
WILL BE ADDED ADMINISTRATIVELY TO THE FINE AND COSTS TO
ARRIVE AT THE TOTAL PAYABLE.

FOR PROSECUTOR	FOR DEFENDANT
REPORTER	CLERK

_____
JUSTICE

DEFAULTED FINE ENFORCEMENT

_____
JUSTICE

■ Provincial Offence Ticket Second Page

ICON
LOCATION
CODE
CODE DE
LOCALISATION
RIII

OFFENCE
NUMBER
N°
D'INFRACTION

FORM 3 PROVINCIAL OFFENCES ACT ONTARIO COURT OF JUSTICE
FORMULE 3 LOI SUR LES INFRACTIONS PROVINCIALES COUR DE JUSTICE DE L'ONTARIO

OFFENCE NOTICE / AVIS D'INFRACTION

I/JE SOUSSIGNÉ(E)

BELIEVE AND CERTIFY
THAT ON THE DAY OF
CROIS ET ATTESTE
QUE LE JOUR DE

(PRINT NAME / NOM EN LETTRES MOULÉES)
Y/A   M/M   D/J

TIME/À (HEURE)

M

NAME
NOM

FAMILY/NOM DE FAMILLE

GIVEN/PRÉNOM

INITIALS/INITIALES

ADDRESS
ADRESSE

NUMBER AND STREET/N° ET RUE

MUNICIPALITY/MUNICIPALITÉ   P.O./C.P.   PROVINCE   POSTAL CODE/CODE POSTAL

DRIVER'S LICENCE NO./NUMÉRO DE PERMIS DE CONDUIRE

PROV
ON

BIRTHDATE/DATE DE NAISSANCE
Y/A   M/M   D/J

SEX
SEXE

MOTOR VEHICLE INVOLVED
VÉHICULE IMPLIQUÉ

1 9

☐ YES/OUI   ☐ NO/NON

AT/À

DID COMMIT THE OFFENCE OF:
A COMMIS L'INFRACTION SUIVANTE :

MUNICIPALITY/MUNICIPALITÉ

CONTRARY TO:
CONTRAIREMENT À :

PLATE NUMBER N° DE PLAQUE D'IMMATRICULATION	YEAR/ ANNÉE	PROV	MAKE/ MARQUE	COLLISION INVOLVED COLLISION IMPLIQUÉE	WITNESSES TÉMOINS	CODE
SECT./ART.		**ON**		☐Y/O ☐N	☐Y/O ☐N	

COMMERCIAL   CVOR / CECVU   C.V.O.R. NUMBER /N° DU CECVU
☐ YES/OUI   ☐ YES/OUI

AND I FURTHER CERTIFY THAT I SERVED AN OFFENCE NOTICE
PERSONALLY UPON THE PERSON CHARGED
JE CERTIFIE EN OUTRE QUE J'AI SIGNIFIÉ UN AVIS D'INFRACTION
EN MAINS PROPRES À L'ACCUSÉ(E)

☐ ON THE OFFENCE DATE
LE JOUR DE L'INFRACTION.
☐ OTHER
AUTRE

SIGNATURE OF ISSUING PROVINCIAL OFFENCES OFFICER SIGNATURE DE L'AGENT DES INFRACTIONS PROVINCIALES	OFFICER NO. N° DE L'AGENT	PLATOON PELOTON	UNIT UNITÉ

SET FINE OF
L'AMENDE FIXÉE DE

$ $

TOTAL PAYABLE

$ $

MONTANT TOTAL EXIGIBLE

TOTAL PAYABLE INCLUDES COSTS AND APPLICABLE
VICTIM FINE SURCHARGE.
LE MONTANT TOTAL EXIGIBLE COMPREND LES
FRAIS ET LA SURAMENDE COMPENSATOIRE
QUI S'APPLIQUÉ

SUMMONS ISSUED. YOU ARE
REQUIRED TO APPEAR IN
COURT ON

Y/A   M/M   D/J   TIME/À (HEURE)

M

ASSIGNATION DÉLIVRÉE. VOUS
DEVEZ COMPARAÎTRE LE

CT.ROOM / SALLE D'AUDIENCE

ONTARIO COURT OF JUSTICE P.O.A. OFFICE AT/
COUR DE JUSTICE DE L'ONTARIO BUREAU - L.I.P. À
279 WELLINGTON STREET, KINGSTON, ONTARIO /
279, RUE WELLINGTON, KINGSTON (ONTARIO)

DATE OF SERVICE IF OTHER THAN OFFENCE DATE
DATE DE LA SIGNIFICATION DE L'AVIS SI ELLE DIFFÈRE DE CELLE DE L'INFRACTION
Y/A   M/M   D/J

■ **Provincial Offence Ticket   Second Page (Reverse)**

IMPORTANT - PLEASE READ CAREFULLY - WITHIN 15 DAYS OF RECEIVING THIS NOTICE, CHOOSE **ONE** OF THE FOLLOWING OPTIONS, COMPLETE THE SELECTED OPTION (SIGN WHERE NECESSARY) AND DELIVER IT (AND PAYMENT WHERE APPLICABLE) TO THE ADDRESS SHOWN ON THE PAYMENT NOTICE. **IF YOU FAIL** TO EXERCISE YOUR CHOICE WITHIN THE 15 DAY PERIOD, OR IF YOU DO NOT APPEAR FOR TRIAL YOU WILL BE DEEMED NOT TO WISH TO DISPUTE THE CHARGE, AND A JUSTICE MAY ENTER A CONVICTION IN YOUR ABSENCE. UPON CONVICTION YOU WILL BE REQUIRED TO PAY THE SET FINE (INCLUDING COSTS) AND THE APPLICABLE VICTIM FINE SURCHARGE. IN ADDITION, AN ADMINISTRATIVE FEE IS PAYABLE IF THE FINE GOES INTO DEFAULT, AND THE INFORMATION MAY BE PROVIDED TO A CREDIT BUREAU

IMPORTANT - VEUILLEZ LIRE ATTENTIVEMENT - DANS LES QUINZE JOURS QUI SUIVENT LA DATE À LAQUELLE VOUS RECEVEZ LE PRÉSENT AVIS, CHOISISSEZ L'UNE DES OPTIONS SUIVANTES. REMPLISSEZ L'OPTION CHOISIE (SIGNEZ LÀ OÙ C'EST NÉCESSAIRE) ET REMETTEZ L'AVIS (AVEC VOTRE PAIEMENT LE CAS ÉCHÉANT) À L'ADRESSE INDIQUÉE SUR L'AVIS. **SI VOUS N'EXERCEZ PAS** VOTRE CHOIX DANS LES QUINZE JOURS, OU SI VOUS NE COMPARAISSEZ PAS VOUS SEREZ RÉPUTÉ(E) NE PAS VOULOIR CONTESTER L'ACCUSATION ET UN JUGE POURRA INSCRIRE UNE DÉCLARATION DE CULPABILITÉ EN VOTRE ABSENCE. EN CAS DE DÉCLARATION DE CULPABILITÉ VOUS SEREZ TENU(E) DE PAYER L'AMENDE FIXÉE (Y COMPRIS LES FRAIS) ET LA SURAMENDE COMPENSATOIRE APPLICABLE. DE PLUS, DES FRAIS ADMINISTRATIFS S'APPLIQUENT EN CAS DE DÉFAUT DE PAIEMENT DE L'AMENDE ET LES RENSEIGNEMENTS PEUVENT ÊTRE COMMUNIQUÉS À UN SERVICE D'INFORMATIONS FINANCIÈRES

① OPTION 1

PLEA OF GUILTY - PAYMENT OUT OF COURT: I PLEAD GUILTY AND PAYMENT OF THE TOTAL PAYABLE IS ENCLOSED (FOLLOW THE INSTRUCTIONS ON THE "PAYMENT NOTICE.")

PLAIDOYER DE CULPABILITÉ - PAIEMENT À L'AMIABLE : JE PLAIDE COUPABLE ET J'INCLUS LE PAIEMENT DE LA SOMME TOTALE À PAYER (SUIVRE LES INSTRUCTIONS SUR L'AVIS DE PAIEMENT).

SIGNATURE

② OPTION 2

TO PLEAD GUILTY WITH AN EXPLANATION: ATTEND THE COURT OFFICE SHOWN BELOW (OPTION 2) WITHIN THE TIMES AND DAYS SHOWN. YOU MUST BRING THIS NOTICE WITH YOU.

PLAIDOYER DE CULPABILITÉ ACCOMPAGNÉ D'UNE EXPLICATION : PRÉSENTEZ-VOUS AU GREFFE INDIQUÉ CI-DESSOUS (OPTION 2) DURANT LES HEURES ET LES JOURS INDIQUÉS. VOUS DEVEZ APPORTER LE PRÉSENT AVIS AVEC VOUS

ONTARIO COURT OF JUSTICE / COUR DE JUSTICE DE L'ONTARIO
PROVINCIAL OFFENCES OFFICE / BUREAU DES INFRACTIONS PROVINCIALES
MACDONALD CARTIER BUILDING, 279, WELLINGTON STREET, KINGSTON, ONTARIO
ÉDIFICE MACDONALD CARTIER, 279, RUE WELLINGTON, KINGSTON (ONTARIO)
BUSINESS DAY 9:00 A.M. - 12:30 P.M. AND 2:00 - 4:00 P.M. / TOUS LES JOURS OUVRABLES DE 9 H À 12 H 30 ET DE 14 H À 16 H
TELEPHONE / TÉLÉPHONE (613) 547-8557

---

③ OPTION 3: TRIAL OPTION

ONTARIO COURT OF JUSTICE
PROVINCIAL OFFENCES OFFICE
279 WELLINGTON STREET
KINGSTON ON K7K 6E1

DEMANDE DE PROCÈS

COUR DE JUSTICE DE L'ONTARIO
BUREAU DES INFRACTIONS PROVINCIALES
279, RUE WELLINGTON
KINGSTON ON K7K 6E1

NOTICE OF INTENTION TO APPEAR IN COURT:
1. I INTEND TO APPEAR IN COURT TO ENTER A PLEA AT THE TIME AND DATE SET FOR TRIAL.
2. I INTEND TO CHALLENGE THE EVIDENCE OF THE PROVINCIAL OFFENCES OFFICER
   ☐ NO   ☐ YES

NOTE: IF YOU INDICATE "NO" ABOVE, THE OFFICER MAY NOT ATTEND AND THE PROSECUTOR MAY RELY ON CERTIFIED STATEMENTS AS EVIDENCE AGAINST YOU.

AVIS D'INTENTION DE COMPARAÎTRE :
1. J'AI L'INTENTION DE COMPARAÎTRE POUR INSCRIRE UN PLAIDOYER AUX DATE ET HEURE FIXÉES POUR LE PROCÈS.
2. J'AI L'INTENTION DE CONTESTER LA PREUVE DE L'AGENT DES INFRACTIONS PROVINCIALES
   ☐ NON   ☐ OUI

NOTE : SI VOUS COCHEZ LA CASE «NON» CI-DESSUS, IL SE PEUT QUE L'AGENT NE SOIT PAS PRÉSENT ET QUE LE POURSUIVANT S'APPUIE SUR LES DÉCLARATIONS CERTIFIÉES POUR PROUVER VOTRE CULPABILITÉ.

SIGNATURE

LANGUAGE AT TRIAL/LANGUE AU PROCÈS :
☐ I REQUEST MY TRIAL TO BE HELD IN THE / JE DEMANDE QUE MON PROCÈS SOIT TENU :
☐ ENGLISH LANGUAGE/EN ANGLAIS   OR/OU   ☐ FRENCH LANGUAGE/EN FRANÇAIS

CHANGE OF NAME OR ADDRESS IF APPLICABLE / CHANGEMENT DE NOM OU D'ADRESSE LE CAS ÉCHÉANT

NAME/NOM

ADDRESS/ADRESSE

(PLEASE PRINT) / (LETTRES MOULÉES)

ICON
LOCATION
CODE
CODE DE
LOCALISATION
RIII

OFFENCE
NUMBER
N°
D'INFRACTION

COMPUTER INPUT / RECORD DOCUMENT
ENTRÉES INFORMATIQUES / REGISTRE DES DOCUMENTS

BELIEVES AND CERTIFIES
THAT ON THE DAY OF
CROIS ET ATTESTE
QUE LE JOUR DE

(PRINT NAME / NOM EN LETTRES MOULÉES)
Y/A   M/M   D/J

TIME/À (HEURE)

M

NAME
NOM

FAMILY/NOM DE FAMILLE

GIVEN/PRÉNOM

INITIALS/INITIALES

ADDRESS
ADRESSE

NUMBER AND STREET/N° ET RUE

MUNICIPALITY/MUNICIPALITÉ   P.O./C.P.   PROVINCE   POSTAL CODE/CODE POSTAL

DRIVER'S LICENCE NO./NUMÉRO DE PERMIS DE CONDUIRE

PROV
ON

BIRTHDATE/DATE DE NAISSANCE
Y/A   M/M   D/J

SEX
SEXE

MOTOR VEHICLE INVOLVED
VÉHICULE IMPLIQUÉ

1 9

☐ YES/OUI   ☐ NO/NON

AT/À

DID COMMIT THE OFFENCE OF:
A COMMIS L'INFRACTION SUIVANTE :

MUNICIPALITY/MUNICIPALITÉ

CONTRARY TO:
CONTRAIREMENT À :

SECT./ART.

PLATE NUMBER N° DE PLAQUE D'IMMATRICULATION	YEAR/ ANNÉE	PROV	MAKE/ MARQUE	COLLISION INVOLVED COLLISION IMPLIQUÉE	WITNESSES TÉMOINS	CODE
		ON		☐Y/O ☐N	☐Y/O ☐N	

COMMERCIAL   CVOR / CECVU   C.V.O.R. NUMBER N° DU CECVU

☐ YES/OUI   ☐ YES/OUI

AND I FURTHER CERTIFY THAT I SERVED AN OFFENCE NOTICE
PERSONALLY UPON THE PERSON CHARGED
JE CERTIFIE EN OUTRE QUE J'AI SIGNIFIÉ UN AVIS D'INFRACTION
EN MAINS PROPRES À L'ACCUSÉ(E)

☐ ON THE OFFENCE DATE
LE JOUR DE L'INFRACTION.
☐ OTHER
AUTRE

SIGNATURE OF ISSUING PROVINCIAL OFFENCES OFFICER SIGNATURE DE L'AGENT DES INFRACTIONS PROVINCIALES	OFFICER NO. N° DE L'AGENT	PLATOON PELOTON	UNIT UNITÉ

SET FINE OF L'AMENDE FIXÉE DE $ $	**TOTAL PAYABLE** $ $ **MONTANT TOTAL EXIGIBLE**	TOTAL PAYABLE INCLUDES COSTS AND APPLICABLE VICTIM FINE SURCHARGE. LE MONTANT TOTAL EXIGIBLE COMPREND LES FRAIS ET LA SURAMENDE COMPENSATOIRE QUI S'APPLIQUE

SUMMONS ISSUED. YOU ARE
REQUIRED TO APPEAR IN
COURT ON

Y/A   M/M   D/J   TIME/À (HEURE)

M

ASSIGNATION DÉLIVRÉE. VOUS
DEVEZ COMPARAÎTRE LE

CT. ROOM / SALLE D'AUDIENCE

ONTARIO COURT OF JUSTICE P.O.A. OFFICE AT/
COUR DE JUSTICE DE L'ONTARIO BUREAU - L.I.P. À

1. HIGHWAY CODE   2. KEY POINT CODE   3. ENFORCEMENT   4. VEH. TYPE

5.   6.   7.   8.

Note: The reverse of the third page is blank and is not reproduced.

◼ **Provincial Offence Ticket   Fourth Page**

ICON LOCATION CODE
CODE DE LOCALISATION
RIII

OFFENCE NUMBER
N°
D'INFRACTION

PROVINCIAL OFFENCES ACT ONTARIO COURT OF JUSTICE
LOI SUR LES INFRACTIONS PROVINCIALES COUR DE JUSTICE DE L'ONTARIO

ENFORCEMENT AGENCY RECORD /
REGISTRE DES DOCUMENTS DE L'AGENCE D'EXÉCUTION

BELIEVES AND CERTIFIES THAT ON THE DAY OF
CROIS ET ATTESTE QUE LE JOUR DE

(PRINT NAME / *NOM EN LETTRES MOULÉES*)
Y/A   M/M   D/J

TIME/À *(HEURE)*
M

NAME
NOM

FAMILY/*NOM DE FAMILLE*

GIVEN/*PRÉNOM*

INITIALS/*INITIALES*

ADDRESS
ADRESSE

NUMBER AND STREET/*N° ET RUE*

MUNICIPALITY/*MUNICIPALITÉ*   P.O./C.P.   PROVINCE   POSTAL CODE/*CODE POSTAL*

DRIVER'S LICENCE NO./*NUMÉRO DE PERMIS DE CONDUIRE*

PROV
ON

BIRTHDATE/*DATE DE NAISSANCE*
Y/A   M/M   D/J

SEX
SEXE

MOTOR VEHICLE INVOLVED
VÉHICULE IMPLIQUÉ

1 | 9

☐ YES/*OUI*   ☐ NO/*NON*

AT/À

MUNICIPALITY/*MUNICIPALITÉ*

DID COMMIT THE OFFENCE OF:
A COMMIS L'INFRACTION SUIVANTE :

CONTRARY TO:
CONTRAIREMENT À :

SECT./ART.

PLATE NUMBER *N° DE PLAQUE D'IMMATRICULATION*	YEAR/ *ANNÉE*	PROV	MAKE/ *MARQUE*	COLLISION INVOLVED *COLLISION IMPLIQUÉE*	WITNESSES *TÉMOINS*	CODE
		ON		☐Y/O ☐N	☐Y/O ☐N	

COMMERCIAL   CVOR / *CECVU*   C.V.O.R. NUMBER *N° DU CECVU*

☐ YES/*OUI*   ☐ YES/*OUI*

AND I FURTHER CERTIFY THAT I SERVED AN OFFENCE NOTICE PERSONALLY UPON THE PERSON CHARGED
JE CERTIFIE EN OUTRE QUE J'AI SIGNIFIÉ UN AVIS D'INFRACTION EN MAINS PROPRES À L'ACCUSÉ(E)

☐ ON THE OFFENCE DATE *LE JOUR DE L'INFRACTION.*
☐ OTHER *AUTRE*

SIGNATURE OF ISSUING PROVINCIAL OFFENCES OFFICER *SIGNATURE DE L'AGENT DES INFRACTIONS PROVINCIALES*	OFFICER NO. *N° DE L'AGENT*	PLATOON *PELOTON*	UNIT *UNITÉ*

SET FINE OF
L'AMENDE FIXÉE DE

$ $

TOTAL PAYABLE
$ $
MONTANT TOTAL EXIGIBLE

TOTAL PAYABLE INCLUDES COSTS AND APPLICABLE VICTIM FINE SURCHARGE.
LE MONTANT TOTAL EXIGIBLE COMPREND LES FRAIS ET LA SURAMENDE COMPENSATOIRE QUI S'APPLIQUE

SUMMONS ISSUED. YOU ARE REQUIRED TO APPEAR IN COURT ON
Y/A   M/M   D/J   TIME/À *(HEURE)*
M

ASSIGNATION DÉLIVRÉE. VOUS DEVEZ COMPARAÎTRE LE

CT.ROOM / *SALLE D'AUDIENCE*

ONTARIO COURT OF JUSTICE P.O.A. OFFICE AT/
COUR DE JUSTICE DE L'ONTARIO BUREAU - L.I.P. À

■ **Provincial Offence Ticket   Fourth Page (Reverse)**

ENFORCEMENT AGENCY NOTES / NOTES DE L'AGENCE D'EXÉCUTION

■ **Provincial Offence Ticket   Last Page**

OFFENCE NUMBER N° D'INFRACTION

PROVINCIAL OFFENCES ACT ONTARIO COURT OF JUSTICE
LOI SUR LES INFRACTIONS PROVINCIALES COUR DE JUSTICE DE L'ONTARIO

PAYMENT NOTICE / *AVIS DE PAIEMENT*

TO PAY THE TOTAL PAYABLE SHOWN, FORWARD YOUR
PAYMENT WITH THIS NOTICE AND THE OFFENCE NOTICE TO
THE ADDRESS SHOWN ON THIS NOTICE. SIGN THE PLEA OF
GUILTY ON THE OFFENCE NOTICE (OPTION 1).

*POUR ACQUITTER LE MONTANT TOTAL EXIGIBLE, FAITES
PARVENIR VOTRE PAIEMENT, ACCOMPAGNÉ DE CET AVIS ET
DE L'AVIS D'INFRACTION, À L'ADRESSE QUI FIGURE SUR LE
PRÉSENT AVIS. N'OUBLIEZ PAS DE SIGNER LE PLAIDOYER DE
CULPABILITÉ SUR L'AVIS D'INFRACTION (OPTION 1).*

MAKE CHEQUE OR MONEY ORDER PAYABLE TO
"CORPORATION OF THE CITY OF KINGSTON" AND
WRITE THE NUMBER OF THE OFFENCE NOTICE ON
THE FRONT OF THE CHEQUE/MONEY ORDER. DO NOT
SEND CASH, CORRESPONDENCE OR POST-DATED
CHEQUES WITH YOUR PAYMENT.
DISHONOURED CHEQUES WILL BE SUBJECT TO AN
ADMINISTRATIVE CHARGE AND THE AMOUNT MAY BE
REFERRED TO CENTRAL COLLECTION SERVICES.

*FAIRE UN CHÈQUE OU MANDAT À L'ORDRE DU «CORPORATION OF
THE CITY OF KINGSTON» ET ÉCRIRE LE NUMÉRO D'AVIS
D'INFRACTION AU RECTO DU CHÈQUE/MANDAT. NE PAS ENVOYER
D'ESPÈCES, NI DE LETTRE OU DE CHÈQUES POSTDATÉS AVEC
VOTRE PAIEMENT.
LES CHÈQUES IMPAYÉS SONT ASSUJETTIS À DES FRAIS
ADMINISTRATIFS ET LES RENSEIGNEMENTS CONCERNANT LE
MONTANT IMPAYÉ PEUVENT ÊTRE TRANSMIS AU SERVICE
CENTRAL DE RECOUVREMENT.*

COMPLETE THE FOLLOWING INFORMATION / *VEUILLEZ DONNER LES RENSEIGNEMENTS SUIVANTS*

NAME / *NOM*

ADDRESS / *ADRESSE*

☐ CHEQUE/MONEY ORDER ENCLOSED
  CHÈQUE/MANDAT JOINT

☐ VISA   ☐ MASTER CARD

CARDHOLDER'S SIGNATURE
SIGNATURE DU DÉTENTEUR DE LA CARTE

CARD NUMBER
N° DE CARTE

0960

CARD EXPIRY DATE (MONTH)   (YEAR)
DATE D'EXPIRATION (MOIS)   (ANNÉE)

SEE BACK FOR MAILING ADDRESS AND INSTRUCTIONS / *POUR CONNAÎTRE L'ADRESSE POSTALE ET LES INSTRUCTIONS, PRIÈRE DE VOIR AU VERSO*

**TOTAL PAID
*MONTANT TOTAL EXIGIBLE*** $ $

■ **Provincial Offence Ticket   Last Page (Reverse)**

REMEMBER TO KEEP A RECORD OF THIS PAYMENT.

N'OUBLIEZ PAS DE CONSERVER UN REÇU DE PAIEMENT

SIGN THE PLEA OF GUILTY ON THE OFFENCE NOTICE (OPTION 1) AND MAIL THE OFFENCE NOTICE WITH THIS PAYMENT NOTICE TO

VEUILLEZ SIGNER LE PLAIDOYER DE CULPABILITÉ SUR L'AVIS D'INFRACTION (OPTION 1) ET ADRESSER L'AVIS D'INFRACTION ACCOMPAGNÉ DE L'AVIS DE PAIEMENT À L'ADRESSE SUIVANTE

PAY TO / *PAYEZ À*

ONTARIO COURT OF JUSTICE | COUR DE JUSTICE DE L'ONTARIO

◼ **Provincial Offence Summons**

ICON
LOCATION
CODE
CODE DE
LOCALISATION
RIII

FORM 6 PROVINCIAL OFFENCES ACT ONTARIO COURT OF JUSTICE
FORMULE 6 LOI SUR LES INFRACTIONS PROVINCIALES COUR DE JUSTICE DE L'ONTARIO

SUMMONS / *ASSIGNATION*

BELIEVES AND CERTIFIES
THAT ON THE DAY OF   Y/A   M/M   D/J   TIME/*À (HEURE)*
CROIS ET ATTESTE
QUE LE JOUR DE   M

NAME
NOM
                                FAMILY/*NOM DE FAMILLE*

            GIVEN/*PRÉNOM*   INITIALS/*INITIALES*

ADDRESS
ADRESSE
                                NUMBER AND STREET/*N° ET RUE*

MUNICIPALITY/*MUNICIPALITÉ*   P.O./C.P.   PROVINCE   POSTAL CODE/*CODE POSTAL*

DRIVER'S LICENCE NO./*NUMÉRO DE PERMIS DE CONDUIRE*   PROV

                                                                          ON

    BIRTHDATE/*DATE DE NAISSANCE*   SEX   MOTOR VEHICLE INVOLVED
    Y/A   M/M   D/J   SEXE   *VÉHICULE IMPLIQUÉ*

1 9   ☐ YES/*OUI*   ☐ NO/*NON*

AT/*À*

                                            MUNICIPALITY/*MUNICIPALITÉ*

DID COMMIT THE OFFENCE OF:
A COMMIS L'INFRACTION SUIVANTE :

CONTRARY TO:
CONTRAIREMENT À :

                            SECT./*ART.*
    PLATE NUMBER   PROV   CODE
    N° DE PLAQUE D'IMMATRICULATION
                             ON

        CVOR / *CECVU*
        ☐ YES/*OUI*

THIS IS THEREFORE TO COMMAND YOU IN HER MAJESTY'S NAME TO   OFFICER NO.   PLATOON   UNIT
APPEAR BEFORE THE ONTARIO COURT OF JUSTICE   *N° DE L'AGENT* *PELOTON* *UNITÉ*
POUR CES MOTIFS, ORDRE VOUS EST DONNÉ, AU NOM DE SA
MAJESTÉ, DE COMPARAÎTRE DEVANT LA COUR DE JUSTICE DE
L'ONTARIO

            Y/A   M/M   D/J   TIME/*À (HEURE)*

                                                        M

        CT.ROOM / *SALLE D'AUDIENCE*   ONTARIO COURT OF JUSTICE P.O.A. OFFICE AT/
                                       COUR DE JUSTICE DE L'ONTARIO BUREAU - L.I.P. À
                                       279 WELLINGTON STREET, KINGSTON, ONTARIO /
                                       279, RUE WELLINGTON, KINGSTON (ONTARIO)

AND TO ATTEND THEREAFTER AS REQUIRED BY THE COURT IN ORDER TO BE DEALT WITH ACCORDING TO LAW. THIS
SUMMONS IS SERVED UNDER PART 1 OF THE PROVINCIAL OFFENCES ACT.
ET D'Y ÊTRE PRÉSENT(E) PAR LA SUITE LORSQUE LE TRIBUNAL L'EXIGERA, DE FAÇON À ÊTRE TRAITÉ(E) SELON LA LOI.
CETTE ASSIGNATION VOUS EST SIGNIFÉE AUX TERMES DE LA PARTIE 1 DE LA LOI SUR LES INFRACTIONS PROVINCIALES.

SIGNATURE OF PROVINCIAL OFFENCES OFFICER
SIGNATURE DE L'AGENT DES INFRACTIONS PROVINCIALES

■ **Provincial Offence Summons (Reverse)**

NOTE TO DEFENDANT

YOU ARE REQUIRED TO APPEAR IN COURT. YOU MAY APPEAR
PERSONALLY OR BY AGENT.

WHEN YOU APPEAR YOU MAY:
    (A)   PLEAD GUILTY TO THE OFFENCE
           OR
    (B)   SET A DATE FOR TRIAL
           OR
    (C)   THE TRIAL MAY PROCEED.

IF YOU DO NOT APPEAR:
    (A)   THE COURT MAY ISSUE A WARRANT FOR YOUR ARREST.
           OR
    (B)   THE TRIAL MAY PROCEED IN YOUR ABSENCE.

REMARQUE AU DÉFENDEUR

*VOUS ÊTES REQUIS DE COMPARAÎTRE EN COUR. VOUS POUVEZ
VOUS PRÉSENTER EN PERSONNE OU PAR L'INTERMÉDIAIRE
D'UN MANDATAIRE.*

LORSQUE VOUS COMPARAÎTREZ VOUS POURREZ :
    (A)   PLAIDER COUPABLE RELATIVEMENT À L'INFRACTION
           OU
    (B)   DEMANDER UNE DATE DE PROCÈS
           OU
    (C)   LE PROCÈS POURRA SE DÉROULER

SI VOUS NE COMPARAISSEZ PAS :
    *(A)   LA COUR PEUT DÉCERNER UN MANDAT D'ARRESTATION
           CONTRE VOUS*
           OU
    (B)   LE PROCÈS PEUT SE DÉROULER EN VOTRE ABSENCE.

**FOR INFORMATION ON ACCESS
FOR PERSONS WITH DISABILITIES, CALL**

**POUR PLUS DE RENSEIGNEMENTS SUR L'ACCÈS
DES PERSONNES HANDICAPÉES**

APPENDIX C

Suspect Apprehension Pursuits Regulation

O. REG. 546/99
IN FORCE JANUARY 1, 2000

1. For the purposes of this Regulation, a suspect apprehension pursuit occurs,

    (a) when a police officer attempts to direct the driver of a motor vehicle to stop;

    (b) the driver refuses to obey the police officer; and

    (c) the police officer pursues in a motor vehicle for the purpose of stopping the fleeing motor vehicle or identifying the fleeing motor vehicle or an individual in the fleeing motor vehicle.

2. A suspect apprehension pursuit is discontinued when police officers are no longer pursuing a fleeing motor vehicle for the purpose of stopping the fleeing motor vehicle or identifying the fleeing motor vehicle or an individual in the fleeing motor vehicle.

3. (1) A police officer may pursue, or continue to pursue, a fleeing motor vehicle that fails to stop,

    (a) if the police officer has reason to believe that a criminal offence has been committed or is about to be committed; or

    (b) for the purposes of motor vehicle identification or the identification of an individual in the vehicle.

(2) A police officer shall, before initiating a suspect apprehension pursuit, determine that there are no alternatives available as set out in the written procedures of the police force established under subsection 7(1).

(3) A police officer shall, before initiating a suspect apprehension pursuit, determine whether in order to protect public safety the immediate need to apprehend an individual in the fleeing motor vehicle or the need to identify the fleeing motor vehicle or an individual in the fleeing motor vehicle outweighs the risk to public safety that may result from the pursuit.

(4) During a suspect apprehension pursuit, a police officer shall continually reassess the determination made under subsection (3) and shall discontinue the pursuit when the risk to public safety that may result from the pursuit outweighs the risk to public safety that may result if an individual in the fleeing motor vehicle is not immediately apprehended or if the fleeing motor vehicle or an individual in the fleeing motor vehicle is not identified.

(5) No suspect apprehension pursuit shall be initiated for a non-criminal offence if the identity of an individual in the fleeing motor vehicle is known.

(6) All suspect apprehension pursuits for a non-criminal offence shall be discontinued once the fleeing motor vehicle or an individual in the fleeing motor vehicle is identified.

4. (1) A police officer shall notify a dispatcher when the officer initiates a suspect apprehension pursuit.

(2) The dispatcher shall notify a communications supervisor or road supervisor, if a supervisor is available, that a suspect apprehension pursuit has been initiated.

5. A communications or road supervisor shall order police officers to discontinue a suspect apprehension pursuit if, in his or her opinion, the risk to public safety that may result from the pursuit outweighs the risk to public safety that may result if an individual in the fleeing motor vehicle is not immediately apprehended or if the fleeing motor vehicle or an individual in the fleeing motor vehicle is not identified.

6. Every police services board shall establish policies that are consistent with this Regulation about suspect apprehension pursuits.

7. (1) Every police force shall establish written procedures that set out the tactics that may be used in its jurisdiction,

(a) as an alternative to suspect apprehension pursuit; and

(b) for following or stopping a fleeing motor vehicle.

(2) Every police force shall establish written procedures that are consistent with this Regulation about suspect apprehension pursuits in its jurisdiction.

8. A police officer shall not discharge his or her firearm for the sole purpose of attempting to stop a fleeing motor vehicle.

9. A police officer in an unmarked police vehicle shall not engage in a suspect apprehension pursuit unless a marked police vehicle is not readily available and the police officer believes that it is necessary to immediately apprehend an individual in the fleeing motor vehicle or to identify the fleeing motor vehicle or an individual in the fleeing motor vehicle.

10. (1) During a suspect apprehension pursuit, a police officer shall consider the tactics for stopping a vehicle as set out in the written procedures referred to in subsection 7(1).

(2) A police officer may only intentionally cause a police motor vehicle to come into physical contact with a fleeing motor vehicle for the purposes of stopping it where the officer believes on reasonable grounds that to do so is necessary to immediately protect against loss of life or serious bodily harm.

(3) In considering the action referred to in subsection (2), a police officer shall assess the impact of the action on the safety of other members of the public and police officers.

(4) Despite subsection (2), a police officer may cause a police motor vehicle to come into physical contact with a fleeing motor vehicle for the purposes of pinning it if the fleeing motor vehicle has lost control or collided with an object and come to a stop and the driver of the motor vehicle continues to try to use it to flee.

(5) Nothing in subsection (2) precludes police officers involved in a pursuit, with assistance from other police officers in motor vehicles, from attempting to safely position the police vehicles in such a manner as to prevent the movement either forward, backward or sideways of a fleeing motor vehicle.

(6) Every police force shall ensure that its police officers receive training about the intentional contact between vehicles that is described in subsection (2). The training must address the matters described in subsections (2) and (3).

11. (1) Every police force shall establish written procedures on the management and control of suspect apprehension pursuits.

(2) The procedures must describe the responsibilities of police officers, dispatchers, communications supervisors and road supervisors.

(3) The procedures must describe the equipment that is available for implementing alternative tactics.

12. (1) If more than one jurisdiction is involved in a suspect apprehension pursuit, the supervisor in the jurisdiction in which the pursuit begins has decision-making responsibility for the pursuit.

(2) The supervisor may hand over decision-making responsibility to a supervisor in another jurisdiction involved in the pursuit.

13. A police officer does not breach the code of conduct when he or she decides not to initiate or chooses to discontinue a suspect apprehension pursuit because he or she has reason to believe that the risk to public safety that may result from the pursuit outweighs the risk to public safety that may result if an individual in the fleeing motor vehicle is not immediately apprehended or if the fleeing motor vehicle or an individual in the fleeing motor vehicle is not identified.

14. Every police force shall ensure that its police officers, dispatchers, communications supervisors and road supervisors receive training accredited by the Solicitor General about suspect apprehension pursuits.

15. A police force shall ensure that the particulars of each suspect apprehension pursuit are recorded on a form and in a manner approved by the Solicitor General.

16. This Regulation comes into force on January 1, 2000.